"This German is a lover of Italian food. Judy Pochini has written with love and expertise. I highly recommend her storied-recipes. Buy the book and make yourself, your family and friends happy by cooking up these delicious meals."

KARIN FINELL, author of *Good-Bye to the Mermaids,* Lost in Hitler's Berlin, UMP Oct. 2006

"Memories of the author as a young woman in San Francisco and of days now gone are interwoven with over two hundred proven, easy-to-follow recipes and culinary tips gathered from four generations of her husband's colorful Italian heritage. The humor and romance of the twenty stories will amuse and inspire you as you create your own elegant Italian dishes."

TOMMIE SPEAR, author of *A Star to Steer Her By*

"What an incredible blend of food and family. This one-of-a-kind book will tickle your palate and funnybone. Enjoy the experience of Italian food and the family story behind it."

JUNE BEHRENS, author of *Missions of the Central Coast* plus seventy-two children's books

"Delicious story. Great read."

KITTY PERI, Arnoldi's Café, Santa Barbara

"The colorful stories and delicious Italian cuisine that Judy presents in *The Frittata Affair* give us the flavor of San Francisco, from times past to times present."

CHARLES CHAMPLIN, author of *A Life In Writing,* 2006; Arts Editor Emeritus, *Los Angeles Times;* long-time instructor, Santa Barbara Writers Conference

"A wondrous gift of life is enjoying an evening with friends, sharing stories and specially prepared Italian cuisine from The *Frittata Affair.*"

JEAN C. WADE, author of *How Sweet It Is . . . Without the Sugar*

The Frittata Affair

Adventures in Four-Star Dining at Home

Buonappetito! Judy

Judy Pochini

authorHOUSE®

AuthorHouse™
1663 Liberty Drive, Suite 200
Bloomington, IN 47403
www.authorhouse.com
Phone: 1-800-839-8640

First published by AuthorHouse 10/31/2007

ISBN: 978-1-4343-4428-1 (sc)

Library of Congress Control Number: 2007907943

Printed in the United States of America
Bloomington, Indiana

This book is printed on acid-free paper.

To Bob Pochini

and his family, whose zest for pursuing excellence

in the culinary arts inspired this book

Acknowledgements

A special thank-you to Bob's sister, Gloria Pochini Riccardi, whose zest, enthusiasm, and expertise in presenting "four-star dining at home" kept Bob on his toes in developing and perfecting his own culinary skills. Also key in helping this book come together, Bob's children, Liane, Jan, Bud, and Gina, contributed great support through their infectious enthusiasm and skill in cooking and entertaining. And Bob's cousin Jack Pochini and Jack's wife Esther provided invaluable input to the description of the Pochinis' Christmas in San Francisco.

This book would not have happened without the prodding of inspirational trainer Marcia Wieder, who stresses the importance of pursuing your dreams.

Jane Trittipo, author of two microwave cookbooks, generously shared her expertise on proper preparation of a cookbook, especially the rules of setting recipes into type. She also helped me learn how to self-publish a book.

At the Santa Barbara Writers Conference I met professional editor and teacher Anne Lowenkopf, who now coaches me in writing memoir style nonfiction. I continue my studies with Anne under the auspices of Santa Barbara Adult Education, and Anne has edited my book. With her professional help and expertise, I feel confident that within *The Frittata Affair* you will find entertaining stories and understandable recipes.

Playing a big role in keeping this project in gear, my long-time friend Stan Lokken has contributed the invaluable service of setting the stories and recipes into type. Along the way, Stan's vigilant attention has caught many of the errors, omissions, misspellings, and inconsistencies that can plague one engaged in such an intricate project. Without Stan's help and enthusiasm, this book might not have continued to completion.

For getting me started on this project to dramatize the stories about the Pochinis, I acknowledge with thanks Gus Slavin, the leader of our Danville-Alamo Writers Group in American Association of University Women, and my Writers Group friends Caroline Sanchez, Vivienne Wong, and Heather Hunter.

Santa Barbara friend and professional photographer Ellin Ostler contributed the magnificent color photos for the book's covers. I especially appreciate her expertise and skill. Computer guru DJ Zayha earned our respect and thanks as he shepherded Stan Lokken and me through the final phases of completing the manuscript. Thanks to Timothy Murphy and the AuthorHouse staff for helping us through the publishing process.

Many other friends and relatives have encouraged me, and I thank them as well. Most of all, I thank the cuisine itself for inspiring Bob to perfect his culinary skills and for inspiring me to write about it.

Judy

About Bob Pochini

"Bob Pochini was the most unusual person I ever met. I enjoyed knowing him, and I admired him. Whether it was cars, cooking, cabinetry, electrical, or anything else that interested him, Bob could do it all well. I've never known anyone like him, and I'm glad I knew him." ... Helen Hogan, client and close friend.

From the time he escaped from his crib, Bob's heritage of Italian American *Genovese* style cooking and cuisine became a lifelong passion. His father Leo and his grandfather Elia, along with his uncle Joe, all worked as the accomplished chefs who purveyed memorable meals at the popular Pochini's Italian Restaurant on Front Street in San Francisco. In 1898, Elia had joined the restaurant and in 1905 became its owner.

But just as Bob was entering the scene in 1934 the restaurant was winding down and closing, perhaps a casualty of the Great Depression. Chef Elia chose to retire; Chef Joe moved to Stockton; and Chef Leo took a post as a bookkeeper for a broker in the city's bustling Produce Market near the restaurant.

In his new job, Leo reported early for work, about 3 a.m., just as he had done at the restaurant. He then closed the office by mid-afternoon, arriving at his home on nearby Russian Hill in plenty of time to prepare the family dinner.

Toddler Robert, fascinated by his father's skillful knife work and deft tossing of the sautéeing vegetables, found himself drawn to his dad's kitchen about the time he had learned to walk and talk, he told me.

"Out! Out!" Leo would say. "Sit on the stairs and stay there. Otherwise, you may not watch."

"But, Dad," Bob would protest. "I want to see—"

"All right, you may stay if you sit there and don't come in here. You may ask questions, and I'll tell you what I'm doing and why."

Thus, to young Bob, cooking seemed a natural interest and occupation for a man at home. And he sat on those steps day after day asking questions and learning all the Pochini versions of North Beach *Genovese* cuisine

Thus it happened that Bob Pochini enjoyed the privilege of training under a master chef, just the way Chef Leo had learned the cuisine from his own father. Bob recalled that his father seldom allowed him the privilege of working as an assistant in the kitchen. I can imagine, therefore, that his mother, Jean, perhaps let her darling son practice in her upstairs kitchen, during intervals when she was not busy preparing the salads and desserts.

So it happened that Bob became an accomplished cook, creating memorable Four-Star quality meals for his family and friends. Not only did he learn all the signature Pochini's Restaurant specialties, he went on to develop innovative new dishes as he perfected his skills.

Cooking may have been my husband's first love, but he had many other pursuits. Cars and engines, music, interior design, real estate, building and remodeling, woodworking, and bartending numbered among the many businesses and pastimes that caught and held his interest.

For more than ten years, as my partner in Judy Hay Interiors of Lafayette, Bob coordinated complaints and any needed repairs, as well as making furniture that we co-designed for ourselves, our family, and our interior design clients.

Automobiles struck his fancy at an early age. A "car nut," he raced them, maintained them, and collected them. He turned his boyhood fascination with cars and engines into his business, becoming both a master mechanic and a master machinist. Starting out as a young entrepreneur, he owned gas stations, auto parts stores, garages, a crankshaft repair shop, and an equipment sales firm in which he was still a partner by the time I met him.

Would he ever have considered owning and operating a restaurant, I once asked. "No," he replied, "too many hours and too much effort to make a living. It's a tough business."

An early starter in auto lore, Bob told me that by age eight or ten he proudly drove the family's 1936 Buick on outings to Stockton (with Dad Leo coaching him, of course). By age twelve, Bob bought his first car for just $10. Because he had no license and could not legally drive his acquisition, he decided to hide it from his parents. He thus did not park it in front of the family's Russian Hill home, but just around the corner. Bob told me that Dad Leo must have sensed that his son might have acquired a car because he would sometimes see Leo peering into the cars parked near Taylor and Union to check the registrations, which by law at that time had to be posted on the steering columns. Leo never did discover Bob's vehicle so the erstwhile driver could enjoy his "wheels" at night while Dad was sleeping.

About that time Bob became friends with a retired mechanic in the neighborhood who repaired cars in his home garage. As an unpaid apprentice Bob worked under that expert, who taught him the craft and helped him tinker with his own vehicle. Soon Bob was building hot rod engines and sneaking out his bedroom window at night to drag-race (as illegal then as it is today) on San Francisco's Great Highway along the coast. While still in his teens, Bob became a professional mechanic, repairing trucks at night for his father's produce marketing firm. By this time, of course, Leo approved of his son's skills. He even trusted Bob to work on the treasured family car.

Bob continued to race and to build race engines as a sideline through the 1970's. He won many trophies with his "supermodifieds," "altereds," and "sprints. " Upon occasion, he even built engines for race boats with great success.

Bob, about age thirty-two, poses with his car and the trophy he won at the Half Moon Bay drag races.

Racer Takes Shape. Bob Pochini, second from right, shares professional expertise with students in the Auto Center Performance Group at Contra Costa College. They are "upping" the speed potential of a Chrysler engine of a racer planned for completion in time for the Spring drag races.
From the Contra Costa Times, December 21, 1967

Years later, in central Contra Costa County, our auto enthusiast became famous for his diagnostic and repair skills, one of our carpet installers later told me. "We called him 'the Italian.' Whenever we had trouble with a car or truck, we'd go to 'the Italian' for a reliable job."

In his late teens Bob avoided the draft by joining the Air Force. It came as no surprise when he was chosen to repair and maintain aircraft engines . Serving in Korea and specializing in fighter planes, Bob experienced many white-knuckle flights on missions against the North Koreans. The canny Air Force made all of its ground crew mechanics fly missions with the planes they repaired (to keep them competent and honest). With those wild experiences Bob grew to dislike flying; he knew so well what could go wrong with the engines, landing gear, and other vital parts of the aircraft that keep them aloft.

Later in his Air Force career, our personable youth worked as a bartender in his "off" hours while serving " stateside." He could build an incomparable Rob Roy, and his stiff Martinis were dangerous as well as memorable. From that period on, he kept a fully stocked home bar from which he purveyed drinks with great skill and genial hospitality.

While he was young, jazz also caught Bob's interest, and he became an aficionado. With San Francisco the jazz center that it was, he enjoyed following such major performers as Vince Guaraldi, Cal Tjader, Dave Brubeck, and many others. For his own enjoyment he played piano and saxophone, but mainly he was an avid, supportive fan. He and I enjoyed many jazz concerts and festivals, and his musician friends used to wave hello from the bandstand and visit at our table between sets.

In keeping with his interest in food, Bob while in his early teens found work as an apprentice butcher for Hyde Street Meat Market, a few blocks from his Russian Hill home. Besides learning to clean out the cases at night and to concoct the hamburger, Bob acquired inside information about the various cuts from the butchers. His bosses shared their many secrets, and Bob made a note of them all. From then on no one could fool him at the butcher's counter! Our many visits to Petrini's in Walnut Creek and Moraga became adventures in which the finicky cook spurred the counter men to find the appropriate cuts for our proposed dishes.

Unlike the typical American husband, my Italian American sweetheart did not play sports or follow them, much to my joy. My days as a "football widow" ended when I married him. He did like to play games, to hunt, and to fish but not just for enjoyment. He played to win and was a sore loser. If he saw that he couldn't win, he would insist on "folding" and then stop playing. One evening after an especially humiliating loss at Trivial Pursuit at the Cohens' house, he pulled our car over to the curb on the way home and announced, "That's enough! I'm so mad I'm walking home!" I thought he had gone nuts, so I pursued, honking and begging him to get back in. Ignoring me, he walked the two miles home, arriving about 40 minutes after I did, a bit cooler in demeanor, thank goodness.

In a previous life (if you would believe in reincarnation), Bob must have had great expertise in electrical energy and machinery of all kinds. He recalled that he showed aptitudes for this early — changing an electrical socket for a neighbor at age four, beginning to learn at age 10 or so, not only about automobiles but also how other machines work.

Because of this, Bob was a woman's dream husband on household repair and maintenance. He could listen to a machine running and say, "Oh, oh, hear that bearing going out!" He even went so far at one point as to rebuild both our vintage electric dryer and dishwasher. A master of many skills, family oriented, a generous giver but sometimes frugal by contrast, a cordial host, a home lover, Bob had a complex and positive approach to life which enchanted me and earned my loyalty. He not only possessed mastery of many skills, he also showed me how to "do it now." He demonstrated his caring and affection in many ways, doing many thoughtful favors, giving generous gifts, lavishing love on his family, maintaining and enjoying a beautiful home, preparing memorable gourmet dinners for me and for our many guests, and caring enough about himself to present an elegant appearance when appropriate.

Best of all for me, Bob relished his self-appointed role of "man behind the woman." With his support I have accomplished much in my careers of interior design and writing. Thank you, Bob, for giving so generously. I do miss you.

Table of Contents

Introduction

When former *Sunset Magazine* trade publications editor Judy Thompson Hay married chef-trained Bob Pochini and started collaborating with him on four-star quality dinner parties for their family and friends, she realized she had a story on her hands. As a scion of a venerated tradition of restauranteurs, Bob not only could prepare the noteworthy cuisine offered at Pochini's Restaurant for 37 years, he could fuse the concepts of "old-country" Italian dishes with the cutting-edge cuisine and ingredients available in San Francisco, Northern California's gourmet capitol.

Early on, Judy started recording the menus of special occasion luncheons and dinners to which she and Bob treated their guests. She understudied Bob as sous chef and began to learn the secrets and techniques of his cuisine. But her perfectionist husband jealously guarded his hard-earned culinary knowledge. Even his children had to show proper humility before he would share his inside information, literally gained by sitting at the feet of his father, the talented and creative Chef Leo. Gaining admittance to Bob's kitchen was a rare privilege. And he definitely did not give away his recipes. After all, one never knew what liberties an untrained recipient might take.

That this travesty of preparation could happen came home to him when he shared just one family secret, the frittata recipe. Read about it in Living From Bite to Bite / The Frittata Affair, the keynote chapter of this book.

When Bob was diagnosed with inoperable cancer he gave Judy permission to reveal some of the secrets of the Pochini's signature cuisine and their approach to Four-Star Dining at Home. This book with its stories and its presentation of the cuisine carries as well the underlying thread of gentle and loving collaboration between trained chef Bob and sous chef Judy as they presented their many festive dinners. *Buon Appetito!*

The
Stories

Old San Francisco scene

The Frittata Affair

Northern Italian Cuisine With Northern California Flair

For over thirty-five years, Pochini's Italian Restaurant served eager San Francisco patrons. Its varied menu of both simple and spectacular dishes offered Northern Italian cuisine with a California flair.

And what distinguishes Northern Italian cuisine from that of Southern Italy? In brief, Northern cooking uses more butter, cream, and cheese. The flavors are subtle, and fresh herbs give dash. Southern Italian food uses more olive oil and tomatoes and is often spicier, with addition of chiles and other strong flavors.

This book is a collection of anecdotes, with recipes, about a love affair that developed into a marriage that blossomed in a shared passion for cooking by my husband Bob, Leo Pochini's son, and me. It focuses on the events and recipes generated by over one hundred years of Northern Italian/North Beach cooking by Bob's *Genovese* Pochini family of San Francisco. They were professional chefs and home cooks who developed a cuisine that reflects classic Genoan dishes yet blends in the flair of California ingredients and cutting-edge stylings.

The characters in the stories include Bob and me as well as Bob's four children— Liane, Jan, Bud and Gina - all of whom have appreciated and cultivated their father's culinary legacy. Key players include Bob's father and mother, Leo and Jean Pochini; and Leo's parents, Elia and

Rosa Pochini, thus making this book a collection of stories about four generations of Pochinis.

The story begins over one hundred years ago, in 1898, when Elia and Rosa Pochini emigrated from Genoa to San Francisco. What prompted them, both thirty-seven at the time, to give up the life they knew for an unknown new land? Rosa especially must have shed tears as she strung her laundry out on the line to dry in the breezy sunshine of Genoa for the last time. Where would she ever find a place as beautiful as this venerable city overlooking the Ligurian Sea? But friends had written of success and prosperity in San Francisco, and her Elia was eager to take up the challenge of a new life in a new country.

Just as they had bid farewell to friends bound for America in the years before, the Pochinis with Elita, twelve, and Dolly, ten, soon found themselves standing on the dock themselves, with trunks and luggage all marked Destination USA. They wrenched themselves away from a throng of family and friends and boarded the ship.

"Will we ever return?" Rosa wondered out loud.

"I hope so, but possibly not," Elia warned. "Better to think about our new country and how happy and rich we will become." Thus, the Pochinis became part of one of the largest mass migrations in recorded history, of Italians to Europe, North America, and South America in the late Nineteenth and early Twentieth centuries.

The Pochini contingent probably arrived in New York and then made their way across country by train. At this writing, no one remembers the exact details of their journey. We do know they settled in the West.

In San Francisco they met Giuseppe Bazzurro, who had preceded them, arriving in 1897 and working for awhile as a "gardener," as the workers in the produce fields surrounding the city were called, before he opened a restaurant. Of special note, the Italians from Genoa, the *Genovese,* reportedly held a monopoly on the farming of fruits and vegetables as well as the wholesale marketing of their produce in the City. Probably the meeting of Pochini and Bazzuro had been pre-arranged, because upon his arrival Elia immediately went to work for Bazzurro in his restaurant at 118 Pacific Street adjacent to San Francisco's Italian settlement near the old Produce District. Elia soon became a partner in the popular restaurant, becoming sole owner in

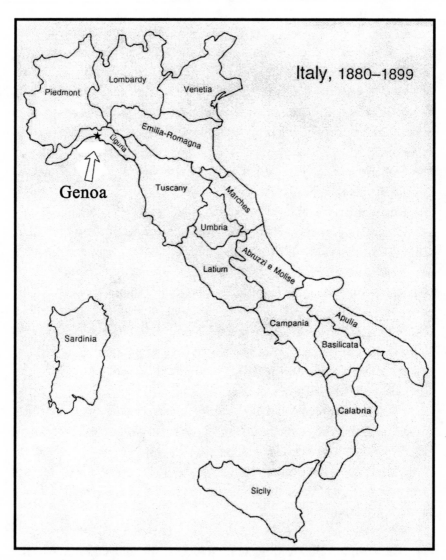

Map of Italy, 1880 -1899. The Pochinis emigrated from the seaport of Genoa on the coast of Liguria.

1905 upon Bazzurro's death, renaming it Pochini's Italian Restaurant, and later moving it around the corner to 618 Front Street, where it remained for the next twenty-nine years.

Two sons, Joseph and Leo, were born in San Francisco after the Pochinis arrived. In the little settlement of North Beach at the foot of Telegraph Hill, the Pochinis and fellow Italians clustered together for sociability and support. The Catholic church, mainly the parish of Saints Peter and Paul, set up a form of settlement house to teach the immigrants survival skills, including the English language and American culture. The Pochinis undoubtedly participated, assimilating successfully into the community. Yet, in North Beach, the Little Italy of San Francisco, they joined others to help preserve the customs, cultures, and traditions they had left behind.

This involved celebrating national holidays of their former home, as well as religious feast days, and even more, the reading of Italian language newspapers and periodicals. Most noteworthy were *La Voce del Popolo* and *L'Italia,* which merged into one daily, *L'Italia,* during the depression (1932). By the 1930's , an "Italian Hour" was offered on the radio. Immigrants, like Rosa Pochini, who developed only limited ability to speak English surely helped keep the Italian-American press in business. For years, *L'Italia* was one of only two Italian dailies in the entire United States, and it was the largest Italian paper west of the Rockies. It continued publication until 1965.

Elia trained his sons in the restaurant business as they matured. This meant having them learn the classic Northern Italian dishes. Shortly before the restaurant closed in 1934, Leo Pochini entered the produce business, but he continued to orchestrate his magical meals for his family and friends on a range in the basement of his Redfield Place home on Russian Hill.

"My father always cooked our meals, and that fascinated me," my yet-to be husband Bob told me one evening as we enjoyed his masterful recreation of a savory Pochini classic, chicken cacciatore with rice. "I was amazed at the dishes he could prepare. By the time I was four, I wanted to get in the kitchen with him and learn. But at that age I was a hindrance, so Dad told me to stay back and sit on the stairs. I could

Sts. Peter and Paul Church, the "Italian Cathedral," on Washington Square.

ask questions if I wanted. I did that for years. He taught me every dish, every secret technique. I literally learned at the feet of my father."

"It sounds as if you had chef's training from a master."

"You've got it."

For years, young Bob persisted in watching from the stairs. Leo's flashing knife action, skillful sautéeing, and deft presentations continued to impress him. "I took full advantage of my father's permission to ask questions," he said. "And I continued asking until I had committed all of the family dishes to memory." Bob told me that he had realized early on that his father cooked dishes unlike any he had tasted at his friends' homes, and that Leo's cuisine was not only more intricate but more savory. He also looked up to his father as a great role model--a totally masculine man who gave considerable skill and commitment to the process of preparing delicious food.

Although Bob never worked as a professional chef, his training under Leo gave him formidable culinary skills. Friends accepted his dinner invitations with joyous expectations.

Later, when I met Leo, I asked him about his years as a chef for Pochini's Restaurant.

"My parents were tough," Leo told me. "Both were exacting, both perfectionists in ingredients, taste, and presentation. My father was especially demanding. At his restaurant I was always cooking under pressure."

"And how did it happen that your father, Chef Elia, became so exacting?" I asked.

"He may have learned in Genoa, before coming here, probably from his father, so I imagine he was put through the same rigorous training and supervision he gave me."

Leo no longer presided over the kitchen by the time I met him. He enjoyed the classic Pochini cuisine as interpreted by Bob and Bob's sister, Gloria Pochini Riccardi; and he gave their dishes his proud approval.

This book includes a major portion of the landmark recipes served at Pochini's Italian Restaurant, brought by Elia and Rosa from Genoa, as well as California recipes developed through the years by the Pochini family chefs and home cooks. The cuisine basically is simple, using lots of fresh produce and fresh meat, fish, and poultry. I present the recipes in simple easy-to-follow steps.

Bob and I began developing *The Frittata Affair* in Fall 1994, several months before he passed away in January, 1995. I am including stories to illustrate his family's warm charm as well as his heritage, this savory cuisine, hoping to tempt you to embrace it for yourself.

Judy Pochini

Food With Love

Ever the innovator, Leo Pochini reversed the tradition of cooking on his first date with Jean Portadino, whom he later married. Bob's mother told me about it one Easter as we were preparing crab meat for her traditional Louis salad.

"A friend had introduced us, and Leo asked me to go to a Sunday afternoon movie. He looked a little like George Raft, only taller and more handsome." A slender lady with gray hair and brown eyes, Jean still savored the romance of life. Bob and I were newlyweds, and she was sharing her own love story.

"Although Leo lived in North Beach area of San Francisco, I lived in the Mission. He came by streetcar all the way from North Beach near downtown and then out on Mission Street to pick me up at my aunt's home above the produce market she owned. Leo and I had plenty of time for conversation all the way into town and back.

"Leo was so polite and friendly, not at all overbearing. He had elegant manners," Jean continued. "So we enjoyed the afternoon. But it was after the movie that the evening became really special." Jean turned to me and smiled as she pried some meat out of a crab leg and added it to our rapidly filling bowl.

"He asked me if I'd like to join him for dinner, and I said yes. And then, you know what he did? He took me to Pochini's, his parents' restaurant, which was closed on Sundays, opened it up, fired up the big

10

range, and cooked a steak dinner just for me." Jean rolled her eyes and gave me a dreamy smile.

"Were you surprised?" I asked. "Did you have any inkling that he might cook for you?" I always did love boy-meets-girl stories, and this one was unusual.

"Yes, I surely was surprised," Jean continued, handing me a whisk and a bowl of ingredients for the Louis dressing. I whisked. She continued.

"Leo went to the huge commercial icebox and pulled out two giant T-bones to grill. While he was firing up the stove, he cut up potatoes, tossed them with a little olive oil, and put them in the oven. He began them raw, didn't precook them, which surprised me. I hadn't seen anyone do that before."

"While he was working on the potatoes, he had me string green beans. Those he steamed until just *al dente*. Then, as I watched, he ran cold water through them so they would stay bright green. I guess that's a chef's secret. When we were ready to eat, he reheated the beans in a skillet with a little olive oil."

"What about the T-bones?" I asked as I tore up the salad greens.

"By this time he was ready to grill those huge steaks. At that point in my life, I liked my steak well-done, and Leo was happy to accommodate me. He did it to just the perfect doneness, of course. And all the time he was cooking he smiled and chatted with me. I must admit I was smitten."

"How romantic. You must have felt giddy."

Jean mused for a moment before replying.

"Yes, it was romantic. I'd had a few boyfriends before but none like Leo. He really made a hit, especially when he set up our table for two by a window and lit a candle. She clasped her hands with joy. "Oh! I had almost forgotten all these details. Can you imagine how impressed I was, at eighteen, to have a date with a handsome man, who happened to be a chef, who was cooking a dinner especially for me, at his restaurant? I could hardly wait for our wedding day."

Oven ~ Fried Potatoes

Use baby potatoes which have been scrubbed well with brush. Cut into bite-size pieces. Toss with olive oil and 1 teaspoon of finely chopped fresh Italian parsley per potato. Place in oiled baking dish. Bake at 350° for about 40 minutes, until you can pierce potatoes easily with a fork. Hold in warm oven until ready to serve.

Sautéed Mushrooms

Select large, firm domestic mushrooms. Scrub well with brush. Place on board stem up and slice 3/8" thick. Heat nonstick skillet. Add 1 tablespoon olive oil and heat. Add mushrooms and sauté, tossing in pan until just brown. **Do not overcook.** Mushrooms should not release juice into pan. Top steak with sautéed mushrooms.

Sautéed Green Beans

Handpick your green beans, one by one. Select for uniform length and girth. Avoid buying beans with blemishes, which would need to be cut out and thus ruin the eye appeal of your beans.

Allow 1/4 pound of beans per person. Wash well in colander and cut off tips and stem ends. Check for strings and remove if necessary. If beans are short, cook them whole. Otherwise, cut beans into two-inch lengths. Place in steamer and steam on Medium until *al dente.* Place in colander and rinse well with cold water to stop cooking process. Beans should be bright green. (If they have turned a dull green, you have overcooked them.) Set aside. Just before serving, heat 1 tablespoon of olive oil in a nonstick skillet. Toss beans in hot oil until heated through. Serve immediately. Optional: Toss beans with slivered almonds for more contrast on the plate.

Grilled Steak

Have butcher cut steaks 1-1/2" thick. One or two hours before dinner, allow the steaks to warm to room temperature. Rub with olive oil. Heat grill or barbecue, so that fifteen to twenty minutes before you plan to serve dinner, it has reached high heat. Place steaks on grill or barbecue and cook on one side until it's charred to your liking. Do *not* turn steaks during this phase, just lift with spatula or fork to check them. After about 5 - 6 minutes steaks should look well grilled on that side. Turn the steaks and grill on the second side 2 - 4 minutes longer, depending on whether you want them rare or well-done. To check doneness, cut into steak with a knife, or press on the steak with index finger. A rare steak will still be pliable, well-done will be firm to the touch. Serve immediately on heated plates.

Portrait of Elia Pochini, circa 1910

BUS. PHONE DAVENPORT 6981   RES. PHONES FRANKLIN 887
                                              PROSPECT 7709

POCHINI'S
ITALIAN RESTAURANT

Banquets and Special Dinners To Order

618 FRONT STREET

Bet. Pacific and Jackson Streets   San Francisco, California

CLOSED SUNDAYS

The Pochini's Italian Restaurant business card

Cravings for Crustaceans

Leo arrived at Fisherman's Wharf early, at eight a.m., just after that morning's crab catch had been cooked. Now the crabbers were pulling the delectable crustaceans out of the vast cauldrons of boiling water and putting them on beds of ice. Clouds of steam enveloped the market, which smelled of the pungent seafood. This sunny day in November marked the opening of the season for Dungeness, the variety caught in the waters of the Golden Gate and highly prized by gourmet and gourmand alike.

Today, opening day, Leo expected the crabbers would have brought in plenty of large ones. He approached Gino, his favorite vendor at this picturesque outdoor market of steaming pots.

"None of your small ones. I want them two pounds or larger, please. Our customers expect an impressive presentation." Leo's voice had power and confidence.

"You can count on me, Leo," Gino shot back, his rubber boots and leather apron already wet with steam. "I always reserve the bigger ones for you. The latecomers get what's left."

"Uncracked as usual?" Gino asked. His powerful build seemed more than adequate to hoist the heavy crab pots out at sea and the cauldrons here on shore.

"Right. I do that my way."

Gino pulled crab after crab from his giant pots, weighed them, and filled two gunny sacks as Leo approved the size of each one.

"Give me half a sack more," Leo requested. "On opening day the entire Financial District comes out."

After hefting the sacks of crab onto his truck, Leo headed for Pochini's Restaurant to start his kitchen duties. Now he would switch roles from burly six-foot tall seafood buyer and hauler to understated co-master of an intricate kitchen.

In his mind Leo reviewed the list of produce he had selected earlier at the wholesale market on Washington Street. "Carrots. Onions. New potatoes. Mushrooms. Zucchini. Crooknecks. Iceberg. Tomatoes. Artichokes. Celery. Peppers. Parsley. *Rapini.* Chard. *Fagioli. Basilico.* Rosemary …"

All would have been delivered by the time he returned to the restaurant. By the time Leo came in bearing the heavy bags of crab, Chef Joe and the kitchen assistant had been working all morning preparing the main menu.

"Ah, *Compa',*" Leo greeted Joe with a quick embrace. Then he started to work on the crab. He and the assistant removed the legs from each crab and placed them cut side down to marinate in shallow bowls of garlic infused olive oil. Soon the kitchen was full of bowls of the marinating legs and ripe with garlic fumes. Then they pried off the "lid" of each crab body to expose the meat and the crab "butter," the yellow deposit inside the body. (Some people pass up the "butter." Others relish it, so Pochini's would serve the "butter" on the side and give diners a choice.) All gray parts were removed and discarded. The bodies then were rinsed and added to the garlic-infused oil marinade. The tops would be replaced for the serving presentation.

Joe meanwhile continued with the main menu items, the normal fare. After the crabs were put in the marinade, Leo paused to check up on things. Chicken Cacciatore? Ready and simmering gently. Polenta? Unmolded, cut into serving portions, and ready to grill. Fresh green beans? The most tender of the season, cooked almost to *al dente,* now cooled with ice water and drained, waiting for a quick reheating with olive oil.

Prawns? Cooked and peeled, waiting for a quick sautéeing with olive oil and garlic. Rice? Partially cooked, ready to bring up once diners placed their orders.

Louis dressing? Ready and waiting to top those salads of tiny bay shrimp or crabmeat with slices of hard-cooked egg, tomato, celery, and iceberg lettuce.

Cuneo's famous Italian sourdough bread? Sliced and ready in baskets to accompany the cracked crab and the Louis salads.

Steaks and chops? Prime, thick, and juicy, waiting in the icebox.

Meanwhile, Chef Elia, recently self-appointed to the post of executive chef, and now manning the reception for Pochini's, had been on the phone all morning. No more chef's uniform for him. These days he dressed in hand-tailored vested suits. As he stood at his post, the sunlight streaming in over the white cottage curtains caught the sheen of wax on his handlebars and the gentle waves of his dark gray hair.

"Mr. Stark? Elia here, over at Pochini's. You told me to call you when I have crab. Well, today's opening day. How many in your party? Fine. See you at noon."

"Mr. Sutro?" "Mr. Edgerly?" "Mr. Pillsbury?" "Mr. ...?"

By 11:30 he had sold all of the crab presentation luncheons. Anyone else could have Crab Louis from the overage that Leo had brought in. And if they sold out, they would tell any disappointed customers to make reservations for the next day.

The opening of the crab season was a big occasion for San Franciscans. At 11:45 the first diners arrived, their mouths watering. Orders were taken for Crab Louis salads for any drop-ins. All of the cracked crab had been reserved.

And in the kitchen Leo and Joe had the platters ready. First they had removed the crab from the oil and garlic marinade. With heavy mallets they had cracked the crab bodies gently, just enough to loosen the intricate honeycomb of shell. They had centered the bodies on the platters of shaved ice and placed the outer shell on each as a cap. Legs had been carefully assembled on boards and cracked and then placed on the platters in natural order around the bodies as if the crab were still whole. Wedges of lemon, sprays of parsley, and radish roses provided garnish.

Promptly at 12:00, a limousine rolled up with sugar magnate Adolph Spreckels and several of his friends.

"Ah, Mr. Spreckels, welcome!" Elia said, taking the gray felt homburgs of the suited and vested party and placing them on the coatroom shelf. "I've saved a table for you right in the window. Come this way. We'll be out with your crab as soon as we fill your drink order."

Once the beverages had arrived at the Spreckels' table, Elia signaled to the kitchen for action. Quickly Leo picked up a platter of crab. Beaming, he carried the platter around the restaurant, showing off his beautiful display of San Francisco's favorite seafood to the diners at each table. After enjoying the many comments of approval, Leo finally took the platter to the expectant group at the Spreckels table and placed it in the center with a grand flourish.

"Ah, Leo," Spreckels beamed. "Another of your culinary triumphs. Thank you."

Once back in the kitchen, Leo joined the others feverishly preparing the remaining platters of crab. They marched into the dining room single file, each bearing a platter and delivering it to one of the fortunate tables. Soon the first deliveries were over; diners resumed their busy hum of conversation, and the restaurant became calm once again. The delicacy, long anticipated over the off-season summer months finally sat on plates in front of them and the patrons were sighing with satisfaction as they cracked the crab legs, extracted the succulent meat, and dipped it in the sauces provided. Quaffs of white wine and bites of sourdough bread gave welcome contrast to the richness of the crab.

After the diners had finished consuming the crab and other specialties, the waiters circulated filling orders for desserts, coffee, and additional wine. Cigars were lit, and people started to relax. Some of the v.i.p. tables pulled out a bit of paper work to review and discuss. Everyone beamed in satisfaction. Tabs were signed or paid. Coats and hats were retrieved. The crowd began to leave.

In the midst of the calm, a limousine pulled up outside. Elia wondered who it could be. He had no further reservations, and particularly none for the crab, long ago sold out. He looked out at the impressive automobile. Who would emerge? He sucked in his breath as he recognized Mr. Madison, a noted attorney. Oh, oh. Had he erred in his note-taking? Had Mr. Madison made a reservation which did not get in the book? If he wanted crab, Pochini's could do it, but it would take some effort.

"Elia!" Mr. Madison greeted him with enthusiasm. "Sorry to pop by so late on opening day, but I was across town, in court all morning and wasn't sure I could get away. Any chance you can take me and my group?" Five of his top legal staff were filing in behind him.

"Of course we can accomodate you," Elia smiled, bowing with elegance. "Sorry about the cigar smoke. You know how it gets, late in the hour. I'll open the door so it will clear. Right this way."

"No need to bother with menus." Madison said. "We're here for the crab, of course."

"Mr. Madison, we will be happy to serve you our special version of cracked crab, but it will take about an hour. Can I interest you and your friends in an aperitif and an appetizer before lunch? That will make the wait go faster."

"By all means," the powerful attorney replied. "After all, we came late. We can discuss our case while you prepare."

Elia dashed into the kitchen to alert Leo and Joe of the emergency. Quickly, they decided to send the dishwasher by taxi to the Wharf for the crab, which they ordered by phone. Fifteen minutes down and fifteen back would make thirty minutes. Maybe the young man could shave it to twenty. Then the crab had to be prepared and marinated. Without the infusion of olive oil and garlic, it just wouldn't taste like the Pochini's famous cracked crab.

Giullio the dishwasher dashed out of the front door and galloped through the final stages of the Pacific Street section of the Produce Market. He dodged handtrucks of produce going into vans for the day's final delivery. All was a cacophony of truck engines revving and idling, horns blowing, men calling, cars threading in and out. Chaos was the order of the day. Reaching the end of the block, Giullio found a waiting cab and hopped in.

Hand trucks of produce clog Washington Street at dawn in the produce market. Hundreds of produce buyers rose before daylight to make purchases from San Francisco's fruit and vegetable dealers.

Photo courtesy of San Francisco History Center, San Francisco Public Library

A. Galli Fruit Co. shared a corner with L. Scatena & Co. at the old produce market. Pochini's Italian Restaurant at Front and Pacific was just a block or two away.

The legendary banker A.P. Giannini began his business career here at age twelve, working for his stepfather Lorenzo Scatena. Giannini went on to found the Bank of Italy, which became the giant Bank of America. Inspired by Giannini's business and financial acumen, Bob and his partner Chuck Clemmons used the banking tycoon's initials, A.P., when they founded AP Equipment Sales many years later. Happily, the two partners achieved financial success with their venture.

Photo courtesy of San Francisco History Center, San Francisco Public Library

Shortly he arrived back at the kitchen entrance with his butcher paper packages of crab. Grabbing them from him, Leo and Joe sprang into action, working with feverish rapidity. Within five minutes, the crabs were in the marinade and the crew was setting up the two platters. Leo and Joe arranged them with a flourish. Twenty-five minutes later, Leo and Joe emerged from the kitchen triumphant with their magnificent offerings. The Madison table, one of the few still occupied at that late hour, oohed and aahed appreciably as they viewed the delicacy.

Elia stood facing Mr. Madison, pardonably proud of this latest feat accomplished by his two well-trained sons.

"Well, Elia, you did it again." The king of the courtroom beamed with approval. "Another incredible culinary favor. I'll never forget you or Pochini's Restaurant. You're the standard bearer for excellent cuisine."

"Thanks, Mr. Madison. We hope you'll come again." Elia gave an understated reply to mask his huge pride. "Whatever you ask, we'll do our best to deliver." Then he retreated to the kitchen with Leo and Joe. *"Madonna!* I think we're all a bit weak in the knees over that one! Congratulations, boys. I knew you could do it."

Note: Material for this reconstructed account was provided to me by Gordon E. Hay, who had been a rising young executive of that day, and by my own experiences in the Financial District, Produce Market and Fisherman's Wharf in later years. .... Judy

Cracked Crab a la Pochini

1 whole fresh crab, cooked but not cleaned, shell intact
1 bulb garlic
1 - 2 cups virgin olive oil
3 fresh lemons (divided)
1 cup mayonnaise
1 6-ounce jar pepperoncini (pickled baby peppers)

Peel garlic cloves and slice. Place in olive oil in medium size mixing bowl. Let stand for an hour if possible. Pull legs off chilled crab. Place in garlic-infused oil "cut" side down, to marinate. (Remainder of legs will "drape" over outside of bowl.) Let "stand" (marinate) for one hour. (Refrigerate in the marinade if longer than one hour). The oil infusion will travel the length of the legs.

Meanwhile, pry "lid" off the crab body. Remove yellow "butter," place in serving dish, and refrigerate. Clean out and discard gray parts inside body, leaving only meat. Place cleaned bodies meat side down into bowl of oil to marinate.

Whisk juice of one lemon into mayonnaise. Place in serving bowl and chill.

To serve, reassemble crab and its legs on a bed of crushed ice or lettuce leaves on a large platter. Replace top on crab's body. Serve with cut halves of two lemons, lemon-mayonnaise, crab "butter," pepperoncini, sourdough bread, and butter. Supply bibs, large napkins, crab-cracking tools, picks, and seafood forks.

This dish is messy! Follow with finger bowls. Serves two or three.

Crab Louis See recipe for Seafood Louis on Page 34.

Intersection of Union and Taylor, Russian Hill, San Francisco

The 900 block of Union Street, where the Pochinis built their home

View of Alcatraz and Angel Island from the 900 block of Union Street

Christmas in San Francisco

Christmas had brought forth San Francisco at its sparkling best. From the bay windows of the Pochinis' spacious home on Russian Hill's Union Street you could see Fisherman's Wharf below and then, Alcatraz and Sausalito across San Francisco Bay. In the distance, white sails as small as the tip of your fingernail glided across the water, some cruising around the Bay, others going back and forth under the dramatic red suspension bridge spanning the Golden Gate. The wind-driven sails seemed idyllic.

Feast preparation, which had begun several days before, hummed along at fast tempo. Noni (Grandmother Rosa) and Auntie Elita had risen early to prepare the soup and begin work on the Crab Louis, the Pochinis' traditional holiday salad. Below the flat and across the back garden, Chef Leo was checking on a giant turkey roasting in his oven, while his wife Jean was bisecting with deft hands two layers of her special chocolate cake Between the four layers she would sandwich her filling of bananas and whipped cream before frosting with satiny chocolate. Their daughter Gloria was stirring the "gravy" (marinara sauce) for the ravioli Noni had made on Christmas Eve. Their son Bob was running errands as requested.

The savory fragrances of the turkey and the marinara sauce blended temptingly with the complex sweet smell of the chocolate and bananas. In between errands, Bob was playing with his lifelong buddy Fred Biagini, who lived next door. Fred's grandfather owned the famous restaurant Fior d'Italia in the North Beach business district, so Fred and his family probably would be having their holiday dinner at Fior d'Italia. Meantime, he was hanging around with Bob and enjoying the hustle-bustle.

By contrast, just 80 miles away, in Stockton, where Chef Joe Pochini and his family now lived, dense tule fog hugged the ground. Visibility: zero in that riverside community. Joe with his wife, Ida, and sons Leo and Jack, would be driving to the The City with their share of special Christmas dishes and desserts. With Chef Elia's retirement and the closure of Pochini's Restaurant in San Francisco, Joseph had taken a job in Stockton, where his wife's relatives lived . Undaunted by the dense fog so usual for Stockton in the winter, Chef Joe and his family would be driving through the Delta to Concord and then around the Bay to the newly constructed Bay Bridge, spanning the Bay from Oakland to Yerba Buena Island and then to San Francisco.

(Sadly, Chef Elia had passed on just the year before, in 1939, so he was not part of this year's celebration.)

Inside the Pochinis' Russian Hill flat, poinsettias bloomed in pots, swags of holly draped the mantel and the door tops, and bunches of mistletoe dangled from the entry light and the double doors to the living room. But the party would not take place here. Instead, the banqueters would hold forth in the social hall downstairs on the ground floor, which also had a magnificent view. The dining table had been carried down. Stretched to the max, it filled the hall. Chairs came from everywhere— bedrooms, the storeroom, even from Chef Leo's satellite home which he had built on Redfield Place, just below the back garden of his parents' home.

"Bob, dear, please run home and bring another chair," Noni called as she double-checked her place settings. "Otherwise, we won't have a place for you," she teased. She had dressed her table in her best cutwork cloth from Italy, along with the fine china, crystal goblets, and sterling that she had acquired over the years as Pochini's Restaurant had prospered. Crystal candelabra dripped with cut bobeches to match the chandelier.

Typical terraced garden below a home, 900 block of Union Street

Bob Pochini and his friend Fred in front of a Redfield Place garage
Photo courtesy of Fred Biagini

Wild area at the end of Redfield Place where Bob and Fred played as children

Liguria Bakery, a venerable North Beach producer of focaccia, now located on the northeast corner of Stockton and Filbert. Bob Pochini was a regular customer and a close friend of Gus Soracco, the founder's grandson.

A mirrored platform on the living room table set off a low bowl filled with holly and red berries from Podesta-Baldocchi, the elegant florist on Grant near Sutter.

At the appointed hour, the guests converged upon the social hall, everyone bearing offerings. In addition to the across-the-garden Pochinis and the Stockton Pochinis, were the San Franciscans, Auntie Irene with her husband, and Auntie Dolly with her husband and daughter. They arrived laden with treasures from their kitchens—antipasto, roast meats, and desserts.

"Merry Christmas, Mama." Chef Joe kissed his mother on the cheek. "We brought roast pork loin from the Rizzos' farm, as you asked. Have you kept those rolls from Cuneo out of Leo's reach? I've looked forward to having at least one or two."

"Season's Greetings," Irene and Dolly chorused as they entered. "Where do you want these desserts? We made baby cream puffs again this year; everyone seems to like them so much."

Bob meanwhile gave a mute high-sign to his cousin Jack, just three years older. "Fred and I have built a fort in the alley. Come on."

Finally, everyone, all of the family, had arrived with their offerings, everything was ready, and everyone was calling for the antipasto. Before the plates of vegetable frittatas could be passed, Bob and Jack vied with each other to see how many morsels each could steal before being caught. Practiced miscreants, each one gulped down six or seven before Leo saw them. "No, no, boys." He slapped their hands playfully. "Please let us have a chance." The merriment continued as platters of salami, prosciutto, copacola, provolone, and smoked jack cheese made their way around the table.

Next came the soup, a creamy cauliflower made by Noni early that morning. "I can detect just a hint of nutmeg. Right, Noni?" Joe asked.

Leo answered for her. "You remember how father always had us put in just a hint. It takes a real palate to figure that one out."

"Here's the offering from Fisherman's Wharf," Jean announced as she served the plates of Crab Louis. "We went down to the Wharf at eight, just as these had finished boiling. You can't get fresher crab."

"And no better Louis salads than Jean's and Elita's," Joe's wife Aida said in admiration. Everyone took a deep breath of satisfaction as the salad plates were cleared.

Next came the ravioli with sauce and grated Parmesan cheese. "Noni, these are your best ever," Jack proclaimed as he finished a second helping. "I agree," Bob echoed. "May I please have more?"

"Hold off, boys," Leo warned as he rose to bring the turkey, roasted to succulent perfection. On a giant platter, he had fanned perfect slices of breast accented by the crisp browned skin . Slices of thigh and leg meat centered the platter, which was garnished by twists of orange and sprigs of Italian parsley from his kitchen garden. Chef Joe, as well, laid out his platter of roast pork with deft precision, fanning the slices and adding garnish. After all, to the Pochinis, presentation was paramount in tempting the diners.

"Me for the white meat." "I want the dark." "Where's the neck? That's my favorite piece." "More celery root, anyone? How about some eggplant?" Platters of crispy fried artichoke hearts, celery root, and eggplant were being passed.

Notably absent from this immigrant Italian Christmas feast: cranberry sauce and dressing. The Pochinis had not embraced either of those traditional American holiday dishes.

"Do we have any rolls left?" Joe asked. "I saw Leo steal at least eight before dinner, and I had to hide the basket before he had eaten them all. I'm amazed, Leo, that you don't weigh a ton. I hope you own a share of Cuneo Bakery so you can profit from such addiction."

Everyone laughed. Before last summer's picnic, Leo had stolen and eaten all of the sourdough rolls before anyone had realized it. Now he was the butt of much teasing, and today lookouts stood vigilant watch over the tempting, chewy buns.

"Well done, everyone," Noni announced as everyone tapered off with satisfied sighs. "Time for you all to get out of here for awhile while we clear things away and set up for dessert. Don't forget to bring your appetites back."

With that, everyone rose and helped clear the table.

"Dad, please take Jack and me for a ride on the Bay." Bob tugged at Leo's sleeve.

"I could take you to Playland at Beach instead. We have time, I think."

"Oh, yes, yes! Playland!." Bob and Jack cried.

"I'm going with you." Jack's older brother Leo announced.

And so everyone departed, some for Playland at the Beach, others for a ferry ride on the Bay, others for a cable car ride down Columbus Avenue to Fisherman's Wharf.

Two hours later, when the revellers returned, they saw a buffet table laden with the dessert makers' finest: Jean's chocolate cake, Irene's and Dolly's profiteroles (tiny cream puffs), dates stuffed with walnuts, assorted biscotti, golden layer cake, and more.

"How can we choose?" Aida asked.

"Don't choose, dear. Try a little of everything. It's Christmas," Noni advised.

The boys, of course, took giant portions and then went back for seconds. They knew that feasts don't happen every day.

After the sweet treats, Leo pulled hot chestnuts from the oven and tossed them directly onto the tablecloth for everyone to shell and enjoy with glasses of dessert wine and coffee.

As the adults settled back for conversation over coffee, the children were excused and returned to Redfield Place to play.

Bob groaned with joyful pain. "Maybe I'll eat less next year."

Recipes:

Cauliflower Soup See Page 130.

Noni's Antipasto See Page 107.

Marinara Sauce See Page 272.

Roast Chestnuts See Page 290.

Noni's Chocolate Cake See Page 289.

San Francisco Seafood Louis

When I arrived in San Francisco in the 1950's, Louis salads usually arrived at our table in large wooden bowls, seemingly filled to the brim with seafood and accompaniments and topped with a tart shrimp-colored dressing. Halfway down into the bowl, we'd come to the end of the "goodies" and find nothing but undressed shreds of whiteish iceberg lettuce. Today I present a Louis on a bed of romaine or mixed field greens. Additionally, I make a point of tossing any "bed" for a salad in a light dressing of extra virgin olive oil and wine vinegar to give my greens taste appeal. Consequently, few of my salad plates return to the kitchen laden with greens.

Dressing
8 heaping tablespoons Best Foods Real Mayonnaise
2 tablespoons extra virgin olive oil
2 tablespoons prepared cocktail sauce
1/4 cup lemon juice
1 teaspoon Worcestershire sauce
1 teaspoon garlic powder

Mix well. Place in refrigerator until ready to serve.

The Seafood
1 pound baby shrimp, fresh, or frozen and thawed or 1 pound shelled crab meat, or ½ pound of each combined
1 tablespoon tarragon white wine
½ teaspoon dried dill weed
2 tablespoons extra virgin olive oil

Thaw shrimp, if frozen, on a dinner plate covered with two paper towels. Midway through the thaw, drain and replace with two fresh paper towels. Blot shrimp well when fully thawed. Toss shrimp with other ingredients and place in refrigerator to marinate.

Shred crab into bite-size pieces as necessary.

<u>The Greens and the Garnish</u>
Mixed field greens or chopped romaine, well drained
Two large tomatoes, peeled and cut into wedges
4 hard-boiled eggs cut into wedges
1 or 2 avocados, peeled and sliced
Celery: 1 small rib for each serving
Lemon wedges

Toss lettuce with oil and vinegar and place on plates. Top with marinated shrimp, or shredded crabmeat or a combination of both, and alternating wedges of tomatoes, eggs, and avocado slices. Decorate each salad with a leafy rib of celery and 2 lemon wedges. Top with a dollop of dressing and pass extra dressing. Makes eight "course" size luncheon salads or four full-meal salads.

How I Met Bob Pochini
and Then ...

Slamming my wine glass down on the nearest table, I huffed out, turning my face skyward and saying, "Well, Lord, why do you get my hopes up and then disappoint me like this? I really thought that this guy was the one."

The circumstances which drew Bob Pochini and me into the same orbit had seemed so fortuitous, up until that moment when I had decided to walk out of the Smokeless Singles mixer. The serendipity leading me to that handsome man with the gray hair and winning smile had all seemed perfect. Now my opportunity to attract him for a date had de-materialized. He hadn't even asked for my number. Defeated and disappointed, I stalked away. It *was* a singles mixer, and he *had* seemed attracted. What had held him back?

The series of events that had prompted me to attend the party flashed through my mind. Somehow I had been led to that scene, and surely he had not appeared there by accident. What people and events had caused our meeting and aborted liaison? Let's see ...

On that day I was wearing a "handed down" ensemble. My sister had made the beautiful Italian print velvet skirt for herself and had paired a top with it. Later she had passed them along to me. I had added a coordinating scarf that I had inherited from our grandmother. In my pre-owned and gently worn ensemble I felt stylish and elegant, and I had experienced a happy and successful day at my interior design job.

My trip home from Berman's Drexel Heritage Showroom in Oakland included a stop at Ed Benstein's upholstery studio in Concord to drop off a roll of fabric. Ed and I conducted our brief business with friendly jollity, and as I was leaving he remarked, "Gee, honey, you look cute tonight." Ed's compliment served as the trigger on the gun shooting me forward. Buoyed with confidence, I decided to drop in on the Smokeless Singles at their Friday night mixer. They met just a few blocks away, at Hobie's Roadhouse on Concord's downtown Todos Santos Plaza. "Ed says I look great," I reflected. "Maybe I should try that singles group just one more time." I had attended their mixer once before and had enjoyed the people I had met. My friend Jeanne Gulick had recommended that group to me, and she was engaged to a man she had met at one of the mixers. So Jeanne figured in this plot as well.

Hobie's Roadhouse on Todos Santos Plaza, Concord

At the mixer I met and chatted with several interesting people. Then I experienced a lull with no one around me. I looked across the room and there stood a handsome gray-haired man with flashing brown eyes and a huge smile. He was speaking animatedly with three women who were giving him their rapt attention. I observed the group and noticed that although the man did not beckon to me he did keep smiling my way as he alternately spoke and listened. *Three women, and I'd be adding a fourth. Pretty stiff odds against even getting close to this guy.*

But I was drawn over to the group. Remembering my cattle-herding techniques as a farm child, I worked myself into the group, edging one woman out as I did so. She peeled off. That left two between me and my goal. One of them finally concluded that she needed a change of company and she left. One other woman, Bob Pochini and I remained. He and I began talking more between the two of us, but my persevering rival had staked him out for herself. She showed strong determination and kept talking and staying. Not wishing to seem impolite to either of us, Bob continued his animated discourse. I found Bob witty, debonair, and polite. He attracted me more than anyone else I had met in years. I had made my Treasure Map and he even looked like the man whose picture I had pasted into my section on romance.

I was hoping Bob would ask for my number and perhaps even for a date. Yes, the other woman and her yakety banter distracted us both, but he did appear to be paying more attention to me. Surely he would find a way to draw me aside or signal me. But he did not. Time passed and nothing happened.

Finally, I decided to give up. That's when I excused myself, slammed my glass on a nearby table, and left.

Disgusted, I strode down the sidewalk toward the parking lot. Then I heard the sound of "human hoofbeats" behind me. "Judy, Judy," a man's voice called as he ran up behind me. It was Bob. Out of breath, he assured me that he wanted to see me again but had not wanted to appear rude to the other lady and ask for my number in front of her. When I had turned to leave he realized then that he would have to make a quick exit in pursuit. After all, he might never see me again. Because Bob was a stranger, I gave him my business card, not my home number.

A week elapsed. No call from Bob Pochini. I began to steel myself against the disappointing possibility that he might not call. One mornimg the following week he did telephone and we set a date for dinner the next Saturday.

On the appointed evening, as I stood at my kitchen sink enjoying the view of Mt. Diablo to the east and tidying up, I heard the provocative "varoom, varoom" of a powerful engine. Down the private lane came Bob driving an elegant, sporty white Datsun 240 Z . Bob himself looked assured and handsome in his Harris tweed sport jacket which set off his muscular build. And that's where his daughter Liane enters the plot. She later told me that months before she had helped him select the Harris tweed as a special-occasion jacket.

Well, that first date was a special occasion. To break the ice, I offered glasses of my finest "jug" wine with crackers and cheese. I decided to introduce my dogs right away, figuring they could help me judge Bob's character. Bob agreed to meet them, so I went to the kitchen door. Katie, the Irish setter, and Mike, the ridgeback/shepherd, bounded in from the back patio. After enthusiastic "hi-di-hi's" and joyous tail-wagging, my two canine pals sat as close to Bob's chair as they could. Bob liked the dogs, and they liked him. He had passed the test.

Over several glasses of wine Bob and I shared a few "opening thoughts." Did he have a dog? Not now, but he had enjoyed Hunter, the mixed breed watch dog who had guarded the ranch he once had owned in Calistoga. We went on to special interests. Cooking? Career scope? Hobbies? The usual exchange.

Then we climbed into that glamorous "Z-car" for the drive to La Tour, a gourmet Belgian restaurant in downtown Concord. "Your table isn't quite ready, Mr. Pochini. How about some champagne while you wait?" At the tiny entrance, crowded with other would-be diners, we exchanged more life details as we sipped our champagne and waited.

"Do you have children?" Bob asked. "No," I replied. " God did not choose to send them my way. How about you?"

"I do. I have four, all college age and older, each just a year apart – Liane, Bud, Jan, and Gina."

"Four in four years," I exclaimed. "Well, that's a clutch you have there! What a challenge it must have been to keep those four in line."

"Oh, you bet! It's been a project ever since they arrived."

The hostess then seated us. The spectacular dinner included potato-leek potage served with flair, house salad garnished with savory cheese puffs, then our entrées. I had the salmon; Bob chose the sweetbreads. For dessert we enjoyed a special chocolate torte. We finished the evening with cordials at T.R.'s, a turn-of-the-century period restoration jazz club in a former bank building on Todos Santos Plaza. The mahogany bar and back bar, relics from California's Gold Country, set off tapestry covered furnishings, and we enjoyed the cool jazz.

Bob not only dressed with dash. He also enjoyed hosting a fine dinner. I felt honored to have attracted him. Did I want to see him again? Yes! As we were driving home, I decided to throw out a little bait. At the Mimosa Café near Berman's in Oakland, impromptu jazz jam sessions were held every Sunday afternoon. I knew Bob liked jazz. He grabbed the lure and reeled me right in. "Yes, why don't we go?"

Bob and I went from that auspicious beginning to a quick knowledge that we wished to see just each other, eventually marrying about a year later. We shared many joyful interests besides jazz, such as camping in trailers and even under the camper shell of a pickup truck, remodeling our homes, building new garages and shops, collaborating on furniture which we mutually designed and which Bob built, entertaining our friends and family with gusto, viewing vintage movies, touring wineries to buy wine for our cellar, and many more. We were together for more than twelve years, exchanging witticisms and pleasantries as we collaborated. I treasured Bob's refreshing wit, his rapt attention to life's details, and especially his prowess in the kitchen. With him as my loving partner in life, business, and romance, I felt inspired to do my most creative and artistic work, whether it was designing a home, coordinating a becoming wardrobe, composing an appetizing salad, or writing a book. He and I played off each other with positive energy that motivated each of us to achieve our best.

Our First Christmas Dinner

Christmas was coming, and our two-month-old romance was blossoming like a giant poinsettia. Bob and I were spending almost every evening together. Yet, at this point, it was too early in our happy liaison for Bob to take me with him to Christmas dinner with his family; and I had my own responsibility to go home to Santa Barbara for Christmas and New Year's with my mother. We thus could not be together on Christmas day.

"Let's celebrate our Christmas early," Bob suggested one evening. "I'll cook a special dinner."

I quickly accepted Bob's invitation. We could be together in spirit only on the actual Christmas day, but we could have our own private banquet ahead of time. That way neither of us would have to worry about whether our parents would accept the newcomer.

I myself knew that my mother would resist Bob's charms, if only for a moment, because he was "foreign," an Italian-American boy who grew up in the ethnic neighborhood of North Beach. Bob's family sounded charming, but they were old-line Italian-Americans. I knew they would scrutinize me carefully before accepting me. I not only had no Italian blood, I was not even a San Francisco girl but a transplant from Phoenix and Santa Barbara. How would they feel about my background?

These were questions we would face after the holidays when the actual moments of moments of introduction came. In the meantime, we could hold a private Christmas revelry without concern for any of that.

Although I had to work on the Saturday before Christmas, Bob did not. He offered to prepare and host the entire dinner without my help. My sweetheart took to his task with enthusiasm, announcing to me that he planned to stage an elaborate party. He kept his menu secret, and the mystery tantalized me.

After work on the appointed evening, I dressed in an elegant long black knit dress and my grandmother's pearls. I wore a black velvet coat, just as if I were heading for the opera.

When Bob opened the door and took in my festive attire, his eyes grew wide.

"Great outfit. Good thing we're not dining out, here in Pittsburg. You look so rich we'd be mugged."

Tempting aromas emanated from the kitchen. I wanted to peek at dinner in progress, but Bob steered me to a seat by the fire. He popped the cork on a bottle of champagne and poured flutes for us.

"Merry Christmas," He toasted as he handed a glass to me.

I smiled back: "Merry Christmas."

Disappearing into the kitchen, Bob quickly returned carrying the most unusual appetizer I had ever tasted– venison pâté. He had found a small piece of leftover venison in the freezer, he explained, and so had devised that extraordinary concoction.

"Your creative pâté delights my palate," I told Bob as I nibbled on a Triscuit spread with the finely chopped, slightly gamey meat in its secret emulsion.

Bob accepted the compliment with pride. "Thanks. I hope it doesn't outshine the dinner."

After our champagne and pâté, Bob led me away from the fire and into the romantically darkened dining room. A single candle lit the table for two.

My host then brought forth bowls of creamy cauliflower soup, warm and savory on that chill and foggy winter night. To accompany the soup, he poured a California chardonnay. We again toasted each other as our shadows flickered on the dimly lit walls. "Merry Christmas."

I wanted to add that I hoped it would be the first of many, but I held back. We were dating each other exclusively, but we were not yet engaged. I did not want to appear premature in my hopes.

Bob then served a small Crab and Shrimp Louis. We talked of the coming Christmas we would spend with our families and then of our planned reunion in Santa Barbara for New Year's. He would arrive by Amtrak on December 29. I had not yet met Bob's parents, but he soon would meet my mother. Hopefully, he would win her approval.

After the salad course, Bob retired to the open kitchen to assemble the main event. What delights would emerge from the covered pots and the closed oven? I wondered. Soon I learned. Bob removed a roast duckling from the oven and skilfully began to carve, first removing the legs and wings and then carving the breast into slices. He placed the duck on our plates. Next he quickly sautéed precooked green beans with a little olive oil and chopped parsley, and served that. Then he uncovered another pot which yielded wild rice with mushrooms. A slice of orange centered with a sprig of Italian parsley provided accent.

"What succulent looking duck," I exclaimed. The presentation was as artistic as it was tempting. I noted the crisp skin and the slightly rare breast meat fanned in slices next to the leg and a sauce giving a bit of sheen.

"*Buon appetito.*" Bob picked up his fork and invited me to start. The beautiful plate of tender, slightly rare duck and its accompanying side dishes delighted my eyes as well as my taste buds. Duck prepared by an Italian chef. Another new dining experience.

"Thank you, Bob, dear. This is magnificent. You couldn't have given me a more generous Christmas gift than this dinner."

"My pleasure. Speaking of Christmas, have you sent your letter to Santa yet ?" Bob was pouring Chateau Diana zinfandel. "Do you have a special wish?"

"Oh, I haven't placed my requests yet. Too busy helping my design clients get their houses ready for the holidays to come up with any wishes for myself. How about you?"

"Bobbie is asking Santa for a new VCR this year. And Bobbie is going to help Santa along with his project by picking it up next week."

My, I thought, this man doesn't mind lavishing a little gift on himself once in awhile. I wonder what he does for others …

"Sounds like a great idea," I commented. "Who but you could know exactly what you want?"

Bob reflected for a moment on his approach to getting exactly what he wanted for Christmas.

"That's the way I look at it." He replied.

Then he rose, removed our plates, and commented on the next course as he strolled into his orderly kitchen.

"Dessert will take awhile, and I can't guarantee it will turn out on the first try. You can kibitz while I work. I'm going to make zabaglione, and it's tricky. Sometimes you have to throw the entire batch away and prepare another."

Despite his disclaimer, Bob knew his way around zabaglione preparation. With a deft hand he combined the eggs, cream, sugar, and Marsala in a double boiler until done to perfection.

"Zabaglione, and made to order just for me. I feel really privileged."

"You should." Bob gave me a commanding look. "I don't make this effort for just everyone, you know."

Bob's zabaglione turned out to be perfect, of course. It tasted creamy and smooth and deliciously rich.

After that, Bob made expresso, brewed in a stovetop pot, rather than an electric machine. Again, my sweetheart worked with skill. He coaxed steaming cups of thick coffee out of the complicated looking contraption. I hadn't had expresso at home before, just in Italy at expresso bars. Bob's interest in serving it at home predated by many years the current rage for pressure-brewed coffees. The first sip was exotic, a true Italian experience right at home.

Picking up a plate of homemade biscotti, Bob led the way back to the family room. He gestured to his well stocked bar. "Amaretto? Galliano?" I chose Amaretto. The nuttiness of the liqueur complimented the sweets and coffee.

"You'll never top this dinner, Bob, dear." I drew him close for a kiss.

Bob's eyes sparkled with satisfaction. He gave me a meaningful look. "I want you to remember me while you're away."

Venison Pâté

2 cups finely chopped cooked venison meat
1 yellow onion, finely chopped
2 cloves of garlic, finely chopped
2 hard-cooked eggs, finely chopped
½ cup ground almonds
1/8 teaspoon hot pepper sauce
1/4 teaspoon salt
1/8 teaspoon ground pepper
2 tablespoons Cognac
Mayonnaise

Mix all ingredients except Mayonnaise. Add just enough Mayonnaise to make a stiff paste. Put in bowl or container. Chill for three hours. Serve as a spread on crackers or baguette rounds. Makes about two cups.

Roast Duckling

One large duckling, 4 to 5 pounds
Salt

Preheat oven to 425°. Remove giblets from cavity of duck. Wash bird well. Pat dry with paper towels. Sprinkle salt inside cavity. Place on rack on roasting pan. Roast at 425° for 30 minutes to render fat. Pour off fat. Reduce oven temperature to 375°. Roast for an additional 2 to 3 hours, for a 4- to 6- pound duck. Duck will be done when a leg moves easily when wiggled. To carve, remove wings and legs, slice breast. To serve, fan slices of breast on each plate, add a leg or a wing. Using a bulb baster, drizzle a slight amount of pan drippings over duck.

Zabaglione

6 egg yolks
2-1/2 tablespoons sugar
1/3 cup dry marsala or sherry
dash nutmeg
1 teaspoon lemon juice

In the top part of a double boiler, beat together the egg yolks and sugar until pale and thick. Beat in remaining ingredients. Set on top of boiler pan base containing gently simmering water. Using a wire whisk or electric beater, beat constantly for 3 to 5 minutes, until mixture is just thick enough to retain a peak for a few seconds. Remove from heat and pour into stemmed glasses. Serve immediately. Makes 4 to 6 servings.

Recipes:
Biscotti See Page 286.
Cauliflower Soup See Page 130.
Sautéed Green Beans See Page 12.
San Francisco Seafood Louis See Page 34.
Wild Rice With Mushrooms See Page 218.

Cordially inviting you . . .
to join us at our
Wedding Reception
on
Sunday, September 18, 1983
at
4:00 o'clock
for a
Champagne Buffet
on the Patio
at
1309 Gragg Lane
Concord, California *

Judith Hay
and
Robert Pochini

"Just Married." *Bob and Judy in the church garden*

The Self-Catered Wedding

Saturday, September 18, 1983 – the wedding day of Bob Pochini and Judy Hay in Concord, California.

At my home, a country cottage on the creek facing majestic Mount Diablo, the entry courtyard and front lawn are set with round tables, blue tablecloths, centerpieces of garden flowers, and ribbon streamers.

It's 1:30. Relatives start to arrive, ready for the caravan to the church. In the small but efficient kitchen, my friend Edith is preparing platters of home-roasted turkey and ham, *crudités* with curried mayonnaise dip, well ripened brie with crackers and grapes, vegetable frittatas, luscious large strawberries with powdered sugar, and special gourmet baguettes of sourdough French bread from Acme in Berkeley.

The small house fills with people, but I'm still dressing. My blue silk dress looks as good today as it did in the salon, my sister tells me, but it's wrinkled. Quick. Off with the dress and steam out the wrinkles. Then I realize I had forgotten to buy navy blue hosiery. Black will not do. So Jean races to Safeway for a pair of L'Eggs hosiery encased in the familiar plastic shell. We just might be ready on time.

Hopefully, this wedding and our self-catered reception will come off without glitches. I reflect on the more than several previous occasions when I had attempted dinner receptions like this. Developed and published by *Sunset* when I worked on staff, the magazine's innovative "Walk-Around Dinner" presents a deceptively simple formula for serving

49

ten to a thousand guests. The secret: put everything from appetizers to desserts out in advance. Then relax while your guests circulate and enjoy your party. Expecting a crowd? Just expand your portions and your party space and invite the guests.

Sound easy? Yes. My previous attempts didn't quite turn out that way, however.

Today, my wedding day, I am presenting a dinner in three courses, appetizers, main dishes, and dessert — the wedding cake. A simple scenario. Nonetheless, I reflect on the past challenges.

Party Number One – a walk-around dinner for fifty in my handsome but tiny two-bedroom rental in Menlo Park. A divorcée on a tight budget, I venture forth with no help, just myself. Consequently, I keep the menu simple – soup concocted by mixing and stirring a dozen cans of broth, vegetable platters served with *Sunset's* recipe for blender bearnaise sauce, sliced ham with special gourmet bread, sliced roast turkey, and wine to accompany all of that. Then, at the end, homemade cookies and a tankard of coffee served in the cleaned-up garage.

As a full-time editor with deadlines to meet, I have only evenings available to prepare in advance for my Saturday soirée. I bake two large batches of cookies one night. The next evening, I tackle the ham, not just an ordinary ham, mind you, but a smoked "country ham" I had carried back from the North Carolina furniture market. At a house party I had attended during the market, such a ham had tasted so delicious. I'd give it a try. Well, "country ham" preparation requires more expertise than I in my naiveté could have imagined. I spend hours wrestling with that giant ham leg and end up with a platter of salty chunks of dry meat – not at all comparable to the fork-tender slices I had enjoyed in North Carolina.

Oh, well. At least I know how to roast a turkey, and that emerges a delicious success. Everything else progresses well the day of the party until I start on the "blender bearnaise" sauce *Sunset* suggests to accompany the special assortment of raw vegetables on their sample menu.

Better not leave that bearnaise sauce until last, I reason. As I blend the first batch, I smell smoke and watch my blender burn out. What a disaster. No time or budget to replace it today. I telephone Hazel, next door, the only neighbor I even know. " May I please borrow your blender?" "Sorry I don't own one." What to do? Whisk or whip the ingredients, I guess. Problem: I don't own a whisk or an eggbeater those days. Another call to Hazel. She has an eggbeater.

But "blender bearnaise" and "eggbeater bearnaise" do not even compare. What to do? Scrap that. Serve lemon mayonnaise with the *crudités*. So I dish up a bowl of that, feeling thankful I have lemons and mayonnaise on hand.

Next come the platters of vegetables. Such fun to arrange. I make two artistic presentations, both centered with my giant mushroom caps. Gorgeous.

Then, time to get the coffee going, I set the urn, cups, and cookies on a festive card table in the garage.

Take a break, Judy. Time to freshen up and change. The soup can wait. And wait it does, for another party. I have run out of time. My "one man band" does not quite make the party -time deadline. Surely, no one will miss the soup. I dodge the cans and stock pot into an empty cupboard, light the candles, and greet my guests with aplomb.

People do circulate as they walk around and enjoy my dinner. The turkey is popular. The ham not so much. My friend Dr. Davy gives me the clue – "What is this strange meat, Judy? Delicious, but oh, so salty."

And my special giant mushroom caps disappear. I guess they have been eaten first until I encounter an officious friend in the living room holding all the caps in a bowl and wielding a knife. "Your mushrooms are too big, dear. I decided to cut them into quarters so they would go further." "Oh, thanks, Cessie. How thoughtful of you."

Well, despite the glitches, that first walk-around dinner establishes my reputation as a hostess.

The next "walk-around dinner " comes a few months later, as a command performance for a designers' conference in San Francisco. The committee decides such an event would put our convention on the map. The big hitch – we have to stage the dinner for three hundred convention delegates aboard *The Harbor Princess* as we cruise San Francisco Bay.

Annabel Post, *Sunset's* foods editor, advises me on quantities. I take the day off and load my car with ten crates of lush produce. Once I arrive home, I realize I have no washing capacity for ten crates, so I improvise – I put it all on the front lawn and spray it with a hose.

Logistics prove a nightmare. No easy parking at the pier. Finally, I get the car unloaded, find a legal parking place in a pricey garage, and run two blocks back to the pier. We start handing the produce, platters of meat, bread, and wine onto the boat. But a throng of party people trample us in our attempt as they also stream aboard.

We find no galley but squeeze into some space in the cabin and do our best. Platters of food disappear before we can get them to the upper deck. Despite these vicissitudes, our "walk-around dinner cruise" makes history throughout the design world.

Unflapped by these challenges, I decide to stage a "walk-around" wedding reception set for just a month later. My bridegroom, Gene Hay, a long-time neighbor, had been widowed a year before when his wife Claire had died of a heart attack. Gene's Walnut Creek garden with its sheltering fruitless mulberry tree provides the setting for our reception for a hundred or so friends and associates. He and I each prepare a ham and a turkey in our separate abodes. In addition, I enlist the aid of two friends to make double recipes of my popular Mexican hominy casserole.

On the day of the wedding my parents drive me from Menlo Park to Walnut Creek with a prepared ham, a roast turkey, bread from the Pink Pastry, and luscious produce from the special Palo Alto greengrocer.

My dad and Gene start carving ham and turkey immediately after we arrive, and my mother sets up shop at the sink preparing the vegetables and strawberries.

All proceeds smoothly until the doorbell rings. In come Kay and Shirley Peakes, who have already begun tippling to celebrate our happy occasion. They are ready for a good time. "Oh, let us help." Shirley grabs a carving knife and attacks a ham. His wife Kay sees the radishes, all washed and ready for the platter. "Oh I'll make radish roses." She elbows my mother away from the sink.

So it happens that my mother washes the remaining five crates of produce in the upstairs bathtub. The day has grown hot, and I need a bath. This does not happen. I become an "unwashed bride."

Does the reception succeed? Of course. We do have a carefree time, and our guests stay for several hours, chatting and munching in the dappled sunlight.

Well, those prior party challenges did prepare me for this occasion. Time to stop reflecting and turn my attention to my self-catered wedding reception with Bob Pochini, who exhibits nervous apprehension about my abilities. I hadn't told him that I'd staged several such receptions before; he might have felt even more nervous. Now he would have to trust my expertise. And expertise I do have by today. My budget, although skinny, does include servers this time; all will go well.

Meanwhile, the living room reverberates with the voices of a standing-room-only throng. Just as I emerge from the bedroom I notice my mother studying the titles in my hall bookcase. She looks at me and smiles. Then she selects a book, carries it into the living room, settles into the sofa, and starts to read. (I later learn that my sis has instructed Mother that if she ever feels nervous she should remove herself from the crowd, grab a book, and start to read.) I guess that works. Mother stays calm.

Bob shows up, looking debonair in his new gray suit. He circulates among his large family and my handful of cousins, greeting everyone with warmth.

I emerge from the bedroom wearing my corsage of yellow rosebuds. I install Bob's matching rosebud boutonniere, pin a white carnation on Paul Riccardi, Bob's nephew and best man, and assist our mothers and my sister Jean with their corsages. We're ready to leave.

I check for a brief moment on my capable friend Edith. I know that her years of experience cooking for the threshing crews on the Missouri farm where she grew up have given her mastery and skill. Yes, Edith has her platter assembly line moving along on schedule. Edith's swift efficiency reassures me. She'll have it all ready by 4:00 with ease.

Time to leave. Bob ushers me to his white "Z-car" (that Datsun 240-Z) and we lead the autocade to the Pleasant Hill Congregational Church, where Rev. Don Rowland greets us. We assemble under the leafy shade of the huge elm in the courtyard. Because the ceremony is brief we and our guests all stand in a semicircle. Then I note our mothers, both well over seventy, a bit nervous and perhaps in need of support. I whisper to the minister, "We need two chairs for our mothers." He beckons to the sexton. The chairs appear. Our mothers sit down. With my sister Jean on my left and Bob's nephew Paul on his right, Bob and I face the minister. Rev. Don had required us to take two counseling sessions, so today we feel at ease with him and with the vows he reads to us. Still, I take a deep breath. It is the third wedding for me as well as for Bob. I particularly feel the sweetness of today's happiness mingled with my sorrow at losing my previous husband Gene after a short but happy marriage. Even though it's my third wedding, I cannot take lightly the vow to "love, honor, and cherish." I begin to feel lightheaded. This is a big step, once again, even though I know Bob so well. When the minister asks, "so long as you both shall live?" I start to weep. Just nine years before, I had lost my beloved Gene to a heart attack after only three years. This sense of potential loss causes me to shake. Then I feel an arm around my waist. A tender reassurance from Bob. I swallow hard and whisper, "I will."

Throughout the ceremony I hear someone behind me sobbing. I hadn't expected anyone else to feel so moved. Who is crying? After the ceremony, I turn around. There sits my answer - Bob's grandson, Nick, reclining in his stroller and sucking on a bottle.

On to the reception. We lead the horn-blowing parade back to Concord. The gentle warmth and lazy sunlight of fall cast a happy glow on the late-blooming zinnias and drifts of oleanders that line our route. At home, a row of pampas grass presides over the lawn with fluffy plumes and reedy cascades. As we arrive, a flurry of happy guests converges on us with congratulations.

Edith has the buffet set with the *hors d'oeuvre* course, including the brie, the *crudités* with curried mayonnaise, and frittatas made with green beans, zucchini, and cauliflower. (We're short almost an entire frittata, though, because daughter Jan's boyfriend has filched most of her offering before she can package it up. Jan apologizes to Bob, but he gives her one of his famous "might have known" looks, nevertheless.)

At the drink table we have tubs icing bottles of champagne, chardonnay, and soft drinks. Bob's son and his sister's three sons will serve.

Bob and I welcome our guests as they stroll into the party. We have no receiving line. This is a "country casual" affair. We take some people around to make sure they meet our mothers, the maid of honor, and the best man. Then we release them to the festivities. Most guests meet and mingle on their own. My friend Gloria arrives with a special casserole of scalloped potatoes for the dinner, and my colleague Claire makes a grand entrance with her intricately carved watermelon basket filled with assorted melon balls. We save Gloria's casserole for later, but we place Claire's offering on the buffet table now to go with the appetizers. The day has warmed, so the cool and refreshing melon balls score a hit.

In the midst of the hubbub, the phone rings. Beulah, my longtime friend and former housekeeper, says she'll wait at the nearby Shell station for someone to help her find us. Gallant Bob offers to go. He soon arrives back with Beulah, who wears her server's uniform and cap with pride. Over the years she would badger me for work as the assistant/server at my dinner parties. Now she has a big-time assignment. Beulah gives me a hug. "Miz Judy, you've sure got a good man in Mr. Bob. I really like him! And, Miz Judy, I just made my Eighty!"

"Congratulations, Beulah. That's great news."

My dear friend and helper then disappears into the kitchen to give Edith a hand. At my previous self-catered wedding to Gene twelve years before, Beulah had come as a guest. This time, however, she plays the role of co-cook and server with great joy.

We end the *hors d'oeuvre* buffet in an hour, and then Beulah and Edith ready the table with the main course. The platters of ham and turkey and the hot casseroles make a handsome presentation. Edith rearranges the raw vegetable platters and includes them as well.

During dinner, Bob and I stroll from table to table to make sure we say hello to everyone. As well as Bob's eight-month-old grandson Nick, the other children are five-year-old Tiffany and seven-year-old Sterling, the offspring of my meditation partners, Randy and Sue. Sterling maintains a quiet dignity while Tiffany scampers around in her party dress and checks all the proceedings. We are the first bridal couple she has ever seen. Even though I'm wearing a short blue dress instead of a long white one, we do have champagne and a wedding cake. She seems thrilled at the prospect of seeing toasts and a cake-cutting ceremony.

Midway through the party, Edith's husband Ray tells me he needs to leave. He'll be back later for Edith, he says. I tell him good-bye. He strolls casually to his brown Dodge and drives away. I later learn that before Ray's departure Son Bud had reported to Bob that he had seen Ray sneak a bottle of champagne out to his car. At Bob's prompting, Bud had then walked over to the Dodge and retrieved the champagne. We now chuckle at the disappointment Ray would feel upon reaching for that bottle of champagne and finding it missing. Guess he will have to resort to Jim Beam.

People continue to mingle. We finish our rounds of greetings. Then we toast each other and cut the cake.

Champagne still flows. The party continues into the evening.

Ray picks up Edith but says nothing. He didn't catch us catching him so we trade no words about it.

Edith and Beulah take good quantities of leftovers. We present the rest to our friends, keeping for ourselves a small buffet assortment and a wedge of cake to freeze for our first anniversary.

My mother and sister and the few close friends stay on, and we share post-mortems. Yes, the party had come off on time and with no hitches. And because it had been self-catered the cost was reasonable.

"Just how much did it cost, dear?" my mother asks. "Oh, about 'X' amount," I reply.

"That's not much at all," she exclaims. "Less than half what your father and I spent for your first wedding."

Silence

"Oh," she exclaims and puts her hand over her mouth.

Judy and Bob at the wedding of Daughter Jan to Harold Speelman (Yes, the reception was self-catered!)
Photo courtesy of Mel Riccardi

Living From Bite to Bite, The Frittata Affair

Shortly after Bob and I married, I helped my friend Delfina give a baby shower for a mutual friend of ours. When I showed up at the party with my special *hors d'oeuvre,* a wheel of brie with fruit and assorted crackers, Delfina gave me a look of displeasure.

Uh oh, I thought, *Delfina seems disappointed, even a bit miffed. What have I done wrong?*

I asked our friend Henrietta to give me a clue. "I think she was expecting you to bring one of Bob's frittatas," she whispered. "In fact, she was counting on it for the unusual gourmet touch."

I shook my head in disbelief. "My goodness, I'm astounded to hear that. Since it's Bob's dish, not mine, and since this party is *my* affair, not his, I wouldn't ask him to cook for it. She really is off base to have expected that."

This incident caused me to muse about Bob's frittatas. I knew they impart a unique and savory taste treat. They had helped establish Bob's reputation as an accomplished cook.

But how had we come to this strange situation with Delfina? I reflected back a couple of years, during the early days of my romance with Bob.

After two or three dates, Bob had invited me over for a home-cooked dinner. He promised that it would be authentic North Beach Italian, so I had readily accepted.

Upon my arrival, Bob offered me a plate piled high with tiny squares of an unfamiliar *hors d'oeuvre,* explaining that it was frittata. I took a piece, golden cauliflower mingled with onion, egg, and grated parmesan. The slightly moist and delicately browned morsel gave off a provocative aroma. At first bite, I enjoyed the crunch of *al dente* vegetables mingled richly with eggs and cheese. The new taste seemed to explode in my mouth.

"Oh! This tastes different from anything I've ever tried. What a treat."

"If you've had frittata before, perhaps it was made with spinach and with lots of egg. This *is* different— less egg. And although spinach frittata did become popular over in The City in recent years, my family has never made frittatas with spinach."

Because I did not yet know much about Bob, I did not realize that evening that when he referred to his "family" he was referring to the cuisine of the trio of chefs who had presided over a San Francisco restaurant, Pochini's, which had purveyed Northern Italian cuisine for over thirty-seven years. Bob's comment on the recipe for frittata did cause me to ponder why "less egg and no spinach" played roles in his version. I'd have to ask for more details when I could.

Meanwhile, after that memorable opener of frittata, Bob's dinner included many additional delights. His wit and sophistication attracted me as well. He obviously knew how to cook and serve a memorable gourmet dinner. Certainly it rivaled the cuisine one could enjoy at a four-star Italian restaurant. Plus, he himself had prepared every dish. No food from a take-out deli had slipped into his menu.

Bob really charmed me that evening with his suave attentions, his witty remarks about life, and his choice of music by such jazz greats as Ella Fitzgerald, Dave Brubeck, and Count Basie, to set the mood of our evening by the fire. My heart was kindled with interest. I looked forward to seeing him again.

Of course, we did see each other again, and again, and again. Dinners in our homes. Dinners out. Jazz concerts. The works.

During our blossoming romance, Bob later served me almost every version of frittata in his repertoire— zucchini, broccoli, celery root, green bean, artichoke heart, and (of course) cauliflower. He even made up a new version with mixed vegetables which he served as a main course accompaniment. Later, after we married, we offered Bob's frittatas at our entertainments, and friends and family not only raved, they came to expect them.

In fact, my friend Delfina, a frequent guest, seemed to live from one frittata bite to another. An accomplished cook in her own right, Delfina touted Bob's culinary abilities to all of her friends.

"Judy is so lucky. She has Bob in her life to cook Italian for her. He makes the best frittata you've ever tasted."

By coincidence, almost every time we entertained Delfina and her husband we had served Bob's "fritt'a," as he called it.

Delfina must have become addicted to Bob's frittatas. Probably that explains why she had hoped I would bring one to her party. She had asked Bob for his recipe many times but he had declined to share it. "I just don't give out my recipes," he had explained.

But Delfina did not give up. She soon mounted a campaign to obtain the recipe. Every time we met at a party she would ask Bob to share it. And every time he would say no, explaining, "I developed expertise by studying with my father, who was a chef for our family restaurant. Unless you study with me, Delfina, dear, you may miss a key ingredient or a special technique. Our cuisine is not yet written out with directions, you see."

Delfina persevered despite Bob's polite refusals. Determined to wear Bob down, each time she saw us she would ask Bob for the frittata recipe. "Please, please, oh, please."

Finally Bob gave in to her pleading. "Okay, I'll give you the ingredients and the quantities, but unless you have hands-on training, I can't guarantee the results."

A month later we ran into Delfina at a party. She raced over to Bob with a triumphant smile. "Dear, I fixed your frittata."

I could see Bob wince. He told me later in private, that he was wondering if she had *prepared* the recipe or if she indeed had "fixed" it, by changing it in some way.

"Yes, darling," she continued. "I decided it could use some meat, so I ground up some salami and added that. It came out very interesting."

Bob and I exchanged glances. He told me later he visualized with combined revulsion and amusement a picture of Delfina not only adding meat, but in fact choosing to regrind a processed meat such as salami for her addition.

"Yes, it must have tasted interesting," Bob and I chorused, rolling our eyes in amazement.

"Are your azaleas blooming yet, Delfina?" I asked, changing the subject. Neither Bob nor I wanted to hear more about how she had "fixed" his treasured recipe.

Ever the cut-up, Bob lifts his little finger to indicate how easy it is to prepare zucchini frittata.

Here are my written instructions on how to prepare delicious frittatas, all tested and retested many times. Note that this type of frittata comes out only 3/8" to 3/4" thick. None includes meat, fish, or fowl!

Asparagus Frittata

1 bunch asparagus
3 extra large eggs or 3/4 cup egg substitute
1 large yellow onion, finely chopped
1 tablespoon virgin olive oil
½ cup grated parmesan or romano cheese
Salt
Pepper
Sprigs of rosemary or thyme for garnish

Preheat oven to 350°. Wash asparagus. Break off lower stems and set aside to use in soup. Cut into ½" long pieces. Place in steamer with water and a pinch of salt. Steam just until *al dente.* Immediately remove from steamer and drain in colander. Chill with ice and running water so asparagus will stop cooking.

Peel onion and chop finely. Heat olive oil in nonstick or cast iron skillet. Sauté onion until limp. Sprinkle with salt and pepper. In large bowl combine onion, asparagus, cheese and **unbeaten** eggs. Turn into 9" x 9" oiled baking dish or pan. Spread evenly and pat with bowl of spoon to flatten mixture in pan. Bake at 350° for 25 minutes, or until frittata is slightly brown on top. Remove from oven and cool to room temperature.

Important: Serve chilled or at room temperature. Cut frittata into 1-1/2" squares and arrange artistically on small plate. Garnish with sprigs of thyme or rosemary.

Squash Frittata

1 pound **small** crookneck squash, or baby zucchini, or medium size zucchini (about two). Cut in half lengthwise. Slice thinly. Add to sautéed onion and sauté slightly until wilted. Proceed as with Asparagus Frittata above.

Celery Root (Celeriac) Frittata

One celery root, medium or large size. Peel to remove stringy outer layer. Cut in half vertically and remove pithy heart. Chop into raisin-size pieces. Steam until *al dente*. Add to sautéed onion in pan and stir-fry for one minute. Proceed as with Asparagus Frittata above.

Broccoli or Broccoflower Frittata

One crown of broccoli washed and stemmed. (Use stems in soup.) Chop fine. Steam five minutes, drain and cool as above. Proceed as in Asparagus Frittata above.

Cauliflower Frittata

One head of cauliflower, florets only, cut into bite-size pieces. Proceed as with Broccoli Frittata above.

Artichoke Frittata

1-1/2 cups prepared fresh baby artichoke hearts, cooked or one 14-ounce package frozen artichoke hearts, thawed and drained, or one 13-3/4 ounce can of artichoke hearts, drained. Do not cook. Cut into fourths or eighths, depending on the size of the hearts. Proceed as above

Green Bean Frittata

Select either small green beans or Romano Italian beans with no blemishes. Wash, string if necessary, and cut off tops. Cut on the diagonal into bite-size pieces. Place in steamer with a small amount of water. Bring to boil on High, then lower the heat and steam for 3 to 4 minutes, testing for doneness. Steam just until *al dente*. Place in colander. Cool with cold running water to stop the cooking process. Proceed as above.

Dinner Will Be a While

We were a little uneasy. Daughter Jan had invited us for dinner in her new home— a flat in a restored West Oakland Victorian. Despite its ongoing gentrification, West Oakland to us meant, "Come here if you dare." Bob and I decided to leave our Mercedes at home and drive over in his well dented Dodge pickup. Chances are it would still have all of its parts after our visit. Jan had asked us to arrive at seven, as it was Thursday, a work day. We guessed that our young career girl was giving herself time to prepare a few things in advance.

Well, Jan did have the sauvignon blanc chilled and the glasses ready. She opened the wine and poured a glass for each of us. Then she toured us through her remodeled flat. "They just finished the kitchen," Jan told us. "For awhile I had only my microwave. I found that microwaves and eggs don't mix. Matter of fact, I'm still recovering from my burn." Jan had gotten in the way of an exploding egg. Our glamorous redhead liked to excel in practical ways, but she didn't always succeed.

Tour over, Jan ushered Bob and me into the living room, poured more wine, and presented brie and crackers. "To tide you over while I cook," she said. Then she pulled her miniskirt into a bell, curtsied, smoothed her ruffled white apron, and left.

We had seen the marinara sauce simmering in the kitchen. Who knew what treat Jan would present with it? Bob settled back into his cast-off recliner, and I lighted on the sprung-out lumpy sofa. We spread brie on the crackers, sipped wine, and admired Jan's chic but funky decor.

Meanwhile, we could see that Casella, the calico cat, was in full crouch watching Gigi the canary in the cage high above.

In just a few minutes, Jan appeared in the doorway, holding a giant Idaho potato. "We're having gnocchi tonight," she announced. "I didn't make them yesterday, no time. But I can do it tonight. Hope you don't mind. Dinner will be just a while." She disappeared back into her culinary domain.

Knowing what we did about the process of making gnocchi, Bob and I stared at her in amazement. Gnocchi from scratch take more than "a while" to prepare. First, you boil the potatoes whole. Then you drain and peel them. Then you mash them and mix with egg and flour. After that you roll the dough into finger-thick ropes and cut into one-inch segments. Then you drop the gnocchi into boiling water and let them cook until they rise to the surface (in about ten minutes). Only after that's done, do you add your sauce and serve. Whew. Quite a process.

"When my sister's friend, Mignon, got a project like that going in Dusseldorf, she and Jean ate around 10 p.m.," I whispered to Bob as Jan returned to her kitchen.

"Oh, no doubt." An experienced gnocchi cook, Bob rolled his eyes in agreement.

We poured another glass of wine and helped ourselves to more brie and crackers.

Meanwhile, Casella had launched her attack on the enticing canary. Gigi sat scolding and screaming from the safety of her cage. Casella used every one of the six toes on her hybrid paws to spring a mighty leap at the out-of-reach cage. But no matter how high she lept that cage was just enough higher. Undaunted, the predatory feline then reconnoitered for the next attack.

With our conversation punctuated by the periodic leaping of the cat and the scolding of the canary, Bob and I reviewed the day's events. That over, we listened for Jan, but heard nothing. Another round of wine, brie, and crackers. Soon we had emptied the bottle and, feeling a bit glowy, had begun planning the remodel of our home. Should we try to build out or up? If we went out, we'd lose a portion of our patio.

But putting a family room in the current master bedroom and creating a new master suite upstairs would not enhance our view. Instead, we'd just see more rooftops.

"Uh, oh. There goes that fool cat again. I've heard of the cat and the canary. Tonight we get the live performance," I noted.

Jan appeared with another bottle of wine but no more food. "Just a while longer," she promised. Then she hastened back to her kitchen. We knew we were not to offer our help. After all, a daughter does have her pride, especially when her dad has been trained by a chef and now cooks like one. And this daughter was striving to impress her dad.

Finally, about nine, Jan announced dinner. Bob and I had drunk most of the second bottle of sauvignon blanc. We hoisted ourselves up with care and staggered a bit as we hastened into the dining room to attack the meal. Jan's starter salad crunched crisply and its dressing had the subtle aroma of tarragon. The gnocchi came out delicate and melted in soft accompaniment to the sauce. Not one tough "pencil eraser" in the lot. Hooray for Jan. Her gnocchi were a success. Her cat didn't get her canary. And she did what she set out to do – show Dad that she, too, could cook.

Gnocchi was a favorite dish of Bob's. His recipe follows. Pair it with Creamy Gorgonzola Sauce, Pesto Sauce, or Marinara Sauce and you'll have a winning starter course or main course. Serve it "tricolore" style by dividing the gnocchi into thirds and using a different sauce on each portion and you'll have a hit, especially as "tricolore" honors the colors of the Italian flag, green, white and red.

Potato Gnocchi See Page 187.
Pesto Sauce See Page 275.
Gorgonzola Sauce See Page 188.
Marinara Sauce See Page 272.

Milanese

Bob bent over to clasp the hand of the chef who had shared his professional and family secrets with him, the agile showman who had made a production of deftly flipping a pair of over-easy eggs, the dad who once could dig up the entire vegetable garden in an afternoon, the pal who had romped with him on the living room rug, the father who now lay listlessly in bed.

No longer strong and vigorous, Chef Leo had suffered a series of strokes. Wheelchair bound and fragile at eighty-four, he lived in a Petaluma nursing home, certainly not a venue in which he would find the gourmet meals he had once enjoyed. His room was colorless and spartan but overlooked a flower-filled garden. We were just completing our visit, brief, because Leo was so weak.

"What can we bring you when we visit next week? Another deli sandwich? Something special I might cook for you?"

Understandably, the old man's eyes lit up at the prospect of a culinary treat. With great effort, he lifted himself closer to Bob and whispered, "Milanese."

"What did you say?" Bob bent forward.

"Mi-la-ne-se." The word came out a barely audible gasp.

Bob sighed. "O.k. I'll do my best. See you next week, Dad."

Once outside Leo's room, Bob groaned. "Oh! What a request!"

"What do you mean? What's the problem?" I was puzzled.

"He asked for Veal Milanese—*his* specialty," Bob replied. "I've tried to make it, but I never did learn to prepare it as well as he. I haven't attempted it in years because it's so tricky. I couldn't refuse what may be Dad's last request, but I don't know whether I'll make it properly. I hope I don't disappoint him."

I had not heard Bob speak of Milanese when referring to his family's repertoire of dishes, and I had never seen him look so anxious when contemplating his role as chef. "You told me some time ago that you have mastered all of your family's dishes." I reminded him. "Your dad wouldn't have asked if he didn't think you could do it."

"That's true." But Bob continued to look worried as he helped me into the car. "He probably wants to enjoy it one last time. I can't fail on this one. I just hope my version will somewhat approximate his."

I was amazed at Bob's fuss over this veal dish. "Why is Milanese so difficult?" We had started our drive home to Concord.

"Well, you see, it calls for thick veal chops, not thin cutlets or scaloppine style medallions of veal. After you have breaded the chops you fry them moderately in a little bit of olive oil so that they brown evenly and slowly. You can't sauté them quickly or they'll burn on the outside and stay raw in the center." We were driving along the Petaluma River en route to Sears Point and the Black Point "cutoff" between Novato and Benicia. The February sunshine and deepening afternoon shadows sculpted the green meadows and voluptuous rolling hillsides.

Bob continued. "It's the process that makes the dish intricate. You literally have to stand over the chops and watch them. Try coordinating that with preparing the vegetable and the rice to go with them and you'll see why it's a challenge to make it all come out at the same time."

I mused over the dilemma as we made our way home past the white herons on stilt legs standing guard over the marshes, ever alert for a piscine meal.

Because Chef Leo had seemed so weak, Bob and I decided to return just two days later. We weren't sure how much longer he had. We visited our fanciest service meat counter to buy beautifully cut, bone-in loin veal chops. Back in the kitchen, I watched intently as my husband carefully dipped the chops first in flour, then in gently beaten egg, and finally, in crushed crumbs of dry sourdough bread. After heating olive oil in a cast iron skillet, he adjusted the fire to medium and gently placed the chops in the pan. As the chops cooked, Bob kept adjusting the heat so that they sizzled only slightly. Whenever they started to pop and sputter (the sound of really hot oil, a sign of high-heat cooking), he turned them down. Every so often, Bob lifted a chop to check the browning process. After they had come to a luscious delicate brown on one side, he then turned them over, taking care not to disturb the crumb coating.

The aroma of the browning veal and the appeal of the golden coating awakened my latent hunger, even at ten in the morning.

"Please make them for *us* soon." I begged.

"If these turn out, I will," Bob promised. He gently placed the meat on a plate, then turned and smiled, "No need to keep them hot. Milanese is one of those dishes that tastes just as good at room temperature as it does warm. In fact, Dad never did serve it really hot because high heat diminishes the flavors."

Before he started preparing the veal, Bob had put on a pot of rice to steam and had prepared some Romano beans (frozen) from our previous summer's garden.

Two hours later, when we entered his father's room carrying the dinner, the eyes of the accomplished chef widened in joyful anticipation.

"You brought the Milanese!"

"I did my best, Dad. Of course, it won't compare to yours..."

I'll always carry in my memory the picture of Leo Pochini, propped up in bed, napkin tucked into his pajama collar, tackling that Milanese. I envied him as the aroma of the crumb encrusted chops entered my nostrils. He gestured with his fork and smiled broadly as he devoured Bob's lovingly prepared dinner.

"Good! Good!" He could not have offered higher praise.

Hearing that, Bob beamed with pleasure and pride. He had passed one more test in his training under a demanding teacher and, more important, he had fulfilled his dying father's request.

Veal Milanese

Veal chops ½" thick (2 per person)
Olive oil
Flour
Fresh herbs for garnish
Packaged seasoned Italian bread crumbs
    or crushed dry sourdough bread crumbs mixed with dried
    oregano and dried thyme
Beaten egg

Wash chops and pat dry with paper towels. Dip first in flour, then in beaten egg then in seasoned bread crumbs until well coated. Set aside. Heat large nonstick or cast-iron skillet on High. Add 2 tablespoons of olive oil and reduce heat to Medium, because you will be browning the chops slowly. Heat oil until it sputters when you shake a drop of water on it. Carefully place chops in pan, allowing plenty of room around each chop. Do not crowd in pan, to give each one plenty of exposure to the oil for even browning. Allow chops to brown slowly on one side, checking them every so often. Once chops have browned to golden on the first side, carefully turn with a cooking spatula and brown them on the other side. Do not cook too rapidly, or the chops will be brown on the outside and raw on the inside. After the chops are done, remove them from the pan and place on heated plates. Garnish with sprigs of fresh Italian parsley, oregano, rosemary, or thyme.

Bob's "Perfect" Steamed Rice

This comes out "perfect" every time (providing you follow the directions)!

1-7/8 cup water
½ teaspoon salt
1 cup long-grain white or brown rice
1 tablespoon butter

Put water and salt in one-quart saucepan. Cook on High without lid until water boils. Add rice. Stir with a fork. Cover. Cook on a *low* simmer for 20 minutes. Fluff with fork and add butter. Serve as soon as possible.

Italian Green Beans

A gardener friend who loved the San Francisco gourmet fare at the venerable Jack's Restaurant (now closed) first introduced me to Italian, or Romano, green beans. They are flat rather than round, and they have a more delicate taste than regular green beans. The best way to acquire them is to grow them in your own garden, as my friend did, or to check the farmer's markets and specialty produce stores during midsummer. The harvest season for Romanos is short and the yield can be sparse, so I recommend freezing extras for dinners later on.

Romano beans - about 1/4 to 1/3 pound per person
Water
½ teaspoon salt
1 tablespoon olive oil

Check the beans carefully and cut off any blemishes. Better yet, select the beans one by one at the market and avoid blemished beans. Cut off stems. Place water and salt in bottom of steamer. Cover and steam until beans are *al dente*. This may take as long as ten minutes, but watch your beans carefully to avoid over-cooking. *Immediately* place the cooked beans in a colander and cool under running cold water to stop the cooking process. Place in cold nonstick or cast-iron skillet with the olive oil. Toss to coat beans with oil. Set aside. Just before serving, heat beans in skillet until properly warm. *Do not re-cook.*

Scintillating Soups

My mother's Irish grandmother taught her to make potato soup, and when I was growing up, that soup warmed our hearts on wintry days. Other than that, Mother's soup skill consisted of opening cans, chicken noodle, tomato, vegetable. When I was ten, Mother taught me how to make Great Grandma Hogan's authentic Irish potato soup. How I enjoyed peeling and cutting up potatoes and onions and turning them into bowls of steaming, satisfying potage. Many years later as an adult, I taught myself how to make cucumber soup in order to use up a bumper crop of Burpee hybrids yielded by my garden. Other than those two varieties, I was clueless about homemade soup.

Bob, on the other hand, had enjoyed many meals of soup from Chef Leo's bountiful pot. And so Bob learned the art of soup preparation from his father. Besides the Pochini minestrone and the basic vegetable soups taught by Leo, Bob also developed the ability to craft vichyssoise, purée of avocado, and many other tempting varieties.

When I saw how easily Bob could concoct a basic vegetable soup that tasted elegantly special, I felt grateful to be his *sous chef* and learn his secrets. If he needed me to chop vegetables or prepare herbs, I was his enthusiastic helper. He taught me how to make homemade soup that could go on the table at once, with the balance to be chilled or frozen for a future first course or main meal.

Bob emphasized one major secret for making vegetable soups– add at least a small amount of butter to enhance the flavors. Even if you are on a low-fat diet, a tablespoon of butter included in a giant pot of soup imparts a rich flavor yet amounts to just a tiny amount per serving. With almost evangelical fervor, Bob promoted this addition of a little butter to most soups. One evening Daughter Gina, in her zealous pursuit of a low-fat diet, served us a cauliflower soup with no butter.

"Everything about Gina's dinner was truly special this evening except for the soup," Bob remarked as we drove home. He had detected the lack of butter. "How can I tell her? I know. I'll have her over next week and serve cauliflower soup with just a touch of butter in it. She's smart enough to get the point."

And Gina did "get it," producing delicious soups with just a *hint* of butter, from then on.

Bob favored thickening his soups with cornstarch rather than flour, to avoid having the soup taste like pan gravy. Cornstarch has a less detectable, more subtle taste than flour.

His soups kept us cozy and pleased our palates on many wintry nights and summer afternoons. Follow these simple recipes and your homemade soups will earn smiles from guests and family.

Asparagus Soup See Page 127.
Broccoli Soup See Page 129.
Cauliflower Soup See Page 130.
Cucumber Soup See Page 132.
Potato-Leek Soup See Page 135.
Minestrone See Page 133.
Zucchini Soup See Page 136.

The Cooking Lesson

Only when the student is ready will the teacher come, to rephrase a popular saying. Bob's daughter Jan, our flamboyant redhead, periodically would ask her dad for his cooking secrets. Knowing Jan's creative penchant for revising at will every item in her life, including recipes, Bob habitually denied her requests. "Jan, you remember that Nono taught our family's dishes to me, father to son. You need to watch how I do things. I'll teach you, father to daughter. When you're ready for that, let me know."

Disregarding Bob's insistence on meticulousness, Jan went off on her own– serving up her versions of ravioli, linguine, soups, and other menu items. No matter how intricate the dish she would try it, and try and try, until she came close to achieving what she would consider success.

Audacious and proud of her cooking prowess (better anyway than that of most of her peers), Jan boldly entered and won a newspaper cooking contest a little while later. She proudly showed Bob and me the front page of *The Contra Costa Times* food section, featuring her recipe, the first-prize winner! The article included a large photo of her in living color, no less.

"Did the paper ask you to prepare your dish so they could take that photograph?" I asked.

"Oh, no. They prepared it, of course," Jan replied, adding, "You know, I never did *actually* cook it myself. I just guessed about the taste and sent it in." This recognition by the *Times* gave Jan even more confidence in her developing culinary abilities, and she continued through trial and error to increase her repertoire.

When it came to *Sima,* though, she finally came back to Bob for help.

"Dad, I've promised Harold I'd make stuffed veal pocket for our Sunday picnic. May I please, please, have your recipe? I can't find it in any of my cookbooks."

"Remember what I told you, dear? No recipes from me without training."

Jan knew when it was time to give in. "O.k. When may I come over?"

Bob had told me many stories about his father, Leo, preparing the daily dinners on the family's range in the Redfield Place basement, below the main quarters, a place where the soot from sautéeing could exit through windows and not soil the formal furniture and draperies upstairs. Just before Jan arrived for her Thursday morning lesson at our home in Lafayette, I asked Bob about those father-son training sessions.

"I suppose you chopped onions and flipped the potatoes in the pan as you stood alongside your dad?

"Oh, no. Dad didn't have the patience for hands-on. He had to get the meal on the table. I first ventured down to his kitchen when I was only four. I was so small that he would have trampled me as he stepped so swiftly from chopping board to skillet to oven. He couldn't let me come too close; he told me I had to stay out of the way, sit on the stairs. I could ask questions and take notes. The stairs thus became my spot for years– the watcher's seat."

"So then, how did you become the accomplished home chef that you are today?" I asked.

"For fourteen years I sat on those stairs almost every day. By the time I left home at eighteen I had every dish and every procedure embedded in my memory. And, from time to time later, Dad did let me cook with him, a rare and special privilege. I held his cooking expertise in great awe, as you know."

Unlike his busy father, Bob as an early retiree now had the leisure to give hands-on training to his daughter. On the appointed day, he and Jan visited the gourmet butcher shop, where they specified a veal breast of mid-size, which would allow a generous pocket for stuffing. Later at home, he showed her how to cut that pocket between the rib meat and skin of the delicate breast. Then dad and daughter together broke up stale sourdough bread into large chunks and soaked them in water. They cleaned and de-stemmed a bunch of chard, chopped it, and steamed it until *al dente*. They chopped and sautéed a large yellow onion. Also, six cloves of garlic. They then combined the onion, garlic, chard, cut-up artichoke hearts, Parmesan cheese and the lightly beaten eggs. Squeezing as much water as they could out of the bread, they put it into the sauté pan to soak up the cooking juices. They then added the bread to the bowl, mixing all ingredients well. After that they spooned this mixture into the pocket they had cut in the veal.

Up until now, stuffing that pocket had presented perhaps the most challenging task. But now they had to sew it shut. Bob threaded a giant cooking needle with twine and handed it to Jan. "Give me a pretty whipstich," he commanded with half a wink. An accomplished seamstress, Jan gamely wrestled with the slippery ellipse of veal. Sticking the needle in was no biggie, but pulling it through presented a challenge, she found. Finally, after much struggling, she finished sewing the pocket shut. Good thing she'd been lifting weights at the gym.

Evrything after that was downhill racing. Bob showed Jan how to rub the prepared meat with olive oil, sprinkle on a little paprika, place it in a baking dish, and roast it at moderate heat until done.

Because *Sima* tastes best at room temperature, it makes an appropriate picnic dish. After Jan's veal breast cooled, she sliced it between the ribs, fanned the slices on a platter, accented the dish with Italian parsley, and she had an impressively festive presentation. The three of us were picnicking on our deck that day, and Jan paused while the *maestro* took the first bite and beamed his approval.

For Jan, that cooking lesson was the beginning of an extensive series of *hands-on* sessions, invaluable for even the simplest of dishes and essential for the intricate ones. Even better, Jan and her dad developed a closer comraderie through their mutual passion for cooking.

Sima (Stuffed Veal Pocket)

1 breast of baby veal, about 2-1/2 pounds
1 bunch Swiss chard
½ baguette stale sourdough French bread
1 large yellow onion
2 tablespoons virgin olive oil, divided
6 cloves garlic, peeled and finely chopped
1/4 teaspoon salt
1/8 teaspoon ground black pepper
1-1/2 cups prepared baby artichokes, cooked
 or 1 13-3/4 - ounce can artichoke hearts, drained
 or 1 14 - ounce package frozen artichoke hearts
1 cup grated Parmesan cheese
6 large eggs
Paprika
Fresh rosemary or Italian parsley for garnish

Have the butcher cut a pocket in the veal next to the ribs and open on one side. Rinse veal and pat dry with paper towels. Set aside. Wash the chard, and discard the stems. Drain on paper towels. Place in steamer over ½ inch of water. Cover. Steam on high until chard wilts. Remove from fire and drain well in colander.

While chard is steaming, soak stale bread in water until well saturated. Peel the onion and chop finely. Preheat nonstick skillet on high. Add 1 teaspoon olive oil to skillet and turn skillet to coat with the oil as it heats. Sauté chopped onion on High until well wilted. Add finely chopped garlic and sauté slightly, taking care not to burn the garlic. Stir in salt and pepper. Place in large mixing bowl. Set pan aside. Place cooked chard on chopping board and cut into bite-size sections with knife. Add to bowl. Cut drained (or thawed and drained) artichoke hearts into fourths and add to bowl. Add grated cheese. Break eggs into separate bowl and break them up slightly with a whisk. Add to other ingredients and mix well.

Thoroughly squeeze water from bread. Place in sauté pan and stir to pick up pan drippings. Mix thoroughly with other ingredients.

Spoon this mixture into the veal pocket until you have filled it, leaving an overlap to allow an edge for stitching.

Thread a large-eye, heavy-gauge cooking or darning needle with kitchen twine. Place stuffed pocket on a non-skid surface, such as a layer of paper towels. To sew, insert the needle at one end, facing up. Push up through the layers of veal. Midway through, you may be able to stand the needle on end and, using two hands, push the veal down onto the needle. Pull the needle and twine through. Overlap the edge of the meat with the twine and start again from bottom to top. Repeat stitches until pocket is fully closed. In essence, you will have "whipstitched" the edge of the pocket to close it.

Brush the finished veal pocket with 1 teaspoon olive oil. Place in shallow roasting pan with ribs down. Sprinkle with paprika. Roast at 350° for about one hour. Veal will be well browned when done. To check for doneness, insert skewer onto breast. Juices should bubble out. Remove from oven and allow to cool to room temperature.

After pocket has cooled, slice crosswise between each rib bone. Slices will be about 1-1/2 inches thick. Remove string. Arrange on serving plate in a fan. Garnish with fresh rosemary or Italian parsley. Chill if you make the pocket well ahead of the meal. Warm to room temperature when ready to serve. Can be eaten out of hand or with utensils, depending on the formality of your occasion. Accompany with a hearty potato or pasta salad along with a green salad and a glass of zinfandel. Serves six to eight.

The Fettuccine Challenge

Before I met Bob, I became a fancier of freshly made pasta. I especially enjoyed Fettuccine Alfredo tossed in a butter and cream sauce tableside at Amelio's in San Francisco. It was served as a separate pasta course or else as an accompaniment to Veal Scaloppine. And occasionally I would procure the fresh pasta from the venerable Genova Delicatessen in Walnut Creek and prepare a special dinner for friends.

Bob brought to our marriage his own penchant for pasta– the fresh kind. As a boy, his parents often had dispatched him from their home on Russian Hill for pasta produced by Cafferata Ravioli Factory in North Beach. At Cafferata, stacks of freshly made "leaves," approximately 8" x 10", were waiting to be cut as ordered– into fettuccine, linguine, or tagliarini, from wide to narrow, whatever the customer preferred. A generous dusting of semolina flour kept the noodles from sticking to each other once cut; and a wrapper of butcher paper protected the pasta until ready to boil.

Once you drop the fresh pasta into the boiling water it cooks in only a few minutes to tender succulence. Tossed with your sauce, it becomes a special main course or a marvelous side dish. No wonder afficionados salivate in anticipation as it cooks.

Bob and I planned our menus around trips to The City for pasta from Cafferata on Columbus, sourdough bread from Cuneo Bakery on Green, and foccacia from Liguria Bakery on Washington Square.

Or we'd stop off at Genova Delicatessen in Walnut Creek for their version.

One day I chanced upon a Macy's ad for an Atlas pasta machine. Aha, I thought. Maybe Bob would like to make pasta at home instead of trekking to San Francisco and Walnut Creek. On that hope, I gave him a pasta machine for Christmas. Bob thanked me politely but I saw no homemade pasta. He evidently had put the machine in the back of his cupboard. No doubt, he may have reasoned, why should he make pasta when he could pick it up on one of his frequent San Francisco trips.

After Bob and I married, however, we became more closely tied to our life in the East Bay. We seldom visited San Francisco except on an occasional day off, which of course included a stop at Cafferata for fresh fettuccine.

Within a year, though, my design career included frequent trips to San Francisco to shop for clients at the Design Center south of Market. Bob began to fancy fresh pasta more and more often. We had found a new purveyor, appropriately named Fettuccine Bros., which had a shop on Russian Hill near the Broadway Tunnel. There, parking was feasible although not easy. Soon Bob began asking me to stop on my "way home." It was five miles across town from the Design Center through heavy traffic to pick up the pasta before I would resume my homeward trek over the Bay Bridge through onerous stop-and-go traffic. Such forays added an hour to my commute time; after two of them, I became fatigued just to think of that jaunt.

On the third occasion, I decided to skip the stop at Fettuccine Bros. I would pick up the fresh pasta at Cook's, a gourmet food and housewares store on Telegraph Avenue in Oakland, just a short detour from my Highway 24 route home.

When I arrived home that evening with my package of pasta I said nothing to Bob about the substitution. After all, fresh pasta was fresh pasta, wasn't it?

Evidently I was wrong. Bob prepared fettuccine with clams, and we sat down to dinner. One bite and he accused me. "This is not from Fettuccine Bros., is it?"

"Well, no," I replied, explaining my substitution and the reason for it.

"No more. It's not the same." He then explained that the Fettuccine Bros. pasta was more delicate and tender; he could tell the difference from the first bite. This puzzled me because any difference I could taste was so subtle I had trouble detecting it. I acknowledged Bob's finely tuned taste buds, but I encourage *you* to follow your own instincts and judge what qualities of fresh pasta please you the best.

After that we limited our fresh pasta purchases to the "approved" stores. But we became so busy that we seldom were able to serve our continuing appetite.

Finally, one day while shopping in an upscale Walnut Creek housewares store, I spied *Pasta Perfecta,* a book telling how to make your own pasta. And the cover featured a handsome Italian chef, dramatically pulling a long sheet of pasta from a machine. My friend Cecilia had told me that Italian men often enjoy competing with each other. I saw that book cover and reasoned, maybe this would work on Bob Pochini. It did.

Bob took one look at the man and his obvious prowess at making pasta and decided to compete. Out came the pasta machine, the food processor, a bread board and a clamp to hold it in place.

From the start, Bob was a natural at producing delectable pasta. Soon he commandeered my drafting board in order to have a surface large enough to handle his generous batches of noodles. He had found a new hobby, and my taste thrills from freshly made pasta would become more frequent.

Progressing from noodles to ravioli was a more complicated project. Bob bought and designed innovative new eqipment for filling and crimping his little pillows. He even pressed into service a plasterer's trowel (new, of course) to smooth the filling surfaces. After many tries, he finally developed a way to keep the ravioli from popping apart as they boiled. Then it was success all the way. He could concentrate on the fillings, feeling assured that the "wrapping" would survive the boiling process.

Best of all, pasta-making took Bob back to memories of his grandmother Noni Pochini. "I remember that she occasionally spent a day making pasta, which she would spread out on the top of her double bed to dry for future use. In fact, I can remember her and others reporting that they had made a 'bed full.' I wish I had her ravioli recipe. It was delicious and delicate. I remember that she used brains, but that's all. Why didn't I pay more attention?"

Yes, we all sometimes wonder why we didn't pay more attention to our family cooks while they were making their specialties. Bob left recipes and instructions among his notes, and here they are.

Fresh Fettuccine See Page 182.
Bob's Ravioli See Page 200.

Catch of the Day

The sign in the window said, "Albacore! Only $1 a pound!" When I saw it, Bob and I were driving through Moss Landing on our way to Sunset State Beach, where we were camping.

"Oh, let's stop and get some," I begged. "I haven't had albacore since I was a girl, and it's so delicious. The fish markets never seem to have it. Or else, when they do, it's so pricey it's beyond our budget."

"O.k., we'll stop," Bob answered. "But you'll find that there's a catch to this bargain that's more than 'catch of the day.' Albacore was never *that* cheap. Even in the old days."

We parked near the tiny fish market, one of the few in the village, and went inside. We saw a case of fresh fish ready for purchase, but no albacore. We hit the counter bell and shortly a fishmonger appeared, his white apron stained from processing fish.

"We're here for the albacore you advertise, but we don't see any."

"Oh, we keep that in the back. It's frozen, you know, and you have to take a whole fish. But they aren't too big – about seven pounds."

We asked to see one, to get an idea of the size of our potential bargain.

"Albacore easily can run seven dollars a pound, so a seven-pounder at seven dollars might be a good buy." I was doing the arithmetic. "This could be a real value."

"We'll see." Bob gave me a skeptical look.

The fishmonger reappeared lugging a slab-hard albacore. To us it looked like a giant, even though he said it was a small one. "Seven dollars, please."

Bob turned to me. "That's a lot of albacore for us to prepare while camping. We don't have a refrigerator, much less a freezer, you know – just an ice chest," Bob protested. But I had my taste buds set for this Pacific coast delicacy. "We could toss what we didn't use."

Bob gave me a quizzical look. Obviously, he was wondering how I could suggest wasting food. He pondered the project a few seconds longer. Then he pulled out his wallet.

As we departed with our frozen catch stashed behind the seat of the pickup, Bob teased me relentlessly about my idea of what constitutes a bargain.

"But a dollar a pound for albacore." I maintained. "You just can't beat that price."

Bob just looked at me and kept driving.

Back at our campground among the pines overlooking Sunset Beach, Bob busied himself with the culinary assignment – albacore dinner. I offered to help, but he said he preferred to work alone and see what he could devise. No running to a corner store for an alternate if he couldn't find a way to cook the fish.

He opened the butcher paper wrapping and placed the stiff creature in the sun to thaw. But September afternoon sunshine on the central California coast provides only mild heat, certainly not enough to thaw out that seven-pound slab of albacore by dinner. What to do? Obviously, the fish was in the "futures" category and we needed an evening meal. I said nothing further and began reading the day's paper. I was in enough trouble already.

After a few minutes, Bob announced that he would find a way to cut off steaks and barbecue them. He asked me to make coleslaw to go with them. He'd work on the rest of the fish the next day, after it had thawed.

Great plans. Executing them was something else. On this trip, we were camping in a shell on the back of our pickup. Bob and I had added amenities, such as a built-in sofa which unfolded to make a bed, custom curtains, a built-in cabinet with a tiny sink, a revolving fan, hooks for our clothes, and even a cocktail table – the ice chest outfitted with a lift-off wooden top. But we had elected to use a Coleman stove for cooking, and that had failed us the night before, in Yosemite Valley, on the first leg of our trip. Tonight we did have the campsite barbecue pit for cooking.

And we had some limited cooking equipment – assorted utensils and a few pots and pans. Bob found a large chef's knife, but it didn't have the serrated edge needed to saw through the solidly frozen behemoth. Using the smooth-bladed knife, he would have to press down, and hard – a feat he could do thanks to his hours of lifting weights.

An expert barbecue chef, Bob figured it would take him an hour to thaw and grill the steaks. This would give me plenty of time to prepare our favorite coleslaw recipe. I even found some sour cream and chopped green onion to make into a tartar sauce.

In our campsite barbecue pit, Bob made a fire with briquettes we had among our supplies. He also cleaned the grill. And he did succeed in cutting off two steaks and thawing them. As the albacore was sizzling on the grill, we wriggled our noses in delight at the savory aromas.

What a memorable dinner we had – grilled albacore with tartar sauce, sourdough bread, and coleslaw. We enjoyed every bite.

The next morning, Bob again busied himself with our albacore caper. By this time, the fish had thawed, so he could bone it and cut it into large chunks. He found red onion, Italian plum tomatoes, and bell pepper in our ice chest, so he concocted a fish stew with white wine. On a trip to Watsonville that day, we bought a fresh loaf of sourdough bread. Albacore stew, what a delicious way to prepare and serve such provender from the sea. We both enjoyed generous servings of the delicacy and still had plenty left for future meals. And we did serve it at home, too. Our seven pound treasure yielded about eight generous servings in all. We came away from that outing with an ice chest full of it.

Did we grow tired of albacore stew? I'll say not. With Catch of the Day becoming Catch of the Week, my budget-conscious *Genovese* spouse delighted in helping me treasure every bite.

Albacore Cacciatore See Page 221.
Nadine's Coleslaw See Page 155.

The Great Turkey

Over fifty turkeys flocked toward us as we stood at the side of their pen and looked through the fence. They probably wondered if we were bringing food. We, on the other hand, were looking *for* food. Mr. Angulo beamed proudly as my mother surveyed the selection.

"I want the biggest tom you have," she announced. We're having a large gathering this Thanksgiving, and I need a gorgeous big bird."

"How's that one over there?" Mr. Angulo pointed to a large tom, fan unfurled, strutting proudly among the hens. "He'll weigh in at 25 to 27 pounds dressed."

"Sold," said my mother. "Can you prepare him today? I'd like to pick him up in a couple of hours."

I stopped hanging on the fence, and my mother began the process of dragging my five-year-old sister, Jean, away from her new fascination, the entrancing big birds.

Back in the not-so-new-but-still-nice '36 Oldsmobile, we drove the two miles home to continue working on the other Thanksgiving treats— Mother's famous sage dressing, yams for candying, potatoes for mashing, cranberries for sauce, cabbage and lime gelatin for salad, and pumpkin for baking into pies.

This was Thanksgiving, we were expecting extra-special guests. My Uncle Elton, Dad's younger brother, was coming with Aunt Nedra, my four-year-old cousin Carolyn and their baby son, Paul. The Elton Cooks lived in Santa Fe and had not come to Phoenix for a visit since their marriage seven years before.

"Thank goodness you're old enough to help me with all of this," Mother remarked as she put me to work chopping walnuts for the salad. I was eleven, so I had been understudying Mother in the kitchen for several years already.

Thanksgiving and Christmas dinners always were our most elaborate feasts, aside from the giant "steak-frys" we enjoyed in the summers. I eagerly worked away at my assignments – cleaning and chopping celery, peeling yams, sorting cranberries – whatever Mother gave me to do. I could hardly wait to see my new baby cousin, as well as my beloved aunt and uncle and Carolyn.

Soon the two hours were up. Mother, Jean and I piled into the Olds to drive back over to the Angulos' for our turkey. We lived in a farming area, but our ten acres consisted of a non-business "gentleman's farm" in the Roosevelt District five miles south of Phoenix. My father worked in town all week; then on evenings and weekends, he and my mother tended the garden and the "farm." The Angulos, on the other hand, worked at least forty acres, raising melons as well as turkeys in order to make their living. We had bought lovely cantaloupes, canary melons, honeydews, and crenshaws from them in the summer. Now we were to become a turkey customer, too.

Mr. Angulo proudly unveiled our dressed tom. "He's a big one, all right, weighed in at 27 pounds."

Mother said thanks. Mr. Angulo helped her load the bird in the back seat and then we took off. Our Santa Fe relatives were driving in that night, so we had to prepare and refrigerate the bird by evening. Then Mother could rise at five on Thanksgiving morning and pop the bird into the oven.

"I certainly don't want to be working on this turkey when the relatives get here this evening," Mother announced. We nodded in agreement. We didn't know then what a close call that would be.

Washing out the cavity and wiping off the skin of our big bird took only a little time. But the task of pulling out the pin feathers, definitely not a pleasantly edible part of a turkey, was to take an endless forever.

Every pin had to come out, of course, and this boy must have had one for each of his twenty-seven pounds.

Pinfeathers on a big old tom don't pull out easily, you know. They were firmly embedded in our bird's flesh. Mother tried tweezers. No luck. Then she tried pliers. A few came out that way. The rest had to be cut out, a painstaking and laborious task. We didn't want to ruin the looks of the skin with holes or tears because, at our dinner, the bird would be presented on a huge platter and carved at the table. He shouldn't be missing big chunks of skin.

"Patience," said Mother as she struggled. "Judy, would you take this knife and see what you can do on this wing. I'll work on the tail." We sweated and strained to extricate those pins. Slowly. Surely. Dad arrived home from the office at 5:30, and we weren't even half done. My, oh, my. He couldn't help because he had to milk the cows. We continued on, stopping only for a quick supper of macaroni and cheese.

After dinner, Dad took my place as the helper. He quickly joined us in our amazement at the difficulty of the task. "Well, we're just going to have to cut some hunks of skin off the tail in order to get these last few out," he announced at 10 p.m.

"I guess so," Mother agreed with a sigh. "Judy, head for bed. We'll wake you up when the cousins arrive."

Almost on cue, the Cooks from Santa Fe drove down our driveway at 10:30. My mother had just stuffed and trussed the bird and placed it in the refrigerator.

"My, what a handsome big bird," everyone said the next day as our giant was presented. "Yes," Mother and Dad and I agreed. "Handsome— and *big!*"

These days, most of us get our turkeys from the supermarket, not only dressed but with pinfeathers removed. The following suggestions for stuffing and roasting a turkey combine the Pochini methods as well as my own developed over many years.

Roast Turkey With Dressing

1 turkey, fresh or well thawed
Stuffing
2 tablespoons olive oil
½ cup white cooking wine
Salt
Pepper

Remove neck and giblets from body cavity. Set aside for use with gravy and dressing. Wash turkey well, inside and out. Pat dry with paper toweling. Season cavity with salt and pepper. Place turkey upside down in large mixing bowl. Spoon stuffing loosely into body cavity. Place turkey on clean preparation surface and loosely stuff crop (just above the breast). Pull skin over crop and fasten with skewers to back of turkey. Close body cavity with skewers. With kitchen twine, lace cavity shut, tie legs together, and truss legs to tail. Lift wingtips up and over behind the back for a natural brace. Rub turkey with olive oil to prevent skin drying. Place turkey on a rack in a shallow open roasting pan. Place a loose "tent" of light weight foil, shiny side down, over turkey to prevent overbrowning. Roast at 325° as indicated on turkey roasting chart, about 3-1/4 hours for 12 pounds. Foil may be removed for the last half hour for a final browning. Spritz with white cooking wine at this time. Baste with pan juices at intervals three times until turkey is done.

Turkey is done when meat thermometer reaches 170°, drumstick moves easily, and juices run clear. Stuffing in a turkey needs to reach 165° to be sufficiently cooked.

Stuffing for Turkey

1 batch prepared cornbread
1 teaspoon dried sage
12 ounces bread dressing mix
1 tablespoon chopped fresh thyme
1-1/2 cups finely chopped onion
1/4 cup butter or vegetable oil
1-1/2 cups finely chopped celery
1 cup liquid

Turkeys vary in cavity size. Allow ½ cup mixed dressing for each pound of poultry. This recipe stuffs a 10- to 12-pound bird. Increase amounts by half again for 15-20 pounds; double for 20-25 pounds. Buy prepared cornbread at the market or make one recipe, or one package of cornbread mix. Cool and crumble into bits. Combine with dressing mix, vegetables, and herbs. Stir in melted butter or vegetable oil. Stir in heated liquid (broth, fruit juice, vegetable juice, or half white wine, half broth) gradually. I prefer butter and broth. Blend lightly. Use more liquid for moister dressing, less for drier. Just before roasting, spoon dressing lightly into neck and body cavities of turkey, allowing room for dressing to expand as it cooks. Fasten neck skin and body cavity with skewers as directed in roast turkey recipe. Allow an hour to stuff, truss, and oil bird. Place on rack in large roasting pan. Roast turkey as directed in recipe for roast turkey. Place any remaining dressing in an oiled casserole dish and place turkey neck on top of dressing. Bake covered along with turkey until neck is done (probably before turkey itself is done). Remove and refrigerate. Reheat at serving time.

Judy's Giblet Gravy

Heart, liver, and gizzard from turkey
1/4 teaspoon salt
White wine (optional)
½ rib of celery cut into fourths
2 tablespoons corn starch
1/4 cup cold water

Wash giblets well and place in saucepan with salt, celery, and water to cover. A bit of white wine may be added if desired. Cover saucepan and bring to boil. Turn heat down and simmer for one hour, or until giblets are well done when tested with skewer or fork. Remove giblets and celery from pan. Discard celery. Chop giblets fine. Return to pan. Set aside until turkey is done. Remove turkey from roasting pan. Skim any fat from pan juices with spoon. Place pan on rangetop on medium heat (for a large pan use two burners). Cook, stirring to loosen browned bits into the drippings. Mix corn starch with water and whisk until smooth. Using large wire whisk, stir as you pour this corn starch/water mixture into the pan. This helps avoid lumps in your gravy. Add desired seasonings. Stirring constantly, bring to boil over medium heat and boil one minute. Taste gravy and adjust seasonings. Note: People who "just don't like giblets" will enjoy this gravy if you take special care to chop those giblets *really fine*. Makes two cups.

Speedy Meals by a Speedy Driver

Just as I drove into our driveway, Bob came out the front door, all smiles. He hurried across the entry courtyard, and motioned for me to stop—not to open the garage door. Unaccustomed to such instructions, I wondered what was up. What was behind the door? What surprise would I see?

He was too late, though. Out of habit, I already had pushed the remote and the door was opening. I saw another car parked in my spot. As the door slowly lifted, I began to identify the car's vintage and make. First I saw the distinctive flat bumper of an older model. Then I saw the radiator grill with the heart-shaped top. Finally, the small propeller hood ornament confirmed my suspicions—it was a 1928 Ford! Well, yes it was, but not exactly. When the fully opened door revealed the full car I saw not a classic '28 Ford but a racy red roadster.

"Ohhh! So you bought yourself a new toy!"

Beaming with joy, Bob escorted me into the garage for a closer look.

The front and rear bumpers and the radiator grill of the car were unmistakably vintage 1928, but the roadster portion was wild and colorful—a "street rod." Its cut-down body had no doors, just smooth sides sporting bursts of orange flames, no fenders, no windows. Behind the seat on a handsomely crafted miniature truck "bed" made of redwood sat the fuel tank—a five-gallon gas can.

I had seen "street rods" like this one at some of the classic car "picnic meets" that Bob and I had attended. Now I saw one sitting in our garage. Of course, such playthings usually have handsomely outfitted souped-up engines with lots of polished chrome fittings. Intuition told me my husband, a former drag-racing champion, would have invested only in a "muscle" car.

As Bob led me to the car I could see how right I was. Knowing the power potential only by guess, I could see that the magnificently polished chrome engine with its blower, as pointed out by my playmate, had big possibilities for speed. And, in case it didn't perform with the desired raciness, Bob as a professional race car builder surely had the know-how to bring that out.

"It's legal, you know. Registered as a '28 because it's built on the original chassis. The body may be fiberglass, and the engine may be a little altered, but it falls within the DMV standards for a '28 car. No catalytic converter, no smog tests. We'll take it out after dinner."

That night Bob had prepared what he considered an "easy" meal– Italian sausages browned in olive oil and finished with a spritz of wine, accompanied by fettuccine with pesto. I prepared a green salad, and with some good zinfandel we had an elegant although swiftly prepared dinner.

Quickly we cleared the table and did the dishes. I changed into slacks and grabbed a visor cap. The car, true to its roadster personality, had no top and no doors. Fortunately, it still had the original running boards, making it relatively easy for me to climb over the side and settle into a bucket seat, a welcome gesture to modernity.

Thankfully, the engine had a modern starter, rather than a crank. Bob turned the key and the roadster sprang to life with an impressively powerful roar.

We rolled down our private lane and out onto the street. I loved riding with Bob because he was a safe although speedy driver, having driven such cars since he was fourteen or fifteen when he had been no stranger to the weekend drag races on San Francisco's Great Highway overlooking the Pacific. Bob knew just how to gun a car's engine while idling at stoplights, egging on drivers of the younger set with their powerful turbo-drives and other advanced speed accessories. He was bad enough when behind the wheel of his Datsun 240Z; now he was a regular devil.

"Let's show this baby to Bob and Emily," he said as he drove his new toy out of our neighborhood and across town.

Along the way, Bob would taunt other drivers as we tarried at stoplights. Varoom! Varoom! He'd race the engine with provocative rhythm. The other drivers would wave and give us "thumbs up," a sign I soon learned means, "great iron." Then a twenty-something guy on a motorcycle dug out as the light turned green and so did we, both making a mad dash to the next light. We won, and the motorcyclist gave Bob a thumbs-up.

"What did we just do?" I asked.

"We raced a motorcycle and won," Bob replied.

"Is that special?"

"Yes. Few cars can out-drag a motorcycle."

I was impressed.

Our friends Bob and Emily, who both had grown up in Manhattan, loved Pochini's new toy. They happily accepted rides in the hot-rod, and returned wide-eyed with joy. For them, as for me, it was their first-ever ride in a rod. Why? We asked each other and then answered in unison, "Because our parents wouldn't let us!"

We admired Bob for having sneaked out of his bedroom window at night to live a secret life among other teenage boys with fast cars in San Francisco.

From that first summer evening jaunt and for the next year or so, Bob and I would clear our brains by taking "roadster rides" after work and on weekends. We took back roads along the north slope of Mt. Diablo, driving past fruit orchards and oak-studded grazing land. We sometimes headed down Danville Boulevard and turned east on Diablo Road to approach the mountain from another side. Most of all, we enjoyed waving to friends and strangers as we drove along. And of course we delighted in the occasional and successful (although illegal) drag races Bob triggered along the way.

Because most of our rides were after-work treats, Bob strove to prepare quick and easy dinners that would take only thirty minutes from start to first bite. Here is a favorite recipe for one of our hurry-up menus of braised Italian sausage, fettuccine with pesto sauce, and a green salad.

Bob poses at the wheel of his new "street rod."
Photo courtesy of Robert Cohen

Braised Sausages

4 - 5 sausages, Italian or other variety
1 tablespoon olive oil
1/4 cup cooking wine

Dry sausages with paper toweling. Using a dinner fork, pierce surfaces of sausages all over. Heat a large nonstick skillet on High. Add olive oil and heat. Place sausages in pan and brown on all sides. Add wine and turn burner to Low. Cover pan and simmer for 10 minutes or until sausages are cooked through. Serves 2 - 4.

In Search of the Giant Zucchini

You know how zucchini in the garden can hide under the large leaves and grow and grow and grow? When you finally find them, they can be huge. My parents considered that an omission in picking, rather than a bonus. Mother knew only how to sauté zucchini with onions and tomatoes, or just to stew slices of zucchini and serve with butter. In those days, we didn't consider using small zucchini raw in salads or for *crudités*; and we had not yet encountered the many other ways to use zucchini – soup, bread, cookies, pickles, frittata, or stuffed with breadcrumbs or sausage – all recipes which use the huge guys as well as the mediums and smalls.

When my parents' Santa Barbara neighbors, the Chachakos family, passed "zukes" of all sizes – from small to giant, over the fence to us, we accepted them politely. Once inside the privacy of our kitchen, we wondered what to do with the behemoths that our Greek friends so proudly had shared. Those over-the-hill monsters can be tough and watery. With regret, we cast them upon our compost pile. But in case we might have been wasting good food, we felt pangs of guilt.

As the years passed, I learned to use those big babies for zucchini cookies and bread. All zucchini gardeners know that the big challenge lies not in coaxing the vines to produce but in finding ways to use the prolific yield.

Stuffed zucchini is a specialty I first enjoyed at the renowned Townsend's restaurant (now closed) on Union Square in San Francisco.

They made the dish from delicate, small squash stuffed with zucchini pulp and crumbs and topped with their special cheddar cheese sauce. How good they were! I ordered the dish often. Then I wanted to try it at home.

Still in my early twenties and learning to cook, I consulted the few cook books I had on hand. No recipes for stuffed zucchini. Undeterred, I forged ahead. I cut out the center of the zucchini to make a trough, chopped up the pulp, mixed it with dry breadcrumbs and egg, stuffed the zucchini and topped them with a cheddar cheese sauce. They really looked appetizing and very much like the Townsend's dish as I popped them into the oven. I figured they might be done in 30 minutes, so I prepared a salad and eagerly anticipated enjoying this new culinary achievement for dinner. But 30 minutes went by and when I pricked them with a fork the zucchini were far from tender. I set the timer ahead 30 minutes and read the paper. Still the zucchini tested hard and uncooked. I had put water in the bottom of the baking dish, as one does with squash, but this evidently did not provide the magic touch. Again, I set the timer for 30 more minutes. After an hour and a half, I was unwilling to wait longer for dinner, so I ate my "creation." Tough and uncooked.

"So much for that." I told myself. I discarded stuffed zucchini as a project and decided to let Townsend's satisfy my desire for that dish.

Years later, after I had married Bob, I finally had a chance to learn what I'd done wrong. At holiday time during the winter, Bob would find small zucchini imported from warmer climes to stuff and serve along with stuffed mushrooms and stuffed bell pepper sections.

In the summer, though, Bob would take one of our home-grown leviathans, cut it in half lengthwise, stuff and bake the halves, and then cut them into sections to serve at our barbecues and picnics.

One bite convinced me this dish tasted as good as it looked. After my disastrous try years before to prepare stuffed zucchini, I was anxious to understudy Bob and learn his secrets. Bob's main trick: **parboil** the squash before you stuff it, just until it becomes *al dente*, not mushy.

Yes, it does help to learn cooking skills from a master. As a beginning cook those many years before, I had failed in my attempt to duplicate Townsend's dish on my own, with no advice, no cookbook, no teacher.

Those trial-and-error days are over, now that I have trained with Bob. Here is a recipe for you to enjoy:

Stuffed Zucchini

1 giant zucchini OR several small or medium zucchini
1/4 teaspoon pepper
1/4 teaspoon garlic powder
4 1"- thick slices dry sourdough bread
1 small onion
2 large eggs
1 tablespoon olive oil
½ cup grated parmesan cheese
Sprinkle of ground paprika
½ teaspoon salt

Wash zucchini and cut in half lengthwise. Scoop out inside pulp and reserve. Microcook on High for six minutes (or parboil) until fork-tender but not mushy. Remove seeds from zucchini pulp and chop fine. Crush dry sourdough bread into crumbs. Peel onion and chop fine. Sauté in olive oil. Add chopped zucchini pulp and brown. Add salt, pepper, garlic powder, and breadcrumbs. In large bowl, mix vegetable/crumb mixture, parmesan cheese, and eggs. Spoon into zucchini shells. Press down firmly. Top with grated parmesan cheese and paprika. Place in large baking pan or dish in 1/4" water. Bake at 350° for 40 minutes, until brown. To serve, cut into 2" wide slices and fan out on platter. Serves MANY.

"This Is Why It's So Difficult to Dine Out"

Just a week ago I finished remodeling the kitchen of my "new" fifty-year-old condo in Santa Barbara. Today I completed installing my equipment in the state-of -the-art space. The latest in appliances and lighting accent granite countertops, tesserae stone backsplashes, and a lighted bar cabinet with liquor and glassware on display, just as Bob would have set it up. Even the dishtowel is on the left and the hand towel on the right, as Bob would have placed them. (Sorry, Bob. We don't have a gas range here, but the smooth electric cooktop heats up fast and in addition provides ample surface for shifting positions of pots and pans.)

Tonight I prepared my first complete dinner in the new kitchen. I decided to make fresh tortolloni, with braised Italian sausages and a side salad. The pasta sauce was a butter and fresh sage concoction with gorgonzola and parmesan cheeses. I'd braised the sausages as Bob had taught me — brown on medium high in a bit of olive oil. Then I spritzed the sausages with a couple of tablespoons of wine, covered, and simmered them for ten minutes.

The garden yielded Mexican sage, so I harvested a dozen medium size younger leaves and chopped them. The sage added a subtle touch to the powerful notes of the gorgonzola.

I made a small salad of fresh tomato wedges and fresh scallions.

Although this dinner could wait for awhile and then be reheated at will, I decided to *"mangia! mangia!"* immediately upon completing it.

With a glass of pinot grigio, I enjoyed every bite. As I dined, I thanked the spirit of Bob for teaching me how to prepare such an elegant and simple gourmet repast.

And then I repeated the words he would say so often when just the two of us at home were enjoying one of our many delicious culinary collaborations:

"This is why it's so difficult to dine out."

I hope that with the help and inspiration of the stories and recipes in this memoir, you, too, will develop a repertoire of simple and taste-satisfying recipes that indeed will make it difficult for you to "dine out" as well.

Buon gusto!
Judy

Recipes:
Tortolloni with Gorgonzola and Sage Sauce See Page 213.
Braised Sausages See Page 95.

The
Recipes

Lamb Cacciatore on polenta

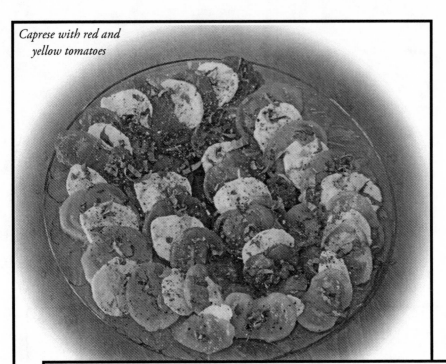

*Caprese with red and
yellow tomatoes*

*Cornish Hen with wild rice and
mushrooms, sautéed green beans*

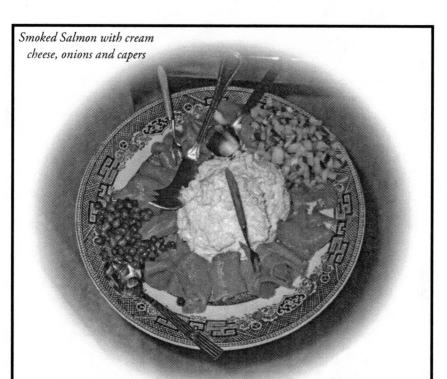

Smoked Salmon with cream cheese, onions and capers

Blood Orange and Avocado salad

Appetizers

Antipasto

In Italy, the hors d'oeuvre *course is termed antipasto (before the meal). But in San Francisco the word antipasto also refers to a popular dish served with the antipasto course.*

This antipasto dish consists of a medley of pickled peppers and vegetables, mushrooms, marinated artichoke hearts, and cooked fish bound together in a complex tomato sauce. Diners pile it onto slices of sourdough baguette. A selection of well cured Italian salami and cheeses often accompanies this savory concoction.

Here are two versions of antipasto, the dish.

Noni's Antipasto

1 large jar hot giardiniera pickles, drained
4 tablespoons extra virgin olive oil
2 4-ounce cans tomato sauce
1 can skinless, boneless sardines, drained
1 4-ounce can button mushrooms or ½ pound fresh mushrooms, washed and cut into quarters
1 8-ounce can pitted ripe olives, drained
1 6-ounce can solid pack tuna, drained and broken into bite-size pieces

Combine giardiniera with olive oil and tomato sauce in 1-quart saucepan. Simmer for 30 minutes on Low. Add remaining ingredients. Simmer 15 minutes. Cool to room temperature. Refrigerate overnight.

Jean Pochini

Antipasto

½ pound fresh small mushrooms
(Canned mushroom caps may be substituted.)
2 6-ounce cans solid-pack tuna
1 large jar of hot giardiniera pickles, drained
1 15-ounce can pitted black olives, drained
1 15-ounce jar green olives stuffed with pimiento, drained
1 8-1/2-ounce jar Italian style pepperoncini, drained
1 4-ounce jar marinated artichoke hearts

<u>Sauce</u>
1 8-ounce can tomato sauce
6 ounces of catsup
5 tablespoons olive oil
2 tablespoons red wine vinegar
1 tablespoon fresh lemon juice
1/4 tablespoon Tabasco sauce

Clean mushroom caps and pat dry. Place in large bowl. Drain tuna and add in chunks. Add vegetables. In separate bowl, combine sauce ingredients. Add to vegetables and tuna. Mix lightly. Refrigerate overnight. Serves 8-10 generously as an appetizer. Accompany with baguette slices.

Stuffed Artichoke Leaves

A prominent Seattle hostess gave a reception in my honor many years ago in her craftsman home overlooking Lake Washington. This simple but showy appetizer was the hit of her party.

2 large artichokes
6 cloves of garlic, peeled
2 tablespoons extra virgin olive oil
1 lemon, cut in half
1/2 pound baby shrimp, divided, thawed and drained
4 ounces cream cheese
2 tablespoons cultured sour cream
2 tablespoons mayonnaise
½ teaspoon prepared horseradish
1/4 teaspoon dried dill weed

Wash artichokes. Cut off stems. Steam in water with garlic, olive oil, and lemon until tender.

Chop half of the shrimp and set aside. Soften cream cheese and whip until fluffy. Add remaining ingredients and mix well. Stir in shrimp.

Pull leaves off artichokes, leaving centermost leaves attached. Leave enough of the bottom on the center so that it will stand upright. Remove choke. Insert one or two flowers using this as a vase. Place in center of two serving plates. Fill the base of each leaf with about one teaspoon or less of the shrimp mixture. Top with one baby shrimp. Arrange in fan shape on plate, like the petals of a chrysanthemum, around the artichoke "vase."

Instruct guests to bite off the end of the leaf with the filling. Keep a discard dish close at hand.

Braesola

Air-cured braesola is to beef what prosciutto is to pork. Braesola is especially popular in the Lake Como area. Here is how they present it.

2 grapefruit, peeled and cut into segments
(Canned grapefruit slices may be substituted.)
1/4 pound braesola, thinly sliced
Extra virgin olive oil

Peel all rind and white outer membrane from whole grapefruit. Cut between inner membranes to get full segments. Set aside.

Arrange four slices of braesola on serving plate. Garnish with three or four grapefruit segments. Drizzle with olive oil.

Bruschetta

Almost unknown in the U.S. until the mid-1990's, bruschetta made a sudden hit. It was devised by Italian housewives as a way to use stale bread. The name bruschetta, pronounced "broo-sket-ah," comes from the Italian bruscare, "to toast." Basically toast rounds accented with garlic butter, bruschetta are topped with mixtures of tomatoes, fresh herbs, truffles, chopped olive tapenade, etc. Best served as sit-down appetizers because they tend to break, lose topping on the table, or spill onto shirt-fronts, bruschetta can be tamed for stand-up appetizers.

I have found that combining topping ingredients into an emulsion solves the messiness problems. Here is a crowd-pleaser:

4 large fresh tomatoes
4 cloves garlic
8 stems fresh basil, divided
2 tablespoons extra virgin olive oil
1/4 teaspoon salt
1 sourdough baguette

Wash tomatoes. Place in tomato press or food mill and process into seedless, skinless pulp. Place in mixing bowl. Peel garlic and purée, using garlic press. Add to tomatoes. Finely chop leaves from four stems of basil. Add to mixture. Add olive oil and salt.

Cut baguette into 1/4 inch thick rounds. Toast lightly. Spread with tomato mixture. Garnish each slice with a basil leaf.

Caravaggio

Like Carpaccio, Caravaggio evidently takes its name from that of a famous Italian artist. Bob and I found the Caravaggio served by a favorite restaurant so delectable that we figured out the ingredients and procured them for our own version to serve at home.

2 pounds beef tenderloin
1 cup mayonnaise
1 tablespoon Dijon mustard
3 teaspoons lemon juice
1 tablespoon Worcestershire sauce
½ teaspoon Tabasco sauce
2 tablespoons beef broth
1 lemon
4 ounces shaved grana cheese
Freshly ground black pepper
Italian parsley for garnish

Rinse beef under cold running water. Pat dry with paper toweling.

Wrap the beef with plastic wrap and freeze about two hours, until meat is very cold but not frozen. Remove wrap from meat. Using a sharp knife or meat slicer, slice tenderloin paper-thin. Set aside to thaw.

Whisk together the mayonnaise, mustard, lemon juice, Worcestershire sauce, Tabasco sauce, and beef broth. Set aside.

On each individual plate, arrange four slices of tenderloin. Top with a squeeze of lemon, the shaved grana, and a grind of pepper. Place a dollop of sauce on the side of the plate. (Pass extra sauce.) Garnish with sprigs of Italian parsley. Serves eight.

Stuffed Celery

My memories of stuffed celery go back to an early age. My Grandma Rose usually served it for holiday dinners and picnics. Grandmother stuffed the celery ribs with a mixture of grated cheddar and mayonnaise. Now I like to go "uptown" with a filling of cream cheese.

1 heart of celery, leaves removed
1 9-ounce tub whipped cream cheese or 1 8-ounce package cream cheese
½ teaspoon chopped fresh Italian parsley
1/4 teaspoon chopped fresh thyme
Paprika to taste.

Wash and trim celery ribs. Cut into 3-inch sections. Pat dry. Set aside. Place unwhipped cream cheese into microsafe bowl. Microcook on High for 30 seconds. Check for spreadability with stirring spoon. Microcook for 30-second intervals until soft or use whipped cream cheese. Fold in parsley and thyme until well mixed. Fill celery sections with cream cheese. Dust with paprika.

Jo's Chicken Liver Pâté

Bob enjoyed serving an elegant pâté for special occasions such as birthdays and wedding anniversaries. This special recipe, as developed by home economist Jo Van Shaick and interpreted by me, is a perennial favorite at receptions following the UCSB Music Affiliates musicales in Santa Barbara. Guests would often confess, as they gathered around the hors d'oeuvre *table, that they enjoyed Jo's pâté almost as much as the music. It helped give a fitting finale to an elegant affair.*

½ pound chicken livers
1 tablespoon olive oil
½ pound mushrooms, washed and sliced
2 tablespoons finely chopped onion
2 cloves garlic, peeled and finely chopped
4 tablespoons unsalted butter
Pinch of ground cloves
1/4 teaspoon salt
1/8 teaspoon pepper

Rinse chicken liver. Place in 1-quart saucepan. Cover with water. Place lid on pan. Poach livers on Low for 15 - 20 minutes. Drain. In nonstick skillet, heat olive oil. Sauté mushrooms on High until soft. Place chicken livers in food processor and pulse until puréed. Add mushrooms, onion, garlic, and seasonings. Purée until smooth. Taste. Correct seasonings as necessary. Chill 1 - 2 hours or longer. Place in decorative serving bowl. Serve with water wafers or toasted baguette slices.

Baby Cream Puffs With Shrimp

A cocktail party at the home of Bob's daughter Liane Pochini Cornell or Gina Pochini Lincoln takes on a super-festive air when arriving guests see a platter of bite-size cream puffs filled with shrimp salad. Here's the recipe, along with tips from these experienced hostesses.

<u>Cream Puffs</u>
1 cup water
½ cup unsalted butter
1 cup all-purpose flour, sifted
4 large eggs

Preheat oven to 400°.

In large saucepan, heat butter with water until mixture boils. Turn heat to Low. Add flour and stir constantly until mixture leaves the sides of the pan and forms a ball, about 1 minute. Remove from heat. Add eggs one at a time, beating after each addition and then continuing to beat until smooth and velvety. (This is a lot of beating.) Drop in portions the size of a walnut onto ungreased baking sheet. You will have 18 portions. Bake until puffed, golden brown and dry, about 15 to 20 minutes. Remove from oven and cool slowly, away from drafts, at least 10 minutes. May be frozen for next-day use.

<u>Shrimp Salad Filling</u>
1 pound bay shrimp, thawed, rinsed thoroughly and dried in paper toweling
1 green onion washed and chopped
2 hardboiled eggs, chopped
4 tablespoons mayonnaise
1 tablespoon catsup
1 tablespoon white wine vinegar or lemon juice
1/8 teaspoon pepper
1/8 teaspoon Tabasco sauce, optional

Place shrimp in mixing bowl. Leave whole or chop if you desire. Add onion and chopped egg. Mix well. In separate bowl, mix mayonnaise, catsup, vinegar, pepper and Tabasco sauce (optional). Add dressing to shrimp mixture a little at a time just until mixture is well coated. Do not "over-dress" the shrimp mixture; that would make your cream-puffs soggy. Chill in refrigerator for 20 minutes, or as long as overnight.

With a sharp knife, cut the tops of the puffs partway off, but leave tops attached. Fill each puff with a heaping teaspoon or so of shrimp mixture. Fold top of puff onto filling. Serve within 30 minutes. Do not let puffs get soggy. 18 servings.

Note that both puffs and filling can be made in advance. Puffs should be filled just before your party, however.

Hearty Deviled Eggs

Deviled eggs always disappear quickly at a buffet. Daughter Jan came up with the idea of topping each one with bacon, another crowd-pleaser. Daughter Gina likes to pipe the yolk mixture into the whites for a dressy effect.

6 large eggs
3 tablespoons prepared mayonnaise
½ teaspoon prepared Dijon mustard
1/8 teaspoon fresh or dried dill weed, chopped
Salt and Pepper to taste
3 slices bacon
Fresh dill weed or Italian parsley

Boil eggs until hard. Allow to cool. Peel. Cut in half lengthwise. Remove yolks and place in bowl. Crumble eggs with fork until finely mashed. Add mayonnaise, mustard, dill weed, salt, and pepper. Mix with fork until fluffy.

On microwave-safe plate, place three paper towels. Lay bacon strips on top of towels. Cover with one paper towel. Microcook on High 3-4 minutes, until well done. Crumble bacon into yolk mixture and blend.

Mound yolk mixture into white "shells," rounding tops. (Or pipe into "shells" with a pastry tube.) Decorate with a tiny sprig of dill or parsley. Serve as an hors d'oeuvre or salad accompaniment. Makes 12 portions.

Mortadella Pinwheels

Cold cuts made into an appetizer? Yes, and oh, so showy on a platter.

8 ounces cream cheese
2 tablespoons grated parmesan cheese
6 slices mortadella, not too thinly sliced

Place cream cheese in microwave-safe bowl. Microcook on High for 2 minutes. Whip with cooking fork. Add parmesan and stir until well mixed. Spread on mortadella. Roll tightly. Wrap in plastic. Freeze for 60 minutes until firm. Cut into 3/8- inch segments, using extra sharp knife. Thaw and serve.

Marinated Mushrooms

Before I met Bob, I learned how delicious this appetizer can be and how easy it is to prepare. I like to take it to pot-lucks, and it always scores a hit. One afternoon I put my chilled bowl of marinated mushrooms onto the counter and left the kitchen to find a serving dish. While I was gone, the unthinkable happened. My roguish Irish Setter discovered that these "veggies" were goood. I caught her in the act of devouring all of them and licking the bowl. Oh, well —

Since that disaster, my friend and mentor Jane Trittipo, the noted author of two microwave cookbooks, has inspired me to "microcook" my way out of a hurried need for a gourmet dish. You can microcook these marinated mushrooms, before church and then chill and marinate then while you attend services. When you return home, they're ready to go along to the church picnic.

1 pound fresh medium-size button mushrooms, scrubbed and blotted on paper toweling
4 cloves garlic, peeled and sliced
2/3 cup extra virgin olive oil
½ teaspoon dried tarragon or 1 tablespoon fresh tarragon leaves, finely chopped
½ cup white wine vinegar
1 tablespoon white balsamic vinegar

Place mushrooms, garlic, olive oil, tarragon, and vinegars in large microsafe mixing bowl or casserole. Cover with plastic wrap or lid. Microcook on High 2 to 4 minutes. Reduce power to Medium and cook 3 to 5 minutes, just until mushrooms are *al dente*. Cool uncovered for 10 minutes. Stir well. Chill mushrooms and their marinade in the refrigerator. Drain and serve in a decorative salad bowl with toothpicks.

Stuffed Mushrooms

Besides his savory frittata, Bob also liked to serve his stuffed mushrooms for an hors d'oeuvre before one of our special occasion dinners. But these versatile treats also dress up an entrée plate as well. The recipe is so simple you'll be tempted to serve it often.

1 pound button mushrooms, washed and scrubbed
½ cup coarse fresh bread crumbs
1/4 cup finely chopped almonds or walnuts
2 tablespoons parmesan cheese, divided
1 tablespoon unsalted butter
2 tablespoons milk
Olive oil
Water

Remove stems from mushrooms and set aside. Place mushroom caps down in an oiled baking dish.

Chop mushroom stems until fine. Place in mixing bowl along with bread crumbs, chopped nuts, and 1 tablespoon parmesan cheese. Melt butter and add along with milk, mixing well. Place a small amount of filling in each cap, making sure filling is evenly distributed among the caps. Top each with a small amount of grated parmesan. Place a small amount of water (2 to 3 tablespoons) in the baking dish. Bake at 350° until mushrooms and filling are heated through and slightly browned on top, about 30 minutes. Serve hot.

Smoked Mussels

Once you discover the mysterious appeal of smoked mussels, you'll want holidays and birthdays to come around often so you will have an excuse to serve them.

For holiday celebrations, Bob and I served an appetizer of smoked New Zealand mussels with champagne. An upscale fish monger or delicatessen usually carries the mussels. Serve with a squeeze of lemon and offer baguette slices as "carriers." A delectable treat.

Polenta Squares With Gorgonzola

Bob developed this recipe after enjoying it at one of our favorite dining spots, Lalime's in Berkeley. It takes a while to prepare, but the savory results make your effort worthwhile. You can prepare the polenta several hours before your dinner and then grill the squares at serving time.

1 recipe for polenta or instant polenta (See Pages 188 and 189.)
2 ounces crumbled gorgonzola
1 tablespoon olive oil

Prepare polenta as directed until it becomes thick but not stiff. Add the cheese along with the butter. Stir well until cheese and butter melt into the polenta mixture. Pour into a well oiled baking dish or onto a large board. Chill in refrigerator for at least one hour until polenta becomes firm. Cut into squares, trapezoids, or triangles. Heat olive oil in heavy cast iron or nonstick skillet. Grill polenta pieces on both sides until golden brown. Remove from skillet and cool slightly if serving as an out-of-hand appetizer. Do not cool if you serve the squares to accompany an entrée or a salad.

Prosciutto/Cream Cheese Pinwheels

Because the prosciutto is so delicate it takes extra effort to roll it with the cheese. The taste, however, will win accolades.

1 12-ounce tub whipped lowfat cream cheese
½ teaspoon Italian herb mix
8 paper-thin slices prosciutto, about 1/4 - 1/3 pound

In microwave-safe bowl, microcook cheese on High 1 minute to soften if necessary. Beat herbs into cheese. Spread 1/8 inch - 1/4 inch layer of cheese on each slice of prosciutto. Roll tightly. Wrap in plastic. Freeze until firm, about one hour. Cut into slices ½ inch thick. Serve when thawed. May be stored in refrigerator.

Prosciutto With Fruit

When asked to bring an appetizer, I often show up with a large platter of prosciutto and melon. The combination tastes delicious, and the melon holds up well on warmer days.

Ask your meat-cutter to give you slices at least four to five inches long. You need the length to give the "wrap" to your fruit. Prosciutto should be sliced so thin you can see your hand through it when held to the light.

Fruit can be 1-1/2-inch chunks of melon - cantaloupe, honeydew, canary, Sharlyn - almost any variety. Or you might like papaya, fresh pineapple, or fresh figs. Prosciutto with figs is top-rated, but fresh figs come around only in late summer and fall. Thus, when I see figs I often plan an event just so I can serve prosciutto with figs.

Prepare the fruit in bite-size pieces. Cut each prosciutto slice in half lengthwise. Wrap a strip around a piece of fruit. Fasten with a round cocktail toothpick. This sounds simple, but it takes patience to do each canapé attractively. Allow plenty of time.

Smoked Salmon Appetizer

Gina Pochini developed her artistry of presentation at the noted All Seasons restaurant in Calistoga. This picturesque treatment for smoked salmon gives her cocktail parties a festive distinction.

Whipped cream cheese
Smoked salmon slices
Chopped red onion
Capers, well drained
Slices of sourdough baguette

On large platter, mound cream cheese in center, or place cream cheese in a small serving bowl. Separate slices of salmon and arrange from edge of cream cheese to outside edge of platter, using two-thirds of space. On remaining one-third of platter, place chopped onions and capers in separate mounds or small bowls. Supply a small serving knife with the cheese, a small serving fork with the salmon and miniature serving spoons for the onion and the capers. Place the baguette slices in a basket near the platter. Guests spread a baguette round with cream cheese and then add the salmon, onion, and capers.

For individual appetizers, toast the baguette slices slightly to keep them firm. Top with cream cheese, salmon, chopped onion, and capers put through a garlic press. This keeps the appetizer controllable and saves your guests the embarrassment of having the bread crumble or the capers drop onto your carpet.

Smoked Salmon Spread

Mincing the capers helps keep them from bouncing off the top of the canape and onto the floor or into a guest's lap.

8 ounces whipped lowfat cream cheese
4 ounces smoked salmon slices
1 tablespoon caper brine
3 teaspoons finely chopped red onion
1/8 teaspoon dried dill weed
1/8 teaspoon dried chervil
1 sourdough baguette, sliced
Capers, drained.

Place first six ingredients in food processor. Pulse until salmon and onions are well pulverized and mixed with cheese.

To serve, toast baguette slices. Spread with salmon mixture. Put drained capers through garlic press into a small bowl. With a small spoon, place a strip of minced capers across the center of each canape.

Stuffed Zucchini Blossoms

Once Bob and I had tried this appetizer we became hooked on it. Sure enough, our zucchini plants had an abundance of blossoms, and we could harvest a few. They wilt easily, so pick blossoms just before preparing them if possible.

12 large zucchini blossoms (with or without baby zucchini attached) (Allow 3 - 4 per person.)
2 large eggs, gently beaten
½ cup all-purpose flour
1 cup dry bread crumbs seasoned with Italian herb mixture
12 "sticks" of easy-melting cheese such as mozzarella or light havarti, about 3 - 4 inches long by 1 inch square
Olive oil

Rinse blossoms. Gently pat dry with paper toweling. In shallow bowl, whisk egg and set aside. Place flour on plate. Place crumbs on a plate.

Heat about 2 tablespoons olive oil in a nonstick skillet. Keep heat on Medium. Fill each blossom with a "stick" of cheese. Dip in flour, then in egg, then in bread crumbs. Gently place in skillet. Fry until golden on all sides, adding additional as needed. Remove from skillet and drain on paper toweling. Serve on small plates as a first course. Makes 12. Serves 4 to 6.

Soups

Asparagus Soup

Bob taught me how to make soup from many varieties of vegetables. This method is so simple you can put a pot of soup on at any season of the year. From asparagus to zucchini, vegetables provide a hearty starter soup or one-dish meal, your choice.

1 bunch fresh asparagus
1 tablespoon olive oil
1 large yellow onion, chopped
1/8 teaspoon black pepper
2 - 14-1/2 - ounce cans chicken broth
1/8 teaspoon ground nutmeg
1 tablespoon butter

Break asparagus stems at point of "no resistance." Cut bottom stems into 1 -inch pieces. Use tops for another dish. In medium size stockpot, heat olive oil on high heat. Sauté onion until transparent. Add pepper. Add asparagus pieces and sauté briefly. Add chicken broth. Bring to boil. Reduce heat. Simmer, covered, for two hours. Add nutmeg and butter. Purée in blender. Process through Foley food mill to filter out the fiber. Serve hot. Butter is needed for flavor. Do not make the mistake of omitting butter in hopes of reducing fat. Cut fat from your diet in another recipe!

Avocado Soup

On a hot summer evening in 1983, Bob courted me with a surprise first course – chilled avocado soup conjured up from his own experience and imagination. Here's his recipe for this refreshing concoction.

2 large avocados, peeled
2 cups chicken broth
4 green onions, cleaned and chopped
1 spray (about 1/3 bunch) of Italian parsley leaves, washed
2 cloves garlic, peeled
1/3 cup lemon juice (about 2 lemons)
1/8 teaspoon pepper
1/4 teaspoon Worcestershire sauce

Put broth in blender. Add green onions. Blend on Low until onions are chopped fine. Add avocados in chunks. Put garlic through press into blender. Add pepper and Worcestershire sauce. Blend. Add lemon juice. Blend. Add parsley. Blend until parsley is finely chopped. Taste. Correct seasonings if you desire. Chill and serve. Makes 4-1/2 cups (4 large servings).

Broccoli Soup

This flavorful soup adds a touch of sophistication to a dinner party, but it also warms the heart on a busy day of projects.

1 tablespoon olive oil
1 tablespoon butter
1 large yellow onion, peeled and chopped
1/4 teaspoon salt
1/8 teaspoon pepper
3 - 14-1/2 - ounce cans chicken broth
1 bunch broccoli, chopped
1/4 teaspoon ground nutmeg

In medium size stock pot, heat olive oil and butter on high heat. Sauté onion until transparent. Add salt and pepper. Add broth and cut-up broccoli. Simmer, covered, one hour until broccoli is soft. Purée with Hamilton Beach in-pot machine or in blender until smooth. Stir in nutmeg. Makes 9 cups, 6 servings.

Cauliflower Soup

Serve this soup as a flavorful course before a dinner of roast pork loin..

1-1/2 tablespoons olive oil
1 tablespoon butter
1 large yellow onion, chopped
1/4 teaspoon salt
1/8 teaspoon pepper
1 large cauliflower, chopped
6 cups chicken broth
Pinch of nutmeg
Italian parsley, finely chopped

In medium size stock pot, heat olive oil and butter on high heat. Sauté onion until transparent. Add salt and pepper. Add cut-up cauliflower and sauté slightly. Add broth. Cover and simmer two hours. Purée with Hamilton Beach in-pot machine or in blender until smooth. Add nutmeg. Makes approximately 9 cups, 6 servings.

Serve garnished with chopped parsley.

Chicken Stock

What a joy it can be to prepare your own chicken meat from scratch when the by-product is a savory stock, soup, or consommé. Use this satisfying result as a stand-alone soup or as an ingredient in sauces or other soups.

1 4 - pound chicken, cut up, unskinned
(Freeze the liver for another use.)
1 chicken gizzard, if available
1 chicken heart, if available
1 large onion, peeled and cut up
2 large carrots, scraped and cut up
1 large stalk of celery
1 bay leaf
1 spray Italian parsley, washed and not chopped
1\2 teaspoon salt
1/4 teaspoon pepper

Wash chicken parts well. Include neck and wing tips as well. Do not remove fat. Place all ingredients in large stock pot. Add just enough water to cover chicken and vegetables. Place on range on High and bring to a boil. Cover pot. Reduce heat to Low. Simmer slowly until meat begins to fall off bones, 2 to 3 hours.

Remove pot from heat. Place chicken and vegetables in a large bowl and refrigerate for other use. Cool pot of broth until it reaches room temperature, about 30 minutes. Place pot in refrigerator and chill until stock turns to gelatin and fat has risen to the top. Skim off the fat. (The fat gives the savory flavor but for health considerations you will want to discard it.)

Serve the soup chilled as consommé or hot as a heart-warming broth. Or use it in a recipe calling for chicken stock. Makes 1 quart or more.

Cucumber Soup

If you have planted cucumbers, you will find your harvest coming along just in time to enjoy this chilled soup an a warm summer day.

4 cucumbers, peeled, seeded, and sliced
6 cups chicken stock, divided
4 green onions, cleaned and chopped
2 teaspoons lemon juice
½ teaspoon dried dill weed
½ teaspoon salt
Dash of white pepper
4 tablespoons Quick Cream of Wheat

Garnish:
Cultured sour cream
Thin slices of unpeeled cucumber or sprigs of fresh dill weed

In large microwave-safe bowl, combine cucumber slices, 3 cups chicken stock, and remaining ingredients. Cover bowl. Microcook on High 8 - 9 minutes, until boiling. Lower power to Medium. Microcook 3 - 5 minutes, until cucumbers are tender. Transfer to a stock pot. Add 3 additional cups chicken stock, stir well, and simmer for five minutes. Cool. Purée with in-pot blender. Chill 2 - 3 hours or more, until ready to serve.

Place in chilled soup bowls. Spoon a dollop of sour cream in the center of each bowl. Accent with cucumber slices or fresh dill weed.

Note: Adapted from Mastering the Art of French Cooking, *Volume Two, by Julia Child and Simone Beck and from* The Everyday Gourmet *by Jane Trittipo.*

Minestrone

This signature Pochini's Restaurant dish presents minestrone as a hearty thick soup, especially warming and comforting on a chilly day. The "drippings" consist of pan juices poured off and saved in the refrigerator or freezer for this use. If you have none, sauté 1 pound of sausage to render off the fat. Remove the meat for another use, then pour 2 cups water into the skillet, scraping bits of meat from the sides. Simmer for 5 minutes, then add to your soup.

2-1/2 cups dried beans (kidney, pinto, or cranberry beans)
½ pound salt pork or pancetta, rind removed and finely chopped
3 medium onions, peeled and chopped
3 cloves garlic, peeled and finely chopped
8 beef bouillon cubes
5 quarts water
2 cups leftover meat drippings
3 tablespoons dried basil
2 tablespoons chili powder
1 bunch Italian parsley, washed and chopped
3 large Idaho potatoes, peeled and diced
3 medium carrots, peeled and diced
3 ribs celery, washed, stringed, and chopped
1 bunch broccoli stems, washed, peeled, and chopped
1 jalapeño pepper, washed, seeded, and finely chopped
2 Anaheim peppers, washed, seeded, and finely chopped
1/4 teaspoon black pepper
1 16 - ounce can tomato sauce
1 6 - ounce can tomato paste
1 pound dry pasta shells
Grated parmesan cheese

First, de-gas the beans: Pick over thoroughly, eliminating any dirt or rocks. Place in large stockpot and cover with water. Cover pot. Cook on High until beans come to a full rolling boil. Remove from heat. Let stand one hour with lid on. Drain in colander. This helps prevent the gastro-intestinal discomfort often associated with beans.

In stockpot, sauté salt pork or pancetta. Add onions and sauté until translucent. Add garlic and sauté briefly. Add bouillon cubes, water, pan drippings, basil, chili powder, parsley, and beans. Bring to bubbling. Turn heat to Simmer and cook for 1-1/2 hours, stirring occasionally to prevent sticking. Add potatoes, carrots, celery, broccoli and chopped jalapeño and Anaheim peppers, plus black pepper. Simmer for one more hour until vegetables are tender. Add tomato sauce and tomato paste.

With a slotted spoon, remove 3 cups vegetables and set aside. Purée remaining soup with in-pot blender until smooth. Return vegetables to pot. Add pasta and cook until it is *al dente*, 10 to 15 minutes or more. Serve in shallow bowls. Pass grated parmesan cheese. Accompany with *crostini* or sliced sourdough baguette. Makes 6 quarts. Serves a crowd. Stores well in refrigerator or freezer.

Nadine's Irish Potato Soup

When I returned from school on chilly Fall afternoons, the oniony aroma of Mother's potato soup drew me to her kitchen. Mother's Irish grandmother taught her this simple "poor man's" soup, a satisfying meal all by itself.

1 tablespoon butter
2 large onions, peeled and chopped
3 quarts water or stock
1 teaspoon salt
6 large Irish potatoes, peeled and cut up
1 quart whole milk (optional)

In large stockpot, melt butter. Sauté onions until translucent and golden. Add water, salt, and potatoes. Bring to a boil. Reduce heat to Simmer and cook for 2 to 3 hours, adding more water if needed. Pulverize potatoes with masher. Check seasonings. If necessary, simmer with lid off until soup thickens. Add milk if desired and heat until blended. Serves four.

Potato - Leek Soup

During the years I worked as an editor for Sunset Magazine *and lived in Menlo Park, my back-fence neighbor would grace my larder with leeks from his garden. "Now you can make soup," he told me, and I did. Years later, Bob treated me to his version of potato-leek soup, a rich and satisfying offering. He would serve it hot on the cool days or chilled on our hot summer days.*

4 tablespoons unsalted butter
1 tablespoon olive oil
1 medium onion, finely chopped
4 - 8 leeks, white parts only, cut in half lengthwise, washed
    thoroughly, and diced (about 1 cup)
4 russet potatoes, peeled and diced, about 3 cups
6 cups chicken stock
1 cup whipping cream
Salt to taste
1 teaspoon finely chopped Italian parsley

In nonstick pot, melt butter and add olive oil. Sauté onion and leeks until golden and transparent. Add potatoes and chicken stock. Bring to a boil. Reduce heat and simmer for 20 minutes or until potatoes are mushy. Purée until smooth with in-pot blender.* Add whipping cream and blend. Check seasonings and add salt if necessary. Serve in heated soup plates and garnish with chopped parsley. Or, for "vichyssoise" style, cool soup to room temperature. Then place pot in refrigerator for several hours until soup is well chilled. Serve in chilled soup bowls with the chopped parsley garnish. Serves six or more.

* If soup seems too thick at this point, add 2 cups of chicken broth.

Zucchini Soup

With summer's bounty of zucchini, you can satisfy appetites with this simple soup. Make it in the morning to serve at lunch, followed by a crisp salad. Refreshing fare for a warm day.

1-1/2 tablespoons olive oil
1 tablespoon butter
1 large yellow onion, chopped
1/4 teaspoon salt
1/8 teaspoon pepper
4 medium size zucchini, washed and sliced
6 cups chicken broth
1 tablespoon fresh thyme leaves, chopped

In medium size stock pot, heat olive oil and butter on High heat. Sauté onion until transparent. Add salt and pepper. Add sliced zucchini and sauté slightly. Do not brown. Add broth. Cover and simmer two hours. Purée in blender or with Hamilton Beach in-pot blending machine until soup is smooth. Taste. Correct seasonings if necessary. Serve in heated bowls and garnish with chopped thyme. Six servings.

Salads

Salad Secrets

After I completed my undergraduate degree work at UCSB, I spent the summer in the beach community of Santa Barbara with my family, resting up from the demanding pressures of my economics studies before launching into a business career.

During this interlude of leisure filled with daily visits to the beach, lunches with friends, and a light load of housework and gardening, I also took up cooking. My passion for developing my culinary abilities focused mainly on salads. Good Housekeeping Magazine *included a comprehensive "salad cookbook" in its June issue that presented a wealth of ideas new to me. I asked my parents for permission to make a different salad every day, and they agreed. What a summer we all had, devouring a tempting, artful looking salad every evening. Over the years, we often reminisced about that delightful "salad summer."*

Here are a few of the pointers I picked up then, and still practice today, from that intensive study of salad making. I have found that with salads, presentation is the big key to eye appeal as well as taste appeal.

1) **Greens**, the "Background" Ingredient: Not every salad contains lettuce or cabbage, but in our American cuisine the majority do. Here's how to deal with them: Buy pre-washed **lettuce or spring mix**. If you do wash your lettuce, be sure to remove all washing water before using it in a salad. Use a salad spinner, roll in paper towels or clean kitchen toweling, or place the greens in a large cotton dishtowel and shake them dry. Bite-size pieces, please. Even the most enthusiastic salad eater gets turned off by unwieldy large leaves or raggedy pieces almost too large to tame for negotiating onto the fork and into the mouth. And torn leaves do taste better than cut ones. The exception to that is a chiffonade of thin crosswise shreds of leaves.

   When you shred **cabbage** for a slaw, make the shred as fine as possible. That's what makes a slaw so tasty, the narrow shreds of cabbage all covered with your special dressing.

2) If you want to add **carrots** for eye-appeal, try shredding them on a coarse grater or in your food processor. Or try cutting a large carrot into thin crosswise slices, and then into quarter-rounds.

3) Unwaxed **cucumbers** just need a thorough washing. If waxed, I like to peel them. Then I score them lengthwise with the tines of a fork to give each slice an appealing serrated edge.

4) **Tomatoes** tossed into salads look pretty and give a satisfying taste when peeled, cut in half through the stem-end and then cut at angles into large bite-size pieces. Although some people prefer to "seed" fresh tomatoes, I think they taste better seeds and all.

   When tomatoes take the spotlight as a "holder" for a stuffing of chicken salad, tuna salad or other substantial fare, you can have the fun of deciding how you want to present them.

   Perhaps the simplest way is to cut a peeled tomato in half and place a scoop of salad on a tomato half, serving one or two halves per person on a bed of greens.

   A more showy approach is to cut a peeled and stemmed beefsteak tomato into sixths, leaving each segment attached at the bottom. You spread the segments apart into a "flower" and place your filling into the center.

   Want to wow the "ladies lunch" crowd? Take a large unpeeled beefsteak tomato and turn it upside down. Cut a spiral slit around the outside. Insert cucumber slices marinated in sour cream into the spiral. Be sure to take a picture of this one; it's a show-stopper first course.

5) How about **bell peppers**, those popular crunchy additions to a tossed salad? I like to cut the pepper in half lengthwise and remove the seeds. Then I cut diagonally across the pepper to make large bite-size pieces. This gives the taste buds more pepper to savor than tiny cubes of pepper, and taste plays a major role in every salad.

6) When I understudied with my Grandma Rose in the kitchen as I was growing up, I joined her quest for learning to make **radish** roses. First you cut a tiny slice off the top and bottom. Then with care you make four thin partial and vertical slices, one on each side of the radish to form your rose. An icewater bath helps the petals

open and stay crisp. These roses add a festive garnish to buffet platters as well as salad plates.

For crunch in your tossed salad, add thin slices of radish.

7) Another crunchy addition, raw jicama, can be peeled and coarsely grated. Or you can toss the **jicama** separately with a creamy dressing and mound it on lettuce leaves.

My San Francisco cousin Louise Kooyman MacDonald taught me two tasty and attractive additions to a salad. For her favorite "company" salad, she would boil a whole unpeeled **celery root (celeriac)** until tender. Then she would peel it, cut it into bite-size pieces and add to her salad greens. For the same salad she would also add diced whites of **hard-cooked egg**. Then she would top each individual salad with sieved yolks of hard-cooked eggs. Glamorous looking and an unusual taste combination.

8) **Celery** should be scrubbed well with a brush. Scrape off any brown coloration. Use a vegetable peeler to remove strings from the outer ribs. Slice diagonally across the rib and add to a tossed salad. This tastes and looks much more appealing than diced celery. Do not discard the yellow heart of celery. Use that and the leaves for a tender treat.

9) **Onions** can overpower a salad if they are pungent. Select red, or torpedo, or sweet yellow or white onions. Peel. Cut in half lengthwise and slice lengthwise or crosswise, as you wish, for pretty slivers to toss with or decorate your salad.

10) **Artichoke hearts**, frozen or in cans, are uniformly tender. Thaw frozen hearts, or chill canned hearts, and cut into bite-size segments. Or prepare fresh baby artichokes. See recipe in the Vegetables section of this book.

11) **Avocados**, the glamour queens of the salad world, have many uses. Peel, cut in half, and stuff. Or slice for garnish. Or mash and add to dressing for a rich effect.

12) **Nuts** can be roasted and, optionally, seasoned before you add them to a salad. Soak shelled nuts in water 10 minutes. Place flat on a baking sheet. Roast at 350° for 10 minutes. Season in a skillet with olive oil, butter, sugar and chili powder. Note: Pine nuts do not need to be soaked first. Roast at 350° for 5 - 10 minutes, watching carefully. Remove when toasty brown.

13) **Roasted vegetables** add dimension and a smoky flavor to salad. Cut Roma tomatoes in half lengthwise. Do not peel. Brush cut side with olive oil. Slice bell pepper, onions, baby zucchini, and Japanese eggplant lengthwise, brush with olive oil, and roast or grill. If you don't have a barbecue available, place vegetables on a baking sheet, spray or brush with olive oil and roast at 375° 30 - 60 minutes, depending on the degree of doneness you want.

Marinated Asparagus Spears

Bob's daughters Jan and Gina joined me in the fun of collaborating on a luncheon for Bob's daughter Liane when she was expecting her son Drew. We decided to present a buffet of easy-to-serve showy salads. Here is Jan's take on a favorite. Plan to marinate the asparagus in advance, preferably the day before your party.

Fresh asparagus spears
Red bell peppers
Balsamic vinaigrette (See Page 146.)

Allow five to seven asparagus spears per serving, depending on the thickness of the spears. You will need enough bell peppers to give you one half-inch cross-section slice per serving. Make enough vinaigrette to provide one cup per pound bunch of asparagus.

Wash asparagus spears gently, taking care not to knock off the tips. Break off tough ends and discard or use in soup. Place asparagus in steamer and steam until just barely tender, 4 to 5 minutes. Lift steamer out of pot and place under cold water to chill asparagus and stop the cooking process. This will keep the asparagus green. Pat asparagus dry with paper toweling. Lay flat in a baking dish. Cover with balsamic vinaigrette. Chill in marinade for several hours. Remove from marinade and place on serving plate or platter in clusters of five or seven spears.

Wash bell peppers and pat dry. Cut crosswise into half-inch rounds. Discard seeds and white membrane. Slip a round over each bunch of asparagus, to give it a "band" much like a sheaf of wheat. Serve on a platter or as individual salads.

Avocado Stuffed With Mushrooms

My friend Cessie Diefenbach served this innovative dish to Bob and me one evening as a salad course, and we enjoyed her offbeat combination of avocado with mushrooms. Here is my re-creation of Cessie's original recipe.

<u>Per Person:</u>
Arugula leaves, washed and drained
2 teaspoons extra virgin olive oil, divided
½ teaspoon white wine vinegar
Splash of balsamic vinegar
½ avocado
1/4 fresh lemon, or 1 teaspoon lemon juice
Fresh ground pepper
3 large mushrooms
1 tablespoon Louis dressing

Shred arugula into bowl. Toss with 1 teaspoon olive oil and vinegars. Place on salad plate. Cut avocado in half lengthwise. Peel and remove pit. Place on arugula. Squeeze lemon juice onto avocado. Grind pepper over avocado and greens.

Scrub mushrooms with brush. Dry with paper towel. Slice. In skillet, sauté mushrooms in 1 teaspoon olive oil. Spoon Louis dressing into avocado half. Then fill avocado with sautéed mushrooms. Serve immediately. Accompany with sourdough French bread.

Avocado Stuffed With Shrimp

Formerly considered exotic fare mainly popular on the West Coast and Florida, avocados now have become "main stream." Shrimp salad in an avocado half is one of my favorite ways to serve them.

Mixed baby field greens, or chiffonade of romaine
Balsamic Vinaigrette (See Page 146.)
½ avocado per person
Dilled Baby Shrimp (See Page 171.)
Lemon wedges
Fresh dill (optional)
Fresh ground black pepper

In salad bowl, toss field greens or shredded chiffonade of romaine with balsamic vinaigrette.

Cut avocado in half lengthwise. Peel each half and remove pit. Place greens on salad plates. Top with avocado halves. Drizzle vinaigrette over avocado halves. Place a scoop of shrimp salad inside each avocado. Garnish each plate with a lemon wedge. Top the shrimp with a sprig of fresh dill if available. Offer fresh-ground pepper.

Bacon, Tomato, Avocado and Spinach Salad

This was Bob's favorite salad. I couldn't make it too often to suit him. It also goes over big at pot-lucks.

1 package baby spinach
6 slices thick-slice bacon, cooked crisp and crumbled
1 large avocado
2 large tomatoes, peeled
Balsamic Vinaigrette (See below.)
Fresh ground pepper

Place spinach in large salad bowl. Add bacon, chunks of avocado, and chunks of tomato. Toss with balsamic vinaigrette. Offer fresh ground pepper. Serves 6 to 8.

Balsamic Vinaigrette

Most of the time, I measure these ingredients directly onto the salad and then toss . For times when you need to pour dressing over the top of a composed salad, you will want to whisk your dressing into an emulsion.

1/4 cup extra virgin olive oil
1 tablespoon balsamic vinegar
1 tablespoon wine vinegar, either red or white
Pinch of dried tarragon

In large measuring cup, place oil and the vinegars. Crumble the dried tarragon between your fingers and add. Using a wire whisk or a fork, mix the ingredients into an emulsion. Pour onto the salad immediately. If you need to let the dressing stand, it will separate. Re-whisk before adding to your salad. Serves two.

Bean Salad

This hearty dish makes an appealing addition to an antipasto platter. Plan to make it in the morning so the beans have plenty of time to absorb the marinade.

1 14-1/2 - ounce can imported canellini beans, drained and
    rinsed
1 14-1/2 - ounce can kidney beans, drained and rinsed
2 green onions, washed and chopped
1 small bunch Italian parsley leaves, chopped
6 cloves garlic, peeled and chopped fine
6 tablespoons extra virgin olive oil
1 tablespoon balsamic vinegar
1 tablespoon red wine vinegar
1 tablespoon white wine vinegar
Juice of one lime (optional)
½ teaspoon salt
1/8 teaspoon white pepper

Place all ingredients in large bowl. Mix well. Chill for several hours or overnight.

Goldberg Bowen Three ~ Bean Salad

Goldberg Bowen was to San Francisco what Fortnum and Mason is to London, a famous purveyor of gustatory delights from around the world. Now out of business, Goldberg Bowen remains a happy memory. When I first arrived in San Francisco, friends insisted that I step inside onto the venerable wood floor to view the display of fried maguey worms in a stack of little jars atop an elegant display case. We passed on the maguey worms, but we did invest in a selection of cold cuts, cheese and the famous Goldberg Bowen Three-Bean Salad. The salad quickly became a favorite of mine. Here is my version.

½ pound fresh green beans
1 14-1/2 - ounce can kidney beans, drained
1 14-1/2 - ounce ceci beans (garbanzos), drained
½ cup extra virgin olive oil
½ cup white wine vinegar
4 ounces gorgonzola or blue cheese, crumbled
½ teaspoon dried tarragon
1/4 teaspoon black pepper.

Wash green beans. Cut off ends and remove strings if necessary. Cut into inch-long sections. Place in steamer and cook until just *al dente*. Drain in colander and cool with running water to stop cooking process and keep the beans green. Drain and set aside. Place kidney beans, cecis and green beans in large bowl. Mix well. Add remaining ingredients. Chill for three hours or more, stirring occasionally. Serves 10 to 12.

Bob's Outrageous Bean Salad

Bob enjoyed preparing this wild concoction for our barbecues. Everyone considers it outrageous because of the giant quantity of garlic it contains. Try it and you'll see what we mean.

1 14-1/2 - ounce can kidney beans, drained
1 14-1/2 - ounce can ceci beans (garbanzos), drained
6 cloves elephant garlic or 1 head regular garlic, peeled and
    chopped
½ teaspoon salt
1/8 teaspoon black pepper
½ cup extra virgin olive oil
½ cup red wine vinegar

Place all ingredients in large bowl. Mix well. Cover bowl. Marinate in refrigerator overnight.

Stuffed Belgian Endive

Bob and I found this on the menu at a quaint neighborhood bistro in Montreal. We decided to include it in our salad repertoire.

2 heads Belgian endive
1 8-ounce tub lowfat whipped cream cheese
½ teaspoon Italian herbs
4 ounces. sliced smoked salmon

Wash endive and separate leaves. Dry with paper towels. Allow cream cheese to come to room temperature. Mix with herbs. Spread the bottom half of each leaf with herbed cream cheese. Top with a small square of smoked salmon. Arrange on serving plate in a fan shape, like the petals of a chrysanthemum. May be served on a large plate for a buffet or on individual serving plates for a sit-down appetizer course.

Blood Orange Salad

I first tasted a blood orange during my growing-up years in Phoenix. I immediately became addicted. Though rare in the U.S., blood oranges are popular in Sicily. When I come across them at our farmer's markets here in California, I jump at the opportunity to serve this salad.

2-1/2 ounces (½ package) spring mix
2 blood oranges
1 small avocado
2 slices red onion, chopped fine

Dressing:
2 tablespoons extra virgin olive oil
1 teaspoon balsamic vinegar
1 teaspoon white wine vinegar
Pinch of dried tarragon
1/8 teaspoon salt

In large measuring cup, whisk dressing ingredients until emulsified. Toss spring mix with half of the dressing. Place on two chilled salad plates.

Peel oranges, removing white outer membrane along with rind and any seeds. Slice one orange on the top of each salad. Peel avocado and slice in a design around the orange slices. Drizzle with remaining dressing. Place a small mound of chopped onion in the center of each salad. Serves 2.

Blue Cheese Salad

I felt inspired to develop this recipe for my dinners at home after enjoying it at the noteworthy Tuscany Ristorante in Westlake, California.

4 Roma tomatoes
1 tablespoon extra virgin olive oil
2-1/2 ounces pre-washed baby spinach, stems removed
2 tablespoons minced red bell pepper
2 tablespoons crumbled blue cheese or gorgonzola cheese
2 tablespoons roasted garlic vinaigrette (Recipe on Page 160.)

Preheat oven to 450°. Wash tomatoes and cut in half. Place cut side up on oiled baking sheet. Drizzle with olive oil. Roast at 450° until soft and brown, about 40 minutes. Cool.

In salad bowl, toss spinach and bell pepper with dressing. Pile in a pyramid on each of two chilled salad plates. Top with crumbled cheese. Place four tomato halves on each plate. Drizzle tomatoes with vinaigrette. Serves 2.

Burrata Salad

Burrata, the soft version of fresh mozzarella, comes contained in its own soft and delectable "rind." After enjoying this salad at Tuscany Ristorante in Westlake I went on a quest for burrata, to no avail. Finally, four years later, I found a cheese shop that carries it, and I made the salad. Do try this when you can find burrata. It's an unusual taste treat.

3 tablespoons extra virgin olive oil
1 teaspoon balsamic vinegar
2 teaspoons wine vinegar
1 slice red onion, finely chopped
1 shallot, finely chopped
Pinch of dried tarragon
3 ounces baby spinach, arugula, or mixed field greens
3 or 4 heirloom tomatoes, peeled and cut into bite-size wedges
4 ounces burrata cheese
Fresh-ground black pepper

Whisk together olive oil, vinegars, onion, shallot, and tarragon. Place greens in large salad bowl. Toss with half of the dressing. Mound on two large plates. Toss tomato wedges with dressing. Arrange on greens. Place a 2 - ounce serving of burrata in the center of each salad. Grind black pepper onto salad as desired. Try to refrain from sighing with joy too loudly while consuming this delicacy.

Caprese

Remember the days when the only mozzarella cheese you could find at the market had the consistency and taste of white rubber? As more and more of us Americans spent time in Italy, we discovered the tender delights of fresh mozzarella. But where could we buy it at home? In the San Francisco Bay Area, the owners of Girapolli in North Beach solved the problem of supply by bringing the husband's father from Italy to produce this delicate cheese and its byproduct, fresh ricotta. Ferrante Cheese started in a Pleasant Hill storefront, and to my delight Mr. Ferrante would pause from his cheesemaking to sell me a pound of mozzarella and a tub of ricotta. Now Bob and I could feast on caprese, a salad composed of fresh mozzarella and slices of fresh tomato. These days almost every upscale market or deli carries fresh mozzarella, so we no longer have to interrupt Mr. Ferrante.

2 ounces of gourmet mixed greens, washed and blotted dry
1/4 cup extra virgin olive oil
1 tablespoon white wine vinegar
1 tablespoon balsamic vinegar
Pinch of dried tarragon
2 large tomatoes, peeled and sliced
1 large "ball" (about 4 ounces) of fresh mozzarella cheese, sliced
1 small bunch fresh basil, leaves only, coarsely chopped
Fresh ground pepper

Place greens in a salad bowl. In a large measuring cup, whisk together olive oil, vinegars and the dried tarragon. Pour a small amount of the emulsified dressing onto the greens. Toss gently until leaves are well coated. Place on chilled salad plates. Alternate slices of tomato with slices of cheese around each plate. Top with basil. Drizzle the remaining balsamic vinaigrette over the salad, making sure you "dress" each slice. Top with fresh ground pepper. Serves 2.

San Francisco Celery Root Salad

My cousin Louise Kooyman McDonald and her husband "Mac" were the first people to treat me to dinner in their home, once I had arrived in San Francisco. The entire dinner brings back happy memories, and the main ingredient in Louise's salad mystified me. I had not tasted it before, so I asked Louise about it. "Oh, that's cooked celery root," she explained. "I substitute it for avocados when they become too high-priced for my budget." Even though the homely looking celery root, or celeriac, has now become more pricey than avocado, I still consider it a welcome way to vary the taste of a salad.

1 whole celeriac (celery root)
1 bag pre-washed field greens
2 hard boiled eggs, chilled
Balsamic Vinaigrette (See Page 146.)
Fresh ground black pepper

Scrub celery root to remove loose dirt. Place in 1 - quart saucepan and cover with water. With lid on pot, boil until celery root is tender when tested with a skewer. Drain and cool. Peel, removing all tough outer membranes. Cut into fourths, then into slices. Chill for at least an hour.

Place greens in large salad bowl. Add celery root slices. Peel eggs. Cut in half. Remove yolks and set aside. Chop whites and add to salad. Toss salad with vinaigrette. Serve on individual plates. Top with sieved egg yolks. Offer fresh ground pepper. Serves 4 to 6.

Nadine's Cole Slaw

My Irish American mother, Nadine Larimer Cook, developed this Western style recipe for Cole Slaw. Bob favored it for our picnics and barbecues and encouraged me to prepare it often. If possible, prepare it several hours in advance to allow the flavors to blend.

1 head of cabbage
2 large avocados, peeled and coarsely chopped
4 tomatoes, peeled, seeded and coarsely chopped
4 green onions, chopped

Dressing:
6 tablespoons mayonnaise
4 tablespoons cultured sour cream
2-1/2 lemons, juiced
1/4 teaspoon Worcestershire Sauce
½ teaspoon paprika
2 tablespoons white balsamic vinegar
1/4 teaspoon coarsely ground black pepper

Wash head of cabbage and remove outer leaves if wilted. Using large French chopping knife, cut cabbage in half lengthwise. Slice cabbage vertically into thin shreds. Periodically, chop a bunch of shredded cabbage across the grain. Transfer to large bowl. Shred entire head of cabbage, omitting the "heart." Add avocados, tomatoes and green onions to bowl.

In 1-quart measuring cup, or small bowl, place ingredients for dressing. Using medium size whisk, fold ingredients together, then whisk until well blended. Add to salad. Using two large spoons, mix well into slaw. Chill. Serve with ham or barbecued meats. Satisfies 12 or more. Store any leftover slaw in refrigerator. Pour off any excess dressing before re-serving.

Marinated Cucumbers

Commercially grown cucumbers tasted bitter many years ago. For this reason, Mother marinated cucumber slices in salted ice water and cider vinegar, and she always peeled them to remove any bitter tasting rind. Years later, as growers offered milder tasting cucumbers, I favored adding them to salads without bothering to marinate them first. Along the way, a close friend of Italian descent suggested I use wine vinegar, olive oil, and celery seed for the marinade. So there we have it, a gourmet taste treat. It works with any type of cucumber. I prefer lemon cucumbers when I can get them; they make a showy offering for a buffet.

**1 or 2 medium green cucumbers or 3 lemon cucumbers, unpeeled
    and thinly sliced (about 2 cups of slices)
1/4 cup extra virgin olive oil
½ cup white wine vinegar
1 teaspoon celery seed
Salt
Fresh ground pepper**

Arrange cucumber slices in large glass pie plate. Top with oil, vinegar, celery seed, and salt and pepper to taste. Chill in refrigerator.

Cucumbers In Sour Cream

This dish makes a big hit at the buffet table, it's so attractive. I also use cucumbers marinated in sour cream to stuff large beefsteak tomatoes. Simply turn the tomato stem end down and cut a spiral slit around the outside, then stuff the cucumber slices into the opening.

1 large cucumber
1/4 cup extra virgin olive oil
2 tablespoons white wine vinegar
½ cup nonfat cultured sour cream
1/4 teaspoon salt
½ teaspoon celery seed
2 tablespoons fresh tarragon, minced
3 green onions, chopped
Fresh-ground black pepper

Wash cucumber well. Score the skin lengthwise with a table fork; this will give each slice a serrated edge. Slice thinly. Place overlapping slices on large platter or two dinner plates.

Whisk oil and vinegar into sour cream until smooth. Add salt and celery seed. Check for taste. Add more oil, vinegar, salt, or celery seed as you deem necessary to adjust flavor. Cut up tarragon with kitchen shears. Fold into dressing. Using a tablespoon, drop dressing onto cucumbers. Smooth to cover cucumbers completely, using back of spoon in circular motion. Top with chopped onions. Grind fresh black pepper onto plate just before serving. Any extra dressing can be refrigerated and used with another cucumber. Serves 10 - 12.

Cypress Club Winter Salad

My friend Dorothy and I became the "ladies who lunch" at least one Wednesday every month, on my day off. We sought out the hottest new gourmet dining venues in San Francisco for our adventures, and the Cypress Club offered this innovative salad, which I have re-created as closely as possible to the original.

4 fresh baby artichokes, prepared as in recipe on Page 255.
½ lemon
3 tablespoons extra virgin olive oil, divided
4 Yukon Gold baby new potatoes
2 tablespoons white wine vinegar or juice of ½ lemon
½ teaspoon ground ginger
4 tablespoons mayonnaise
1 cup pre-washed baby spinach, stems removed
1 small spray baby arugula *
1 tablespoon fresh pickled ginger **, finely chopped
2 ounces smoked duck or turkey breast, shredded

Wash artichokes. Place in steamer. Squeeze lemon over them and add lemon to steamer. Drizzle with olive oil. Steam until pierced easily with a fork, about 30 minutes. Drain and chill. Cut in half. Scrub potatoes and cook whole. Chill. Cut in half. In large measuring cup, whisk vinegar, olive oil and ginger into mayonnaise. In large salad bowl, toss spinach, arugula, and pickled ginger with 4 tablespoons of dressing.

Place on 2 chilled salad plates. Cut artichokes and potatoes. Place on salad cut side up. Fold 1-1/2 tablespoons of dressing into smoked duck or turkey. Place in center of each plate. Drizzle remaining dressing over artichokes and potatoes. Serves 2.

* Check your local farmer's market or specialty greengrocer for baby arugula.
** Available at Asian foods markets.

Floating Salad

This unusual salad adds a touch of glamour to a summer buffet or picnic spread.

1 large or 2 medium size tomatoes
1 small cucumber, lemon cucumber preferred
1 red or orange bell pepper, seeds removed
1 red or torpedo onion, peeled and cut into 8 thin crosswise slices
    (about 2" of onion)
Fresh ground black pepper
1 spray fresh thyme broken into small sprigs
1 cup water
1 cup white vinegar

Peel tomatoes and slice vertically. Slice cucumber and bell pepper crosswise into rounds. Pull onion slices apart into rings.

In large glass bowl, place a layer of tomato slices. Top with a grind of pepper and sprigs of thyme. Follow with layers of cucumber, bell pepper, and onion rings. Top each layer with pepper and thyme. Continue layering as appropriate. In large measuring cup, mix water and vinegar. Pour over salad. Chill one hour or more. Serve with slotted spoon. Serves 2 to 4.

Roasted Garlic Vinaigrette

Although you need to allow plenty of lead time to prepare this dressing, the oomph the roasted garlic will give to your salad makes it worth the effort. Roasting the garlic cuts its pungency.

1 head garlic, roasted and peeled
1 tablespoon balsamic vinegar
3 tablespoons red wine vinegar
½ cup extra virgin olive oil
3 tablespoons minced red onion

Cut off the top eighth of the entire (intact) head of unpeeled garlic. Place on a baking sheet. Roast at 350° until cloves are soft (30 to 60 minutes, depending on the size of the garlic). Remove from oven. Allow to cool. Squeeze each clove to force the soft garlic out of its skin.

Place vinegars and olive oil in a blender. Add onion and garlic. Whirl until emulsified. Use immediately on salad or store in refrigerator for future use. Whisk to re-emulsify before adding chilled dressing to salad. Will keep in refrigerator for about a week.

Goat Cheese Patties

Daughter Gina Pochini Lincoln makes these to dress up her party salads.

1 log goat cheese
Extra virgin olive oil
Dry bread crumbs

Carefully remove wrapping from cheese. Slice into 3/8" thick segments. If cheese patties crumble, moisten with 2 or 3 drops of olive oil and reshape. Dip each cheese pattie into olive oil, then into crumbs, coating each side. Place on oiled baking sheet. Bake at 225° for ten minutes. Using spatula, slide gently onto top of salad. Serve while still warm.

Orange/Avocado/Red Onion Salad

Oranges provide a welcome change from tomatoes during the winter season. For ease of preparation, choose a seedless variety, such as a navel orange.

1 large navel orange
2 tablespoons extra virgin olive oil
1 teaspoon white balsamic vinegar
2 teaspoons white wine vinegar
Pinch of dried tarragon
2-1/2 ounces of prewashed spring mix
½ avocado, peeled and sliced lengthwise
2 slices of red onion

Rinse orange. Peel with a knife, removing rind and all white membrane. Cut crosswise into six slices.

In measuring cup, whisk together olive oil, vinegars, and tarragon.

In small salad bowl, toss the salad greens with half of the dressing. Place on two chilled salad plates.

Place three orange slices on each salad. Place sliced avocado in a fan design. Separate onion slices into rings. Top orange and avocado slices with onion rings. Pour remaining dressing over all. Serves 2.

Panzanella

I applaud Italian cooks who devised this clever way of turning day-old bread into a gourmet dish. Best when chilled before you serve it, but plenty o.k. if you want to devour it right away. (You can vary the taste by using leftovers and odds and ends to accompany your torn bread.)

2 Roma tomatoes, peeled and chopped
2 tablespoons chopped red onion
2 tablespoons chopped red bell pepper
2 tablespoons roasted garlic vinaigrette (See recipe Page 160.)
2 tablespoons pesto sauce, fresh or bottled (See Page 275 for
    recipe.)
4 thin slices of day-old Rustic Ciabatta bread, torn into bite-size
    pieces
1 tablespoon extra virgin olive oil, optional
Romaine lettuce, washed, dried and cut crosswise with scissors
    into a chiffonade

In large salad bowl, toss vegetables with roasted garlic vinaigrette and pesto sauce. Add bread and toss until well coated. Taste. If bread seems dry, add the extra olive oil. Chill one hour in refrigerator. Make the chiffonade of lettuce by rolling three romaine leaves lengthwise into a "cigar" then cutting into thin shreds with kitchen scissors. Place on cutting board and cut across the shredded leaves. Put a portion of chiffonade on each of four chilled salad plates. Put a mound of panzanella on each plate. Serves 4.

Papaya and Avocado Salad

Exotic flavors of avocado and papaya blend well in this showy salad. The seeds of the papaya provide the rich dressing.

1 medium size papaya
1 avocado
5 ounces prewashed spring mix
Papaya Seed Dressing (See below.)
1 tablespoon pomegranate kernels or dried cranberries.

Peel papaya and cut in half lengthwise. Scoop out seeds and set aside for dressing. Cut papaya into lengthwise slices. Peel avocado and remove pit. Cut into lengthwise slices.

Prepare dressing. In salad bowl, toss greens with a small amount of dressing. Place on chilled plates. Arrange papaya slices on greens like the spokes of a wheel. Place avocado slices in between. Drizzle with dressing. Accent the center of the "wheel" with pomegranate kernels or dried cranberries. Serves 4.

Papaya Seed Dressing

Sybil Henderson, an exotic fruit marketer and expert, introduced me to this recipe. This versatile concoction uses the papaya seeds, which I formerly had thrown away. Equally glamorous on fruit or green salads, it also makes an excellent meat marinade.

1 tablespoon fresh papaya seeds
1 cup white wine vinegar
½ cup sugar
1 teaspoon dry mustard
1 teaspoon seasoned salt
2 cups extra virgin olive oil
1 small red or yellow onion, minced

Cut a papaya in half and scoop out the seeds. Discard membrane. Place vinegar in blender. Add sugar, mustard, and salt. Turn blender on low and gradually add olive oil and onion. Add papaya seeds and blend *only* until they are cut to the size of coarsely ground pepper. Pour into dressing jars or bottles and store in refrigerator.

Pasta Salad Putanesca

Putanesca, the naughty term referring to the indolent manner of a "lady of the evening," is used to express how little effort it takes to assemble this simple pasta dish.

1 tablespoon salt
2 tablespoons extra virgin olive oil, divided
4 ounces dry pasta, such as angel hair, penne, or fusilli
2 teaspoons white wine vinegar, divided
Fresh ground black pepper
2 cloves garlic, peeled, and put through press
2 garlic presses full of drained capers, put through press
1 teaspoon whole capers, drained
½ teaspoon anchovy paste
1/4 cup marinated sundried tomatoes, coarsely chopped
4 ounces sliced olives, drained
½ red bell pepper, finely chopped
1/3 torpedo or red onion, finely chopped

Fill large stock pot two-thirds full of water. Add salt and 1 tablespoon oil. Bring to rolling boil. Add pasta and stir well. When pasta and water again come to a boil, reduce heat to Low. Cook slowly for time noted on package, until pasta becomes *al dente*. Drain in colander. Return to pot. Toss with 1 tablespoon olive oil, 1 teaspoon vinegar, and fresh ground pepper. Add 1 tablespoon olive oil, 1 teaspoon vinegar and remaining ingredients. Mix well. Chill for at least two hours. Serves 2 - 4.

Pasta Salad With Shrimp

Bob and I prepared many picnics for ourselves and friends. This salad was one of Bob's favorites. It transports well in a cooler, and it adds a refreshing note to the menu on a warm day.

1/4 pound salad shrimp, thawed, drained, and blotted dry with paper toweling
1 tablespoon salt
2 tablespoons extra virgin olive oil, divided
8 ounces dry fusilli pasta or 10 ounces cheese tortellini
½ red bell pepper, seeded and chopped
2 tablespoons chopped Italian parsley
6 tablespoons chopped red or torpedo onion
1 tablespoon lemon zest
Juice of one large lemon
1/4 cup mayonnaise
1 tablespoon chopped marinated sundried tomatoes
1 tablespoon white wine vinegar
1 teaspoon balsamic vinegar
½ teaspoon salt
1/4 teaspoon pepper
½ teaspoon dried dill weed

Thaw and drain shrimp on paper towels. Drain. Pat dry with a paper towel. Set aside in refrigerator.

Fill large stock pot two thirds full of water. Add salt and 1 tablespoon olive oil. Bring to a full rolling boil on High. Add pasta and stir. Bring back to a boil. Reduce heat to Low. Cook on low 6 - 10 minutes, or until *al dente*. Drain in colander. Place in large bowl. Toss with 1 tablespoon olive oil. Chill 2 hours. Add remaining ingredients and mix well. Chill one more hour. Serves 8 - 10.

Persimmon and Avocado Salad

Hachiya persimmons not only look pretty on the tree, these large and slightly pointed fruit ripen to a juicy sweetness. Combined with another exotic, the avocado, persimmons make an attractive tropical salad for fall parties.

Romaine lettuce
White wine vinaigrette
2 Hachiya persimmons or any other available variety, completely ripe
1 avocado
Papaya seed dressing (See Page 163.)
2 limes

White Wine Vinaigrette
2 tablespoons extra virgin olive oil
1 teaspoon white wine vinegar
½ teaspoon white balsamic vinegar

Whisk together until an emulsion forms.

Rinse romaine leaves and dry thoroughly. Roll several leaves together. With kitchen shears, cut leaves crosswise into a chiffonade. Place on cutting board and chop in half along spine of leaves. Place in salad bowl. Toss with white wine vinaigrette. Place on chilled salad plates.

Select persimmons which are firm but ripe, not mushy. Peel and cut in half and slice. Arrange by half-persimmon portions on individual salad plate in a fan on top of the lettuce. Peel avocado. Cut into fourths lengthwise. Slice each section into four or five slices and intersperse with persimmon slices. Drizzle papaya seed dressing over all. Garnish each plate with a lime half. Serves 4.

Sautéed Portobello Mushroom Salad

The large and super-large portobello mushrooms work well as dramatic accents in salads. Here, we serve them warm atop a chilled salad. My Santa Fe cousins Paul and Dona Cook gave kudos to this glamorous and delicious presentation.

1/4 cup extra virgin olive oil
1 tablespoon balsamic vinegar
1 tablespoon white wine vinegar
Pinch of dried tarragon
4 ounces mixed baby greens, washed and blotted dry
1 red bell pepper, washed, seeded, and chopped
2 ounces goat cheese
½ cup pecan halves, roasted
1 tablespoon olive oil
4 portobello mushrooms, washed, scrubbed, stems removed
Black pepper

Whisk together extra virgin olive oil, balsamic vinegar, white wine vinegar, and dried tarragon. Toss in salad bowl with baby greens, bell pepper, and crumbled goat cheese. Place on chilled salad plates. Decorate edges of salad with pecan halves.

In large nonstick skillet, heat olive oil. Sauté whole mushroom caps on each side until heated through. Place on top of salad and serve. Grind pepper over salad. Serves 4.

Bob's Red Potato Salad

This was Bob's favorite version of potato salad. We served it often at summer picnics and barbecues on our deck. Our guests liked it, too – we seldom had leftovers.

2 pounds small red potatoes, scrubbed and cut into bite-size
    pieces
2 tablespoons extra virgin olive oil
3 hard-boiled eggs, chopped
1/4 bunch Italian parsley, chopped
2 tablespoons chopped fresh arugula (optional)
4 tablespoons mayonnaise
1 tablespoon dijon mustard
3 tablespoons white wine vinegar
Salt and pepper to taste

Cook potatoes until just *al dente*. Do not over-cook. Drain in colander. Place in bowl. Toss with olive oil. Allow to cool to room temperature. Add remaining ingredients and mix well. Add salt and pepper to taste. Chill 2 - 3 hours in refrigerator. Serves 8 - 10.

Romaine Salad

The toasted "chili nuts" give an unexpected taste and texture to this salad.

½ bunch romaine leaves, washed and patted dry
1 small avocado
½ lime, Bearss or Mexican variety preferred, or 1/4 lemon
1/8 teaspoon salt
1/4 red bell pepper, washed, seeded, and chopped fine
4 tablespoons extra virgin olive oil, divided
1/4 cup pecan halves
1 teaspoon sugar
1/4 teaspoon chili powder
1 teaspoon red wine vinegar
½ teaspoon balsamic vinegar

Roll 3 romaine leaves together lengthwise. With kitchen shears, cut crosswise into a chiffonade. Place on cutting board and cut along the length. Put into large salad bowl. Repeat until all leaves are used. Peel and dice avocado. Sprinkle with lime juice and salt. Add to bowl along with chopped bell pepper.

In nonstick skillet, heat 1 tablespoon olive oil on Low. Add nuts and stir to coat. Sprinkle nuts with sugar and chili powder and stir until nuts are warm and well-coated. Add to salad. Add 3 tablespoons olive oil along with the vinegars to bowl. Toss. Serves 2.

Scala's Salad

Microwave cookbook author Jane Trittipo and I enjoyed this salad for lunch at Scala's in San Francisco one January day. I took notes so I could try it at home. Here is my version..

Baby green beans – 5 or 6 per person
3 fresh yellow or red beets which when cooked and cubed will
    make about ½ cup
2 tablespoons white wine vinegar, divided
3 - 4 tablespoons olive oil, divided
Red onion, sliced into rings, 1/4 cup or less
½ rib of celery thinly sliced crosswise, to make 1/4 cup or less
3/4 head 5" diameter radicchio, thinly shredded, as for coleslaw
1 Belgian endive thinly shredded (optional)
1 tablespoon finely chopped Italian parsley
½ large avocado, cubed
2 - 3 ounces of chevre (fresh goat cheese), crumbled
4 chilled salad plates
Freshly ground black pepper

Boil green beans until *al dente*. Drain in colander and rinse with lots of cold water to stop cooking process.

Boil whole beets until tender. Cool, peel, and cut into ½ " cubes. Marinate in refrigerator for several hours in white wine vinegar and olive oil vinaigrette, about 1 tablespoon olive oil to ½ tablespoon wine vinegar.

Slice onion and celery. Shred radicchio and endive. Chop parsley. Place in salad bowl. This may be done several hours in advance and chilled. Just before serving, peel and cube avocado and add to bowl. Whisk remaining oil and vinegar into vinaigrette, reserving 1 tablespoon. Toss salad with vinaigrette. Add beets and marinade. If using red beets, this will turn everything red, of course, a plus in appearance. Place salad mixture on the four chilled plates. Top with green beans and goat cheese. Pour remaining vinaigrette over top of each salad. Grind fresh black pepper over salads to taste. Serves four.

Dilled Baby Shrimp

This is my favorite "stand-alone" shrimp salad.. I made this for daughter Liane's baby shower and placed large scoops on leaves of Bibb lettuce for an easy-to-serve offering at our salad buffet. When I became a San Francisco resident in the 1950's, our fish markets carried fresh shrimp from San Francisco Bay. Now that such a delicacy has been "fished out," the markets instead offer "previously frozen" baby shrimp, thawed and ready to use.

1 pound baby shrimp, thawed, drained, and patted dry
Juice of 1 large lemon
1 tablespoon white balsamic vinegar
4 tablespoons extra virgin olive oil
½ teaspoon minced dill weed, fresh or dried
1 head Bibb lettuce leaves, washed and spun dry

Place shrimp, lemon juice, vinegar, olive oil, and dill in mixing bowl. Stir gently until well mixed. Cover with plastic wrap. Marinate in refrigerator for 2 to 3 hours. Arrange lettuce leaves on plates or on large serving platter. Place a large scoop of shrimp on each leaf. Or use a scoop of this shrimp as accent in the center of a composed salad. For a glamorous touch, place a scoop of shrimp on a tomato half or into a tomato "blossom." Serves 8 - 10.

Spinach Salad

Fellow guests at a Newcomers Club potluck devoured this with enthusiasm. I left the party with an empty bowl.

½ package (5 ounces) prewashed baby spinach, stems removed
2 slices thick bacon, cooked and broken into bits
3 tablespoons grated parmesan cheese
2 ounces gorgonzola cheese, crumbled
1-1/2 ounces pine nuts, toasted
4 tablespoons extra virgin olive oil
2 teaspoons red wine vinegar
2 teaspoons balsamic vinegar
1/4 teaspoon dried tarragon
Fresh ground black pepper

In large salad bowl, combine spinach leaves, bacon bits, cheeses and pine nuts. In large measuring cup, whisk together olive oil, vinegars, and tarragon. Add to salad and toss gently. Grind black pepper over salad and toss once more. Serve.

Spinach Salad With Pears

I first enjoyed this salad at a gourmet restaurant operating in one of Emeryville's upgraded warehouse spaces near San Francisco Bay. The innovative and delicious mix of ingredients inspired me to serve it for guests. It also travels well to a potluck. Carry the dressing separately and add it just before serving.

8 ounces pre-washed baby spinach

2 or 3 firm ripe pears, preferably Bosc, comice, or red Bartlett, unpeeled

½ lemon

3 ounces crumbled gorgonzola cheese

½ cup chopped nuts, preferably walnuts or unblanched almonds, toasted and then chopped

1/4 cup extra virgin olive oil

1 tablespoon white balsamic vinegar

1 tablespoon wine vinegar

1/8 teaspoon tarragon

Place spinach in large salad bowl. Cut pears into bite-size pieces into small bowl. Toss with the juice of the lemon to prevent pears from turning brown. Add to spinach. Add cheese and nuts. In large measuring cup, mix together oil, vinegars and tarragon. Whisk well until emulsified. Pour onto salad and toss. Serves 4 – 6.

Judy's Summer Salad

This attractive salad catches the spirit and flavor of summer when hot days give that "full bloom" feeling. By not "firing up" your oven or your range, you conserve your air-conditioning budget.

2-1/2 ounces pre-washed baby spinach, stems removed
1 ounce arugula leaves, washed and blotted dry
3 tablespoons sunflower sprouts
10 large mushrooms, washed , blotted dry, and cut into quarters
Balsamic vinaigrette (See recipe on Page 146), divided
2 large tomatoes, peeled and sliced
½ avocado, peeled and sliced
1 lemon cucumber or 2" of green cucumber, washed and sliced,
    then cut into quarter slices
Fresh ground pepper

In large salad bowl, toss spinach, arugula, sprouts and mushroom quarters with 3 tablespoons dressing. Arrange on chilled luncheon or dinner plates. Alternate slices of tomato with slices of avocado in a circle around the plate. Mound cucumber chunks in center. Drizzle with remaining vinaigrette. Grind pepper over all. Serve with cold cuts and foccacia and you have a complete "no-cook" meal. Serves 2.

Marinated Tomatoes

Before fresh mozzarella cheese became available at our nearby markets, causing the current rise to popularity of caprese salad, I often would serve marinated tomatoes. In summer, when giant beefsteak tomatoes become available, this salad has winning appeal, either as a separate course or as a showy platter at buffets and casual barbecues. Slices of red tomatoes alternated with yellow tomatoes give a showy, dramatic color contrast.

Large beefsteak or heirloom tomatoes, peeled and sliced
Large yellow or golden tomatoes (optional), peeled and sliced
Balsamic vinaigrette dressing with tarragon (Page 146.)
Green onions, cleaned and chopped, tops and all
Fresh basil leaves, chopped or cut with kitchen shears (optional)
Fresh ground black pepper
Fresh herbs for garnish
Basil leaves or sprigs of thyme

Place sliced tomatoes in a circular design on platter. Alternate red with yellow or gold if you are using two colors. Drizzle a generous amount of balsamic vinaigrette dressing on the tomatoes. Sprinkle chopped onions and basil over all. Add a generous grind of black pepper. Chill in refrigerator or on a bed of ice for at least one hour. Garnish with basil leaves or sprigs of thyme at serving time.

Tortolloni Salad

Tortolloni are the "big brothers" of tortellini. This hearty salad makes a good main course for lunch.

2 tablespoons extra virgin olive oil, divided
1 tablespoon salt
1 9 -ounce package fresh cheese tortolloni
1 15 - ounce jar artichoke hearts in water, drained and cut into
    quarters
4 tablespoons sundried tomatoes marinated in olive oil, not
    drained, cut into strips
½ red bell pepper, finely chopped
½ medium size red onion, coarsely chopped
½ red bell pepper, sliced, for garnish
Small spray Italian parsley, washed, for garnish

<u>Dressing</u>
3/4 cup mayonnaise
Juice of one lemon
2 teaspoons anchovy paste
4 tablespoons extra virgin olive oil
1/8 teaspoon white pepper
½ teaspoon garlic powder
1/8 teaspoon salt

In large stockpot, bring 3 quarts water, 1 tablespoon olive oil, and salt to boil. Add tortolloni and stir. Bring to a rolling boil. Reduce heat to Low. Cook length of time as directed on package. Drain in colander. Place in large mixing or salad bowl. Toss with 1 tablespoon olive oil. Add artichoke hearts, sundried tomatoes, chopped bell pepper, and chopped onion. Mix well.

In large measuring cup, combine dressing ingredients. Whisk until smooth. Use ½ cup of dressing on salad. Add more if desired. Chill at least 2 hours. Garnish with bell pepper slices and Italian parsley. Serves 4 - 6.

Tropical Tuna Salad

This unusual combination of flavors adds a festive touch to an al fresco summer lunch at home.

1 6-ounce can solid white albacore tuna packed in water, drained*
1 tablespoon toasted sunflower seeds
1/8 teaspoon cumin
1/8 teaspoon black pepper
3 tablespoons mayonnaise
2 tablespoons extra virgin olive oil
Juice of ½ Bearss lime
1/4 teaspoon dried tarragon
2-1/2 ounces mixed baby salad greens
½ small cantaloupe, seeded and sliced
1 small avocado, peeled and sliced

In mixing bowl, break up tuna with fork. Add sunflower seeds, cumin, pepper, and mayonnaise. Mix well. Set aside.

In large measuring cup, whisk together olive oil, lime juice, and tarragon to make a vinaigrette.

Place greens in salad bowl. Toss with half of the dressing. Place on two chilled luncheon plates. Top with alternate slices of cantaloupe and avocado. Place a large scoop of tuna mix in the center. Drizzle salad with remaining vinaigrette. Serves 2.

* Or substitute a 6 - ounce jar or can of imported tuna packed in olive oil, drained. Flake with a fork and use in salad without sunflower seeds, cumin, pepper, or mayonnaise. The olive oil from the tuna may be used in the salad dressing if you choose.

Pasta, Gnocchi
and
Polenta

Artichoke Pasta

One day while browsing among the fascinating offerings at Walnut Creek's Oakville Market (sadly, now closed), I came across artichoke pasta. I decided to prepare it with artichoke hearts and accent it with the rich, creamy texture of macadamia nuts. This dish made an immediate hit. If you're in a hurry, frozen or canned artichoke hearts will work. If you can plan in advance, do prepare a batch of fresh hearts to include in this dish. I of course prefer the fresh baby artichokes, and they are worth the effort to prepare them!

1 8-10-ounce package imported artichoke pasta
1 tablespoon salt
2 tablespoons olive oil, divided
1-1/2 to 2 cups prepared fresh baby artichokes, cooked or 1 14-ounce package frozen artichoke hearts or 1 13-3/4-ounce can artichoke hearts in water, drained
1/4 cup unsalted Macadamia nuts, coarsely chopped
3 tablespoons crumbled gorgonzola cheese
1/3 cup grated parmesan cheese
Freshly grated black pepper (optional)

Fill large stock pot with water. Add salt and 1 tablespoon olive oil. Bring to a rolling boil. Add pasta. Stir gently. Bring back to a boil. Boil on Low until pasta is almost *al dente*. See package for suggested time. Slowly pour pasta into colander to drain. Gently return to pot. Cut artichoke hearts into quarters and add with nuts, gorgonzola and 1/4 cup of parmesan. Stir *gently*. (This pasta is delicate when cooked and subject to breaking apart.) Serve on plates. Top with remaining parmesan and a grind of pepper if desired. Serves 2 - 4.

Fresh Fettuccine

Here is the method Bob devised for using the Atlas pasta maker that I had given him. Now we didn't have to alter our commute to purchase fresh pasta. We could enjoy our own "in-house" version whenever we wished.

Prepare pasta according to the directions for Ravioli, Page 200. Once you have 8 sheets, or leaves, set the cutters on the machine to the width specified for the type of pasta you want — fettuccine, linguine, tagliarini, etc.

Flour a large piece of butcher paper or a wax-paper-covered sheet of newspaper. As you run each sheet of pasta through the machine, lay the noodles out flat on the paper. Take care not to overlap the noodles. Sift a little flour on top. Set aside.

To cook, heat to boiling a stock pot of water. Add 1 tablespoon salt and 1 tablespoon olive oil. With both hands, lift the pasta from the paper to make sure the strands are separate. Place in pot and stir gently. Bring to a boil, turn down the heat to Low and start to time the cooking process. Cook until pasta tastes just *al dente,* "to the bite." Drain in colander. *Do not rinse.* Return to pot if cooking a hot dish. For salad, leave pasta in colander to cool.

Note: Pasta may be made in larger amounts and dried for future use. Use a rack for drying. Or lay the pasta strands on a counter, table, or even on a bed, and allow to dry. Store in large jars or Ziplock plastic bags.

Fettuccine Alfredo

Bob and I enjoyed this Roman dish, and we both knew how to prepare it. By the time we met and married; however, our diets did not include pasta sauces so decadently high in fat. I include this recipe in our book, however, because it pairs so well with veal and is a mainstay of elegant dining.

1 tablespoon salt
1 tablespoon olive oil
9 ounces fresh fettuccine
6 tablespoons butter
1-1/2 cups whipping cream, divided
1 cup grated parmesan cheese
Fresh ground pepper

Fill large stock pot with water. Add salt and olive oil. Bring to a boil. Add fettuccine. Return to a boil on High. Cook, uncovered, until pasta is *al dente*. Drain in colander. Return to pot and set aside.

In a large nonstick skillet, melt butter. Stir in ½ cup whipping cream. Bring to a boil on High. Cook, stirring occasionally, until butter and cream are blended and bubbles form. Reduce heat to Medium and add fettuccine. Toss with 2 forks until pasta is thoroughly coated with sauce. Add the cheese and toss to coat. Add the remaining cream in 1/3-cup portions, tossing fettuccine well after each addition. Keep tossing as needed until noodles absorb the sauce. Serve immediately. Grind fresh pepper over each serving. Serves 4 to 6.

Fettuccine With Mushrooms and Arugula In White Wine Sauce

16 ounces fresh fettuccine, separated into strands
1 pound fresh crimini mushrooms, scrubbed and sliced
8 ounces fresh arugula leaves
1 tablespoon salt
3 tablespoons olive oil, divided
1 tablespoon butter
1/4 cup white wine
1 tablespoon corn starch
2 tablespoons capers, drained
Shaved grana or fresh parmesan cheese
Freshly ground black pepper (optional)

In large nonstick skillet, sauté mushrooms in 2 tablespoons olive oil, just until mushrooms are softened. Add butter and melt into mushrooms. Reduce heat. Immediately add wine. Set aside.

Fill large stock pot with water. Add salt and 1 tablespoon oil. Bring to rolling boil.

Add fettuccine and stir gently. Return to boil. Boil on Low 3-5 minutes until pasta is *al dente.* Drain in colander. Return to pan. Add mushrooms.

Return skillet to fire and stir in cornstarch until blended. Simmer five minutes until reduced by half. Add to pasta. Add capers. Toss all together gently. Serve warm topped with shaved cheese. Grind black pepper on top. Serves 2 – 4.

Fettuccine With Pesto Sauce

This makes a satisfying accompaniment to spicy entrées. Try it with braised Italian sausages or chicken parmigiana.

1 tablespoon salt
2 tablespoons olive oil, divided
9 ounces fresh fettuccine
Pesto sauce
Parmesan cheese, grated

Fill large pot two-thirds full of water. Add salt and 1 tablespoon olive oil. Bring water to a rolling boil. Add fettuccine. Boil 3 - 4 minutes until fettuccine is *al dente*. (Remove a noodle from the water and bite into it to see if it's done to your taste.) Immediately remove pot from range. Pour contents into colander placed in the sink. Do not rinse pasta. Once pasta has drained, return to pot. Toss with 1 tablespoon olive oil to help keep strands separate. Toss with pesto sauce and grated parmesan. Pass extra grated parmesan. Serve hot.

Pesto Sauce: See recipe on Page 275.

Fettuccine With Smoked Salmon

The Italian flag colors of green, white, and red give this dish a festive appeal.

1 tablespoon salt
2 tablespoons olive oil, divided
9 ounces fresh spinach fettuccine
1/4 large red onion, finely chopped
2 tablespoons capers, drained
4 ounces smoked salmon slices, cut into bite-size sections
4 ounces cream cheese, cut into bite-size cubes
1/4 cup grated parmesan cheese
1 spray Italian parsley
Fresh-ground black pepper

Fill large stock pot two-thirds full of water. Add salt and 1 tablespoon olive oil. Bring to a rolling boil. Separate fettuccine into strands. Drop into boiling water. Stir gently to make sure strands are separated. On Low, bring back to a slow boil. Cook until *al dente* 3 - 4 minutes. Drain in colander and return to pot. Toss with remaining olive oil. Add onion, capers, salmon, and cream cheese. Mix gently. Heat in pot until warm. Serve on heated plates. Sprinkle with parmesan cheese. Garnish each plate with a sprig of parsley. Add fresh-ground pepper. Serves 2 - 4.

Potato Gnocchi

Allow plenty of advance preparation time for this dish.

Before Bob and I were married, I enjoyed a birthday party for his mother Jean at the Greenbrae home of Gloria and Mel Riccardi, Bob's sister and brother-in-law. During the cocktail hour, Gloria excused herself to cook the gnocchi. "Oh, my, Gloria is brave," Jean remarked. "She's daring to cook gnocchi for a crowd. I've had them fall apart in the water and become glue." Gloria's gnocchi stayed intact, and I felt impressed with her success.

Two years later, after Bob and I were married, I asked him to prepare gnocchi. "You prepare most of the other Pochini Restaurant classics. How about gnocchi?" I asked. Bob confessed he had not attempted to make those delicious little dumplings. He promised to try.

2 pounds russet potatoes, scrubbed, unpeeled
2 egg yolks
1-1/2 teaspoons salt
1-1/3 cups unbleached flour, more or less

Use firm, dry potatoes. Cook whole in boiling water until tender. Drain and peel. Return potatoes to the saucepan. Shake over low heat until dry. Press through a ricer into a large bowl. Or break up with a fork. Mash the potatoes until smooth. Mix in the egg yolks and salt. Add just enough of the flour to make a dough. This will depend on the moisture in the potatoes. Use as little flour as you can to bind the dough. Do not overwork the dough. It should be soft - but not at all sticky.

On a lightly floured surface, roll portions of the dough into finger-thick ropes. Cut into 1-inch lengths. Gently roll each piece with the back of a dinner fork to create light ridges. Fill large stock pot with water. Add 1 tablespoon salt. Bring to a rolling boil. Gently place the gnocchi, a few at a time, into the pot, removing them with a slotted spoon a minute or two after they rise to the surface. Drain well and transfer to a warm platter. (Or refrigerate or freeze for future use.)

Serve on heated plates with pesto sauce, marinara sauce, or creamy gorgonzola sauce. For *Gnocchi Tricolore* in the colors of the Italian flag, divide gnocchi into thirds. Sauce each third with pesto, marinara, and creamy gorgonzola. Arrange in thirds of red, white, and green on each plate. Garnish with sprigs of fresh basil.

Gnocchi With Gorgonzola Sauce

Yes, this is rich, but it's so satisfying. The gnocchi with their delicate texture set off the slightly "gamey" punch of the gorgonzola.

½ cup whole almonds, shelled
2 ounces crumbled gorgonzola cheese
½ cup half-and-half, "soured"
1 tablespoon cider vinegar (optional)
4 tablespoons nonfat whipped cream cheese
1 tablespoon salt
1 pound potato gnocchi or potato/spinach gnocchi
3 tablespoons grated parmesan cheese, divided
1 spray Italian parsley, finely chopped

In food processor, whirl almonds until ground medium fine. Add gorgonzola and pulse until well blended. Use leftover soured half-and-half. Or "sour" the half-and-half by stirring in the vinegar and allowing it to sit for 10 minutes. Add to processor and pulse until blended. Add cream cheese and blend. Set aside.

Fill large stock pot two-thirds full of water. Add salt. Bring to a rolling boil. Add gnocchi and boil on Low until all gnocchi rise to the top of the pot, about 2 - 3 minutes. Drain in colander. Return to pot. Add enough sauce to coat gnocchi well, plus a little extra sauce. Do not let gnocchi "swim" in sauce; save any extra sauce for another use. Stir 2 tablespoons of grated parmesan into gnocchi and sauce. Heat on Simmer/Low until warm. Place on serving plates. Top with remaining parmesan. Decorate with sprinkles of the chopped parsley. Serves 2 - 4.

Lasagne al Forno

This recipe adapts well either to the "no-boil" or fresh lasagne noodles, as well as other pre-prepared ingredients. Most cooks use the dry noodles.

1 tablespoon salt
2 tablespoons olive oil, divided
1 pound dry lasagne noodles
    or 12 - 15 fresh pasta "leaves," uncooked
    or 1 pound "no-cook" lasagne noodles
1 pound fresh mushrooms, scrubbed and sliced
4 cups marinara sauce, either "house made" or prepared
4-1/2 ounces fresh spinach, washed and drained well
½ bunch fresh basil
1 pound ricotta cheese
1 pound fresh mozzarella ovolini, sliced
3 ounces chopped prosciutto
1/4 cup grated parmesan cheese
Fresh herbs for garnish

To prepare dry lasagne noodles, fill large stock pot with water. Add salt and 1 tablespoon olive oil. Bring to a rolling boil. Add noodles one at a time. Stir gently. On Low, return to a boil, boiling gently until *al dente*, about 10 minutes. Remove pot from heat. With slotted spoon, remove each noodle from water, draining and keeping it intact as you do so. Place individual noodles on waxed paper until you are ready to assemble the dish.

Or, consult your "no-boil" or "fresh" lasagne package and prepare lasagne noodles as directed.

Heat 1 tablespoon olive oil in nonstick skillet. Sauté mushroom slices until *al dente*. Add to marinara sauce and set aside. In food processor, pulse spinach and basil until finely chopped. Add ricotta and pulse until well mixed.

Oil 9"x13" baking dish or pan. Place thin coating of sauce on bottom. Top with lasagne noodles, another layer of sauce, one-third of the mozzarella slices, one-third of the prosciutto, a layer of lasagne noodles, sauce, spinach/basil/ricotta mixture, a layer of lasagne noodles, sauce, mozzarella slices, a layer of lasagne noodles, sauce, ricotta mixture, noodles, and sauce. Top with the grated parmesan cheese. Cover with aluminum foil, sealing sides of container well. Bake in preheated 375° oven for 45 minutes, or as package may direct if you have used "no-cook" lasagne noodles. Remove from oven. Remove foil and let stand for 10 minutes. Cut into squares and place on heated plates or pasta bowls. Garnish with sprigs of fresh herbs. Serves 8 - 10.

Linguine With Artichokes

Crazy about Fettuccine Alfredo? Here is a similar dish without the butter and cream.

1 tablespoon salt
3 tablespoons olive oil, divided
½ pound fresh linguine or fetuccine
1-1/2 to 2 cups prepared fresh baby artichokes, cooked,
    or 1 14-ounce package of frozen artichoke hearts
    or 1 13-3/4 -ounce can hearts of artichoke in water, drained
4 - 5 ounces prepared artichoke/lemon pesto (½ of a 9 -ounce
    tub)
6 tablespoons grated parmesan cheese, divided
4 tablespoons toasted pine nuts
Fresh ground black pepper
1 red bell pepper, seeded and sliced

Fill large stock pot with water. Add salt and 1 tablespoon olive oil. Bring to a rolling boil. Add pasta. Boil on Low until *al dente*, per package directions on length of time. Drain in colander. Return to pot. Cut artichoke hearts into quarters. Add to pot along with pesto, 4 tablespoons of the cheese, pine nuts, and several grinds of pepper. Toss gently to mix. Serve on plates or in bowls. Top with remaining cheese and decorate with bell pepper slices. Four servings.

Linguine or Angel Hair Pasta With Crudarola Sauce

Developed by Chef Francesca, the contessa who owns Villa Pambuffetti, a charming small inn located in the Umbrian hilltop town of Montefalco.

8 - 10 Roma tomatoes
2 stems fresh basil, leaves only, chopped
2 - 3 stems fresh oregano leaves, chopped
8 - 10 fresh mint leaves, chopped; use wild mint if available
1 spray Italian parsley, chopped
8 arugula leaves, chopped
4 green onions, chopped
1 dried Japan chile, seeded and chopped
2 large cloves garlic, peeled
1 tablespoon salt
3 tablespoons extra virgin olive oil, divided
9 ounces fresh linguine or imported dry angel hair pasta
8 ounces fresh mozzarella cheese, cubed
4 tablespoons grated parmesan, divided
Fresh ground pepper
Extra fresh herbs for garnish

Put tomatoes in colander. Pour 2 quarts of boiling water over the tomatoes to loosen skins. Peel, seed, and chop. Place in large bowl. Add chopped fresh herbs, arugula, onions, and chile. Put garlic through press into bowl.

Fill large stock pot with water. Add salt and 1 tablespoon oil. Bring to rolling boil, add pasta. Return to boil on Low. Cook until *al dente*, 1 - 4 minutes. Drain in colander. Return to pot. Add uncooked sauce and mix well. Add fresh mozzarella cubes and 2 tablespoons parmesan and mix well. Heat slightly on Low. Serve on heated plates. Top with additional parmesan cheese and a grind of fresh pepper. Garnish with fresh herbs. Serves 4.

Orecchiette With Parma Sauce

The lean, air-cured, Italian ham, prosciutto, comes from Parma, a rocky region where the hogs feed on the sparse vegetation and stay svelte, slim, and almost fat-free. The "little ears" shape of the orecchiette complements the thin slivers of ham in the creamy cheese sauce.

1 tablespoon salt
2 tablespoons olive oil, divided
8 ounces imported orecchiette ("little ears")
½ cup grated light Havarti
6 slices prosciutto, finely minced
½ cup grated parmesan cheese, divided
4 tablespoons Italian parsley, finely chopped

Sauce:
2 tablespoons corn starch
2 cups milk, regular or low fat
4 tablespoons unsalted butter
½ tablespoon salt
1/4 teaspoon pepper

Fill large stock pot with water. Add salt and 1 tablespoon olive oil. Bring to a rolling boil. Add pasta. Stir well. Bring back to a boil. On Low, boil slowly until pasta is *al dente*. Drain well in colander. Return to pot. Toss with 1 tablespoon olive oil. Set aside.

Sauce: In saucepan, mix cornstarch with milk until smooth. Add butter, salt, and pepper. Stirring constantly, bring to a boil over Medium heat. Boil 1 minute. **Or,** microcook on High, stirring three or four times with fork or wire whisk for 3 - 5 minutes, until mixture boils. Boil 1 - 2 minutes.

Add Havarti and 1/4 cup parmesan cheese to sauce and stir until cheeses melt. Add prosciutto and parsley and stir well. Pour sauce over orecchiette and stir well. Reheat if necessary. Serve in pasta bowls. Top with grated parmesan cheese.

Busy ~ Day Pasta

This dish requires a minimum of food preparation. It goes from pantry to table in thirty minutes or less.

1 tablespoon salt
3 tablespoons extra virgin olive oil, divided
½ pound imported dry pasta
5 cloves of garlic, peeled
1/4 teaspoon coarse grind black pepper
1 14-1/2 - ounce can "ready-cut" tomatoes, undrained
½ bunch Italian parsley, chopped
1 3-ounce package pre-washed baby spinach
4 tablespoons crumbled gorgonzola cheese
4 tablespoons grated parmesan cheese, divided
½ teaspoon dried Italian herb blend
2 tablespoons pine nuts, toasted

Fill large stock pot with water. Add salt and one tablespoon olive oil. Bring to rolling boil. Add pasta. Boil on Low until *al dente*, about 11 minutes. Drain in colander. Return to pot. Run garlic through garlic press and add. Toss with remaining 2 tablespoons olive oil and pepper so that pasta is well coated. Add tomatoes and liquid, parsley, spinach, gorgonzola, 2 tablespoons of parmesan cheese, herb blend, and pine nuts. Toss until well mixed. Return to fire and reheat. Serve immediately. Top with extra parmesan. Makes 3 - 4 servings. Also good chilled as a pasta salad.

Pasta With Fava Beans and Olives

Now that fresh fava beans become available in season the innovative cook can develop a new taste combination such as this.

1 tablespoon salt
1 tablespoon olive oil
½ pound imported spaghettini
½ pound fresh fava beans, shelled
2 tablespoons minced red onion
1/4 cup toasted pine nuts
Fresh ground black pepper
½ cup grated parmesan cheese, divided
1 6- ounce can small pitted ripe olives

Fill large stock pot with water. Add salt and olive oil. Bring to a rolling boil. Add spaghettini. Boil on Low until *al dente*, 5 - 10 minutes. Drain in colander. Return to pot.

Meanwhile, cook beans in water until *al dente*. Cool. Remove outer skins from beans. Reheat beans by microcooking on High for 30 - 60 seconds. Add to pasta. Add drained olives, onion, pine nuts, pepper and 1/4 cup parmesan cheese. Place on serving plates and top with remaining parmesan cheese. Four servings.

Impromptu Pasta

Raid your garden in midsummer for a feast.

½ pound fresh large mushrooms, scrubbed and cut into sixths
3 tablespoons olive oil, divided
12 - 16 fresh green beans, strings removed, cut into 2 - inch
    segments
1 tablespoon salt
1 pound angel hair pasta, fresh or dry
1 large yellow tomato, peeled and diced
1 large red tomato, peeled and diced
1/4 large torpedo onion, peeled and coarsely diced
2 ounces blue cheese or feta cheese, crumbled
2 tablespoons sliced almonds
1/4 cup grated parmesan cheese, divided
2 cloves of garlic, peeled
Fresh-ground black pepper
Sprigs of fresh basil

Scrub and cut up mushrooms. Sauté in 1 tablespoon olive oil until *al dente*. Do not over-cook. Remove from heat and set aside. Steam green beans until crisply done. Drain in colander. Shower with cold water to stop the cooking process. Set aside.

Fill large stock pot with water. Add salt and 1 tablespoon olive oil. Bring water to a rolling boil. Add pasta and on Low, bring back to boil. Cook pasta until just barely *al dente*, 40 - 60 seconds. Note: Angel hair is delicate and should not be overcooked. Drain in colander (separate from beans). Return to pot. Toss with remaining olive oil. Add tomatoes, onion, blue cheese, mushrooms, almonds, green beans, 2 tablespoons parmesan, and garlic put through a press. Warm gently. Serve on heated plates. Top with extra parmesan cheese and a grind of pepper. Garnish each plate with a sprig of basil. Serves 4 - 6.

Penne With Chicken and Artichokes

This off-beat combination of chicken with artichoke hearts and Macadamia nuts results in a tempting taste treat.

1 tablespoon salt
2 tablespoons olive oil, divided
8 ounces imported penne pasta
1/4 cup grated parmesan cheese, divided
½ cup roasted chicken, "pulled" into small shreds
1/4 cup dry-roasted salted Macadamia nuts, chopped
1-1/2 to 2 cups prepared fresh baby artichokes, cooked
    or 1 14-ounce package of frozen artichoke hearts
    or 1 13-3/4-ounce can hearts of artichoke in water, drained
    and cut into fourths
Pinch of mixed dry Italian herbs
Freshly ground black pepper

Fill large stock pot with water. Add salt and 1 tablespoon olive oil. Bring to a rolling boil. Add pasta. Stir well. Bring back to boil.. On Low, boil slowly until *al dente*, about 10 minutes. Drain well in colander. Return to pot. Toss with 1 tablespoon oil and 2 tablespoons of the cheese. Add chicken, nuts, artichoke hearts, and herbs. Toss well. Place servings on plates. Cover with paper towels and microcook on High for 1 minute. Top with remaining grated parmesan and a grind of pepper. Serves 2 - 4.

Penne With Coteghino

Even today, few supermarkets carry coteghino, a flavorful Italian sausage. You can make a point of asking for it at a deli in the "Italian section" of your city.

1 tablespoon salt
2 tablespoons olive oil, divided
8 ounces imported penne pasta
1 pound coteghino sausage*
½ large yellow onion, peeled and diced
1 4-ounce can sliced black olives
2 Italian peppers, seeded and chopped or 1 green bell pepper
Fresh ground black pepper
1/4 cup grated parmesan cheese
2 ounces light Havarti, grated

Fill large stock pot with water. Add salt and 1 tablespoon olive oil. Bring to a rolling boil. Add pasta. Stir well. Bring back to a boil. On Low, boil slowly until *al dente*, about 10 minutes. Drain in colander. Return to pot. Slice sausage into half-inch thick rounds. Then cut into quarters. Heat 1 tablespoon oil in nonstick skillet. Sauté sausage, turning often. When browned, remove with slotted spoon and add to pasta. Reheat drippings in skillet. Stir well to loosen bits of sausage. Add onion and sauté until translucent and slightly brown. With slotted spoon, remove from skillet and add to pot. Add olives, chopped peppers, and several grinds of pepper. Toss to mix and heat slightly. Add cheeses and toss well. Place servings on plates. Cover with paper towels and microcook on High for 30 seconds. Makes 2 - 4 servings.

* Usually available at a full-service Italian deli.

Polenta

Yes, this dish does resemble our old-fashioned cornmeal mush, but Italian cooks use it as an appetizing alternative for rice or pasta. It works well grilled as an appetizer or soft as a base for sauce, cacciatore, sausage, or a medley of vegetables. Unlimited possibilities abound. Bob and I especially liked soft polenta as a base for his famous chicken or lamb cacciatore.

You can buy polenta, the coarse Italian corn meal, at Italian specialty markets. The cooked version of the Italian corn meal is also called polenta. Over the years, many experts have developed easy-cook methods for preparing polenta — double-boiler, microwave, or instant. Purchase instant polenta at your Italian market or deli. Most tasters conclude, however, that the traditional slow-cook method gives best control over texture and taste. Here is the slow-cook method that Bob developed.

1 cup polenta
1/8 teaspoon salt
4 cups water, divided
1/8 teaspoon pepper
1 tablespoon butter

Place polenta, salt, and 2 cups water in 2 - quart saucepan. Stir well, *in one direction only,* to avoid lumps, and then stir in this same direction during the entire cooking process. Place on Medium to High heat, continuing to stir until mixture comes to a boil. Turn heat to Low. Continuing to stir, add water 2 tablespoons at a time. Stir after each addition, cooking until mixture thickens after that addition. Then add more water, stirring and allowing to thicken after each addition, until all water has been added. Continue to stir and cook for about twenty to thirty additional minutes. Mixture should be thick but not stiff. Add pepper and additional salt if necessary. Stir in butter. Hold on Low heat for no longer than 10 minutes until time to serve. Or pour into well oiled baking dish or onto large board. Cut into squares or triangles to serve. May be made in advance and chilled then reheated.

Instant Polenta

Yes, instant polenta does take less time to cook , but still it stiffens quickly. Don't make the mistake of serving some and then leaving the rest in the pot. Pour it out of the pot into a flat dish or onto a board.

4 cups water
2 teaspoons salt
2 teaspoons olive oil
8 ounces <u>Beretta</u> instant polenta

Pour water into a non-stick saucepan. Add salt and olive oil. Bring water to a boil. Boil for two minutes. Remove from heat. Quickly pour in polenta, beating with a whisk or wooden spoon. Return the pot to the heat. Cook 5 - 6 minutes on Medium High, stirring constantly. Remove from heat. Let polenta settle for one minute. Pour into a well oiled baking dish or onto a board. Serve immediately. This makes a stiff polenta. For softer polenta, increase water to 5 cups. Serves 5 - 6.

Bob's Ravioli

Several ravioli factories have operated in San Francisco's North Beach for many years. Chances are, Pochini's Restaurant served ravioli made by one of them. As Bob was growing up, his parents sent him to Cafferata on Columbus for ravioli or fresh pasta cut to order.

From the 1960's on, while Bob was living in central Contra Costa County, he procured his ravioli from Mrs. Molino's factory on Pleasant Hill Road. In the 1980's, after Mrs. Molino passed away, Bob taught himself the art of ravioli making. Here's his basic recipe and method.

<u>Filling</u>
1 frying chicken, about 4 pounds
1/3 pound prosciutto, chopped fine
1 bunch spinach leaves, washed, drained and chopped fine
1/4 cup grated romano or parmesan cheese
1 large egg
1-1/3 cup fresh or canned chicken broth
1 tablespoon olive oil

Remove giblet package from chicken cavity and set aside for another use. Wash chicken well under cold water. Pat dry with paper towels. Truss chicken. Rub with olive oil. Place on rack in roasting pan. Roast at 325° until internal temperature reaches 180°. When done, leg will jiggle easily. Remove chicken from oven and cool until easy to touch. Cut into pieces and remove skin. Remove meat from bones and chop into small bits. Place in large bowl. Add prosciutto, spinach, cheese, egg, and broth. Mix well. Cover with plastic wrap and store in refrigerator.

<u>Pasta</u>
2 extra-large eggs
2 cups *unbleached* flour
1 teaspooon olive oil
1/3 cup water

Place eggs, flour, and olive oil in food processor. Pulse until blended, about 10 times. While processor is running, add water. Pulse until dough forms a ball. Remove from processor and place on a large well-floured board. Roll dough in flour and form a ball. Cut ball in half with a sharp knife. Gently flatten one half. Crank through pasta machine set on "1." Dust both sides with flour. Fold ends into center. Crank through machine. Repeat this process four more times (six times total). Keep flouring so dough does not stick to the rollers. Repeat process with remaining dough. You will have two pieces.

Reset machine to "2." Roll each piece through twice. Reset machine to "3." Roll through once. Reset machine to "4." Roll through twice. Reset machine to "5." Roll through twice. Cut each piece in half. Flour well. You will have four pieces. Reset machine to "6." Roll through once.

Cut each sheet in half. You will have eight sheets. Cut each to the size of your ravioli press or template. (Bob devised and made a 5" x15" x ½" template with 12 circular openings 1-1/4" in diameter. He used heavy gauge plastic. (See photograph.)

Place a sheet of pasta on the ravioli press. (If using a template, place a sheet of pasta on the floured board and place the template on top as shown in photo.) Fill each opening with the chicken mixture. Tamp the filling into the opening with the bottom of a shot glass. Using a new, clean plasterer's trowel or the edge of a large spatula or knife, remove excess filling. Brush water onto dough between filling and around the edge of the rectangle. Flour one side of a second sheet of dough. Turn over and brush entire sheet with water. Place wet side on filled sheet. With fingers, press top of second sheet on unfilled area. Using top of your ravioli press (or a custom made wooden press 4-1/2" x 12-1/2" with 12 openings 1-1/2" square), push down hard to seal top sheet to bottom sheet. Cut with a ravioli cutter, checking the seal on each edge as you cut. Place onto floured boards for storage. (Ravioli factories place prepared ravioli on gently floured cardboard sheets called "cards." They sell the ravioli by "cards.") Set ravioli aside. Makes about 2 dozen ravioli. May be frozen for future use. Any excess dough or trimmings may be re-processed gently and cut into noodles.

<u>Sauce</u>
3 tablespoons unsalted butter
3 tablespoons flour
2 cups marinara sauce, warmed in microwave or small saucepan
1/4 cup dry sherry
1/4 cup whipping cream

In nonstick skillet, melt butter. Whisk in flour to make a roux. Whisk in marinara sauce. Add sherry and whipping cream and blend. Keep warm.

<u>To cook and serve ravioli</u>
Fill large stock pot with water. Add 1 tablespoon salt and 2 tablespoons olive oil. Bring to full rolling boil. While water is boiling, gently slip ravioli into pot. Do not stir. Boil ravioli until they rise to top. With flat ravioli lifter, remove to heated plates or pasta bowls. Top with sauce and freshly grated or shaved parmesan or grana cheese. For color garnish with sprinkle of finely chopped Italian parsley. Utter a triumphant sigh of satisfaction of your job well done and enjoy!

Meatless Filling for Ravioli or Manicotti

Bob enjoyed presenting both ravioli and manicotti with this delicious filling.

½ package (2 ounces) spinach, washed and drained
1-1/2 pounds ricotta cheese
1/3 cup grated parmesan cheese
1 large egg
½ teaspoon salt
1/8 teaspoon black pepper

In food processor, pulse spinach until finely chopped. Add remaining ingredients. Pulse until well blended.

The Ravioli lesson: Bob folds a sheet of pasta.

Bob cranks the pasta sheet through the machine while Gina and Liane look on.

Gina folds a sheet.

Gina cranks it through.

Bob places a template for filling on a sheet of pasta.

Bob fills the template.

Bob tamps the filling down with a shot glass.

Ever the innovator, Bob scrapes off extra filling with a clean, new plasterer's trowel.

Liane cuts the finished ravioli.

Bob lifts the cooked ravioli out of the pot with a slotted spatula made by Chef Leo.

Rigatoni With Eggplant

Inspired by a dish I first enjoyed at Square One (now closed) in San Francisco. Be sure to cook the eggplant until it's soft, thus allowing its flavor to blend well with the other ingredients.

1 tablespoon salt
4 tablespoons olive oil, divided
12 ounces imported rigatoni
1 red onion, finely chopped
3 cloves garlic, peeled and finely chopped
1/4 teaspoon salt
1/8 teaspoon pepper
2 Japanese eggplants, washed and sliced crosswise into rounds
1 cup marinara sauce
2 tablespoons fresh basil leaves, coarsely chopped
3 tablespoons grated parmesan or romano cheese, divided
Sprigs of Italian parsley

Fill large stockpot with water. Add salt and 1 tablespoon olive oil. Bring to rolling boil. Add rigatoni. Stir well. On Low, return to boil and cook until pasta is *al dente*, about 8 - 10 minutes. Drain in colander, shaking colander to dislodge water that might remain inside the pasta tubes. Return to pot. Toss with 1 tablespoon olive oil to keep rigatoni from sticking together. Set aside.

In large nonstick skillet, heat 2 tablespoons olive oil. Sauté onion and garlic until onion becomes translucent. Stir in salt and pepper. Add eggplant slices and sauté until browned. Add marinara sauce. Simmer until flavors blend and eggplant becomes soft, not chewy. Toss with rigatoni and 2 tablespoons of the parmesan or romano cheese. Serve on heated plates. With kitchen scissors, add shreds of basil leaves to top of pasta. Top with remaining cheese. Garnish with parsley. Makes 6 servings.

Rigatoni and Italian Sausage

Rigatoni is much loved by Italian cooks because its ribs and tubular shape attract sauce handsomely.

5 or 6 Italian style sausages
1 large onion, finely chopped
3 - 4 cloves of garlic, finely chopped
1 large bell pepper, seeded and chopped
1 8-ounce can tomato sauce
1 large tomato, peeled, seeded and chopped
1 tablespoon salt
2 tablespoons olive oil
1 17-ounce package imported rigatoni
1/4 cup grated parmesan or romano cheese

Cut sausages into 1-inch slices. Remove casings and discard. In large nonstick skillet, sauté until crumbly (10 - 15 minutes). With a fork, break up sausage as it cooks. Tip skillet so that drippings run to one side into a pool. Allow to cool until fat congeals on drippings. Skim off fat. Return to heat. Add onion and garlic and sauté with the sausage until onion becomes translucent. Add bell pepper and sauté 2 - 3 minutes. Add tomato sauce. Simmer about 45 minutes until sauce thickens. Add fresh tomato. Simmer five minutes more. Set aside.

Fill large stock pot with water. Add salt and olive oil. Bring to a rolling boil. Add pasta and stir well. Return to a boil. On Low, boil pasta slowly until *al dente*, according to time suggested on package. Drain in colander, shaking to remove water. Reheat meat sauce. Pour into pot. Add pasta. Stir well. Add cheese and stir once more. Serves 4 - 6.

Bob's Spaghetti a Vongole With Clams

During our early married years, a San Francisco Italian chef moved his trattoria to Concord. Our friend Cecilia discovered his little place and introduced us to it. Cecilia found the vongole to be a savory treat, and we agreed. Bob immediately reached into his repertoire to come up with this version. In Italy, we Americans get frowned upon because of our penchant for sprinkling cheese on our seafood. Some restaurants even forbid it, in fact. But personally, I like this dish with lots of parmesan cheese. (So there!)

1 tablespoon salt
1 tablespoon olive oil
1 pound imported spaghetti
½ pound unsalted butter
6 cloves garlic, finely chopped
1/2 pound fresh baby clams, shelled,
    or fresh minced clam meat
    or 1 pound baby clams in the shell
    or 1 pound can baby clams
    or 1 6-1/4 -ounce can minced clams
1 8-ounce bottle clam juice
1/3 bunch Italian parsley, finely chopped
1/4 cup grated parmesan or romano cheese
Black pepper, coarsely ground, to taste

Fill large stock pot with water. Add salt and olive oil. Bring to rolling boil. Add pasta. Boil on Low until *al dente* — about 10 minutes. Drain in colander. Return pasta to pot.

In 1-quart saucepan, melt butter. Add garlic and sauté. Add clams or clam meat and clam juice and heat through. Add to pot of pasta. Add parsley and cheese. Toss well together. Serve topped with black pepper. Pass extra cheese. Makes 4 - 6 servings.

Spaghettini Side Dish

This makes an excellent accompaniment to barbecued Italian style sausage.

1 tablespoon salt
3 tablespoons olive oil, divided
1 pound imported dried spaghettini
½ cup sun dried tomatoes, reconstituted 4 green onions, chopped
  in olive oil, julienned 1/4 cup grated parmesan cheese,
  divided
1/4 cup crumbled gorgonzola cheese
1/4 cup toasted pine nuts or chopped almonds

Fill large stock pot with water. Add salt and 1 tablespoon olive oil. Bring to a rolling boil. Add pasta. Boil on Low until pasta is *al dente*. Drain in colander. Return to pot. Toss with tomatoes, gorgonzola, nuts, onions, 2 tablespoons parmesan cheese, and 2 tablespoons olive oil. Toss well. Place in center of heated plates. Add one or two barbecued Italian style sausages on the side. Top pasta with remaining grated parmesan.

Tagliarini With Asparagus

After a winter of dishes made of squash and root vegetables, the arrival of asparagus brings much joy. I especially like to serve it with pasta in a combination of ingredients such as this.

1 tablespoon salt
2 tablespoons olive oil, divided
8 ounces imported dry tagliarini
1 pound fresh asparagus
1/4 cup toasted almonds, chopped
3 tablespoons chopped red onion
4 medium mushrooms, scrubbed and sliced
3 tablespoons crumbled gorgonzola cheese
1/4 cup grated parmesan cheese, divided
Freshly ground black pepper

Fill large stock pot with water. Add salt and 1 tablespoon olive oil. Bring water to a rolling boil. Add tagliarini and stir. Bring back to a boil on Low heat. Cook pasta until *al dente*, 8 - 10 minutes. Drain pasta in colander. Return to pot. Toss gently with remaining olive oil. Set aside.

Wash asparagus and snap off large ends. (Save ends for soup if desired.) Cut asparagus stalks on the diagonal into 1 - inch segments. Add to pot along with almonds, onion, mushrooms, gorgonzola cheese, and 2 tablespoons parmesan cheese. Toss gently while reheating on Low. Serve on heated plates. Top with grated parmesan and a grind of pepper. Serves 2 - 4.

Tortolloni With Gorgonzola and Sage

Tortolloni are the big brothers of the diminutive tortellini, a circular pasta reportedly designed to represent navel of Venus, the goddess of love. Legend says that a man so admired the beauteous Venus that he spied on her in the bath in an attempt to view her beauty. But the modest goddess so draped her garments while bathing that our Peeping Tom saw only her navel. Smitten by what he saw, the peep fashioned a pasta to resemble as closely as possible the famous navel of his beloved. This pasta originated in Bologna, where it's a favorite to this day.

3 tablespoons extra virgin olive oil, divided
1 tablespoon salt
8 ounces tortolloni, fresh or dry
2 tablespoons butter
1 tablespoon chopped fresh sage leaves
3 tablespoons crumbled gorgonzola cheese
Grated parmesan cheese
Fresh ground black pepper
Sage leaves for garnish

Fill large stock pot with water. Add 1 tablespoon olive oil and salt. Bring to a rolling boil. Add pasta and stir. Return to boil then reduce heat to Low. Continue boiling until *al dente*, 5 minutes for fresh pasta, 5 to 10 minutes for dry. Drain in colander. Return to pot.

In small skillet, melt butter. Add sage and toss to warm sage. Add butter and sage, plus gorgonzola to pasta. Toss until well mixed. Heat slightly if necessary. Serve on heated plates. Top with grated parmesan and pepper. Garnish with sage leaves.

Rice and Grains

Risotto Milanese

Bob enjoyed preparing this classic Pochini's Restaurant dish. In fact, he used the restaurant's pot for doing so. He liked to serve risotto in place of a pasta course, before the entrée. I would clear the soup or salad course from the table and engage our guests in conversation while we waited in patient but eager anticipation for Bob's masterpiece.

1 ounce dried porcini mushrooms
4 cups unsalted chicken stock
1/4 teaspoon saffron threads
1/4 cup extra virgin olive oil
½ cup minced onion
1 cup arborio or carnaroli rice
½ cup grated parmesan cheese, divided
Salt and freshly ground black pepper

Place dried porcini in a small bowl. Cover with boiling water. Let sit one hour. Remove porcini from bowl. Rinse under running water to remove grit. Strain soaking liquid through a coffee filter. Reserve liquid.

Bring stock to a boil. Add mushroom soaking liquid and bring back to simmer. Pour off one cup broth and add saffron. Set aside.

In a large deep pot, heat olive oil. Add onion and sauté until golden. Add rice. Stir until rice is coated in oil. Stir in reserved saffron-stock. Keep stirring until liquid is absorbed. Add porcini stock one ladle at a time, stirring after each addition is absorbed and rice is tender but still firm inside (about 30 minutes). Use only as much stock as you need to achieve the desired creamy texture in the rice. (If you run out of stock before rice becomes creamy, add water one ladle at a time as before.)

Stir in mushrooms. Add 1/4 cup grated parmesan. Season with salt and pepper to taste. Serve in heated pasta bowls or on heated plates. Pass extra grated parmesan.

Wild Rice With Mushrooms

Bob served this glamorous side dish often with Cornish hens, roast duckling, and other game-type entrées. Wild rice is not a true rice but the seed from a plant which grows wild in the Upper Midwest. I have been told that this culinary delight is not cultivated and that harvesting rights belong to the indigenous tribes who live in its growing region..

1 cup wild rice
4 cups water, divided
1 teaspoon salt
5 tablespoons butter, divided
2 tablespoons olive oil
½ pound button mushrooms, scrubbed and sliced

Put rice in mixing bowl and add water to cover. Let stand for a few minutes. Pour off any foreign particles that may have risen to the top. Drain rice completely. Repeat this process two more times. Set rice aside.

Meantime, bring 2 cups water and salt to boil in a large saucepan. Add the rice and 4 tablespoons butter and cover. Reduce heat to Low and cook without stirring until rice is tender, approximately 40 to 60 minutes, until all water has been absorbed. Makes 3 cups.

In nonstick skillet, melt butter, add olive oil, and heat. Add sliced mushrooms and sauté until mushrooms are *al dente* and just begin to release moisture. Stir into rice and serve.

Main Courses

Albacore Cacciatore

This impromptu stew, concocted by Bob on a camping trip, brings home the true meaning of cacciatore, a stew made with the "catch of the day" from hunting or fishing.

3 - 6 pounds albacore, either fresh or frozen and thawed
1 large onion, peeled and coarsely chopped
1 large bell pepper, washed, seeded, and coarsely chopped
2 stalks celery, strings removed, cut into 1/4" slices
4 Roma tomatoes, peeled, seeded, and chopped
1 tablespoon olive oil
½ teaspoon salt
1/8 teaspoon pepper
1 bay leaf
1 teaspoon fresh thyme leaves, chopped or ½ teaspoon dried thyme
2 cups dry white wine

In large pot, heat olive oil.. Sauté onion until translucent and golden. Add bell pepper and celery and sauté slightly. Add tomatoes, salt, pepper, bay leaf, and thyme. Stir well. Add wine. Heat to simmer. Cut albacore into 1" by 2" chunks. Add to pot. Bring stew to simmer on Low. Cover pot. Simmer for 20 to 30 minutes, until albacore flakes easily with fork and vegetables are tender. Serve in heated soup plates. Accompany with sourdough bread. Serves 6 to 8.

Calamari "Rings"

When abalone was plentiful years ago, only knowledgeable Italian fishermen ate squid, or calamari. Today, calamari has become a profitable catch. The mantels became steaks, replacing our prized abalone. The small mantels are stuffed, like pasta tubes, or cut into the now familiar rings to be fried or used raw in salads. Once you develop a taste for calamari, you'll become a devotée. I first had calamari "rings" many years ago, when I worked for Sunset Magazine. A colleague had persuaded a fisherman in Monterey to give him an unmarketable squid or two rather than throwing them away. He brought them back to Sunset headquarters, where the foods editors prepared the rings.

1 pound fresh or frozen calamari legs cut into "rings"
2 eggs, beaten
All - purpose flour
Salt
Pepper
4 tablespoons olive oil
Lemon wedges or slices
Tartar sauce
Prepared seafood sauce

Thaw calamari. Blot dry with paper toweling. Beat eggs with whisk until lemon colored. Pour a layer of flour onto a plate. Season with salt and pepper. In large nonstick skillet, heat 2 tablespoons olive oil. Dip rings first into flour, then into eggs, then again into flour. Fry in oil just until golden. Do not overcook or the calamari may turn onto "rubber." With slotted spoon, remove calamari from pan and put on a plate covered with a paper towel to blot up any excess oil. Add the remaining oil to the pan if necessary and continue until all calamari has been fried. Serve family style and pass lemon and sauces. Or "plate," giving each person a portion garnished by lemon and a small helping of each sauce.

Calamari Steaks

Once abalone became almost extinct and thus priced out of reach, Bob and I found the frozen and pounded calamari mantels a tasty substitute.

1 pound frozen calamari steaks
2 eggs, slightly beaten
All-purpose flour
Seasoned dry bread crumbs
1 tablespoon olive oil
Wedges of lemon
Tartar sauce, optional

Thaw steaks and blot with paper toweling. Place beaten eggs, flour, and bread crumbs in flat bowls or deep plates as large as or larger than the steaks.

In nonstick skillet, pour olive oil and heat on Medium. Dip each steak first into flour to coat both sides, then in beaten egg, then into bread crumbs, coating well. Fry slowly until golden brown on one side. Turn with spatula and fry other side. Remove from pan immediately. Do not overcook. Place on heated plates. Serve with wedges of lemon and tartar sauce, if desired.

Add a serving of steamed rice and a green vegetable and you will have "plated" an appealing entrée.

Cioppino

Bob peers into a cauldron of cioppino. The giant pot put in years of service at Pochini's Italian Restaurant; but, lacking a lid, Bob pressed a new hubcap into service. Notice the wine cork inserted into the valve stem opening.

For a true culinary adventure, you'll enjoy shopping for and preparing cioppino, the famous Italian seafood dish. (Warning: This project is not for the squeamish.) Daughter Jan proposed a cioppino party one summer day. Initiated into the mysteries of fresh seafood markets in Oakland's Chinatown, Jan proposed to take Bob and me on a quest for truly fresh fish and shellfish — live in tanks. Ducking down stairways into wet, murky, smelly, and mysterious basements, we bought a crab, which we carried home alive, live shrimp and mussels, a cod from the "live" tank, and the large fish head so necessary for flavor and consistency. We watched one proprietor don a huge glove and pull out just the crab we wanted. Then he tied the potentially lethal pincers and wrapped it in paper for the trip home. At another stall, the owner pulled our fish out of the tank, then killed, skinned, and fileted it. Once we procured our seafood, we drove straight home to Lafayette, where our commodious kitchen could accommodate three eager and industrious cooks.

We used a large cauldron from Pochini's Restaurant, but we had no lid large enough to cover the pot. Ever ingenious, Bob found a new Chevrolet hubcap among his treasures. He cleaned that thoroughly, then put a wine cork in the valve stem opening to make the lid tight.

1 2-1/2 - pound live crab
½ pound medium-size uncooked shrimp
1 large fish head
1 pound fresh mussels
1-1/2 pounds fresh codfish, cleaned and fileted
2 tablespoons olive oil
2 tablespoons butter
1 large onion, peeled and chopped
1 large leek, washed free of dirt and chopped
1 head of garlic, peeled and finely chopped
1 8-ounce can tomato sauce
2 cups dry white wine
1 bottle (8 ounces) clam juice
1 6-ounce can pitted ripe olives, drained
1 small carrot, peeled and diced
1 stem of saffron, crushed
1 spray of fresh thyme leaves, chopped
1 bunch Italian parsley, washed and chopped

Kill and clean the crab. Wash well. Break it into pieces. Wash shrimp and fish head. Drain on paper towels. Scrub mussels to remove beard. Cut cod filets into 2 - inch chunks.

In giant stockpot, heat olive oil and melt butter. Sauté onion and leek until golden and translucent. Add garlic and sauté slightly. Add tomato sauce, wine, clam juice, olives, carrot, saffron, thyme, and parsley. Stir to mingle. Reduce heat to Simmer. Add seafood. Cover pot. Simmer for two hours, shaking pot occasionally. Check pot to make sure it has sufficient liquid. If not, add more wine.

Serve in large flat soup dishes. Accompany with crusty sourdough bread. Drape a large napkin around the neck of each guest. Provide large bowls for the shells, as well as seafood forks, crab crackers, etc. *Mangia! Mangia!* Serves 6 - 8.

Pasta With Mussels Vongole

This takes an hour or more to prepare. Allow plenty of time. Farm-raised mussels are available all year.

Pasta:

1 tablespoon salt
3 tablespoons olive oil, divided
½ pound imported cappelini or spaghettini
½ teaspoon garlic powder

Pesto Sauce:

1 bunch fresh basil, leaves only
1/4 cup extra virgin olive oil
8 cloves garlic coarsely chopped
1/4 cup grated parmesan cheese

Broth:

2 cups dry white wine
2 cups water
1 cup extra dry vermouth
4 green onions, chopped
1 lemon with entire rind, halved
Leaves from several sprigs of fresh thyme, chopped
1/4 teaspoon dried dill weed
3 tablespoons butter
Dash of black pepper
6 - 10 cloves garlic, minced
1 bunch Italian parsley, rinsed and tied with twine

Mussels:

2 pounds large farm-raised mussels

Pasta and Pesto:

Fill large stock pot with water. Add salt and 1 tablespoon olive oil. Bring to rolling boil. Add pasta. Boil on Low, until pasta is *al dente*. Drain in colander. Return to pot. For pesto, blanch basil with boiling water. Cool with ice water to stop cooking action. Pour olive oil into blender. Add blanched basil and garlic and grind on Low until leaves become tiny bits. Add parmesan cheese and blend. Add to pot with pasta. Mix gently. Cover and set aside.

Mussels in Broth:

Pull the beard from each mussel. Scrub briefly under running water, rubbing mussels together to remove any debris. Place broth ingredients in large stock pot. Bring to a boil. Add mussels and cover pot. Bring back to a boil, then reduce heat and simmer for 5 - 7 minutes, occasionally stirring with slotted spoon. When mussels open, remove from pot and keep warm. Remove parsley and discard. Pour broth through strainer into another large pot. Return to original stock pot and boil again until broth is slightly reduced.

To serve, reheat pasta. Place in individual serving bowls. Distribute cooked mussels around edge of pasta. Ladle 2 to 3 tablespoons of broth around edge of pasta onto mussels. Pass extra grated parmesan cheese and chunks of sourdough bread for dunking. Serves 3 - 4.

Bob's Garlic Prawns Sauté

Bob and I made the mistake of ordering sautéed prawns as an entrée one weekend in the restaurant of an historic hotel in California's picturesque "gold country." The penurious proprietor gave us only four prawns each. Upset by such a stingy excuse for an entrée, Bob rushed to the market upon our return home. He prepared and served this generous version, and it became one of our favorite dishes. As an optional accent, decorate each plate with a few baby green beans or asparagus spears.

12 - 16 prawns or jumbo tiger shrimp
2 - 4 cloves garlic, finely chopped
1 tablespoon olive oil
1/4 cup white wine
1 lemon

Pat prawns dry. Chop garlic. Heat oil in non-stick skillet. Add prawns and garlic. Sauté on Medium 1 - 2 minutes. Note: Keep heat <u>medium</u> to avoid browning or burning garlic, which turns it bitter. Add white wine and sauté 1 additional minute. Serve with or over rice. Squeeze lemon on prawns. Serves 2.

Seafood Crepes

Bob owned a crepe maker so he could make crepes from scratch. You can cut down on the lengthy preparation time for this dish by purchasing fresh crepes at your full-service market or deli.

1 recipe Bob's Velouté Sauce (Page 227)
½ pound cooked shrimp, fresh or thawed and blotted dry, shells removed
1/2 pound crab meat, either fresh or frozen and thawed, cut or pulled into bite-size pieces
8 fresh crepes
Lemon wedges

Oil a 9" x 13" baking dish. Place a small layer of sauce on the bottom. Mix the shrimp and crab meat together in a bowl.

Place a prepared crepe lengthwise across the dish. In the center of the crepe, spoon the seafood mixture along the length. Top with two or three small ladles of sauce. Roll crepe along the length of the filling. Repeat until all eight crepes have been filled. Top with remaining sauce. Place in preheated 325° oven. Heat for approximately ten minutes, just until sauce is bubbly. On heated plates, place two crepes per plate. Decorate with lemon wedges or slices. Accompany with steamed spears of baby asparagus and steamed baby carrots.

Shrimp Jambalaya

I first enjoyed this dish as prepared and served by San Franciscan Beverly Falkenburg in 1955. I have adapted it to include the ingredients we use and enjoy today.

1 red onion, finely chopped
1 clove garlic, finely chopped
2 tablespoons olive oil
1-1/2 cups finely diced ham
1 pound baby shrimp
1-1/2 tablespoons butter
1 cup long grain white rice
1 teaspoon salt
Cherry tomatoes, halved
1-1/2 cups bottled clam juice, fish or chicken stock, or water,
    boiling hot
½ bell pepper, finely chopped
4 Roma tomatoes, seeded and finely chopped
3 sprigs parsley, finely chopped
Cayenne pepper to taste

Sauté onion and garlic in oil. Add ham and shrimp and sauté briefly. Add butter and melt. Add raw rice and sauté. Add rest of ingredients. Cover pan. Simmer 20 to 25 minutes until rice is done. Garnish with cherry tomato halves. Serves 4 to 6.

Crab Jambalaya

I enjoyed this dish at the renowned Postrio Restaurant in San Francisco and then developed my own version.

Substitute 1 pound shredded crab meat for the shrimp. Omit parsley. Top each serving with two or three crab legs which have been sautéed in butter or with a serving of broiled or fried striped bass. Garnish with cherry tomato halves. Serves 4 to 6.

Roast Beef

Petrini's, our favorite San Francisco style full-service butcher, had franchises in markets near us. Before we would settle on our choices, Bob and I would stroll along the cases, eyeing the specials to decide what we could afford. A butcher would ask Bob, "What would you like today?" Bob would reply, "Oh, today we're just looking. The re-fi on our house hasn't come through yet."

Roast sirloin, rolled and tied, was Bob's favorite. Petrini's sold top quality sirloin, and we didn't mind paying a little extra for it.

1 boneless top sirloin beef roast (about 3-1/2 pounds), rolled and tied at intervals
2 tablespoons olive oil

Rub roast all over with olive oil. Place on rack in large roasting pan. Let stand on counter until roast reaches room temperature.

Place on a lower rack in a pre-heated 325° oven. For rare, roast for 1 hour 15 minutes, approximately, until a instant-read meat thermometer reads 115° to 125° when inserted at several spots. For medium-rare, increase time to 1 hour 30 minutes until the instant-read thermometer registers 135° to 145°. For well done, increase time to 35 minutes per pound, to achieve an instant-read temperature of 160°. Remove from oven and cover loosely with foil. Let stand for 10 to 15 minutes before carving.

While the beef would be roasting, Bob often would find room in the oven for a baking dish of Oven-Fried Potatoes (see recipe), an appropriate accompaniment to the roast.

Barbecued Chuck Blade Roast

One of Bob's favorite offerings for our family meals on hot summer evenings was barbecued chuck blade roast. First cut blade chuck comes off the beef just one knife blade cut away from the tender and more expensive rib and contains a large portion of the tender "rib eye" muscle, normally sold as "market steak." Yes, the blade does contain some muscles other than the "eye," but these are a continuation of the same muscles found in the rib (which we often enjoy as part of a prime rib roast). Because the price was reasonable, my thrift-minded husband enjoyed barbecuing this tasty meat almost every week. We used the leftovers in burritos.

1 chuck blade pot roast, 2" to 3" thick
2 tablespoons virgin olive oil
Coarse ground black pepper

Rub roast with olive oil and pepper. Let it sit unrefrigerated until it comes to room temperature.

Barbecue over hot coals, or on High in a gas barbecue, until roast is well seared on one side, about 8 minutes. Turn over and continue grilling, another 8 minutes or so, until instant-read meat thermometer registers 135° for rare. Place on serving board and cut into thin slices.

Calf's Liver

Mother made me eat my liver whether I wanted to or not. In fact, she would brag to her friends about holding my nose and shoving it down my throat. To this day, I shy away from fried liver, even with onions, a dish my parents enjoyed almost every week. Despite my aversion to liver, the smell of it frying with onions does conjure up happy memories of home to me. I still avoid fried liver, however.

One day, though, Bob wanted a dinner of liver for his health.. The nearby market had calf's liver, which I consider the best. Bob coached me in preparing it. By golly, it tasted good! Here's his simple recipe.

Sliced calf's liver
2 tablespoons olive oil
1 or 2 eggs, broken into a flat bowl and whisked to blend
Yellow cornmeal, poured onto a flat plate

Rinse liver and pat dry with paper toweling. In nonstick skillet, heat olive oil on Medium. Dip liver in eggs, then in cornmeal to coat well. Place in skillet. Fry slowly until browned on one side. Turn and brown on the other side. When golden brown, serve immediately.

Accompany with country-style fried potatoes and onions and a green vegetable.

Pollo Cacciatore
Hunter's Chicken Stew

This is a Pochini's Restaurant signature dish. Bob prepared it often for special occasion dinners.

1 2-1/2 - pound frying chicken cut into serving size pieces
2 tablespoons olive oil, divided
1 large onion, chopped fine
3 cloves garlic, chopped fine
1 pound fresh mushrooms, sliced
1 14-1/2 - ounce can chicken broth
1 6 - ounce can tomato paste
18 ounces (3 tomato paste cans) dry red wine
3 tablespoons chopped fresh Italian parsley
1 teaspoon finely chopped fresh oregano
1 teaspoon finely chopped fresh thyme
1 16 - ounce can pitted small ripe olives
1/4 teaspoon salt
1/8 teaspoon ground pepper

Wash chicken and rinse out cavity. Pat dry. Cut into serving size pieces. Then cut each piece, except the wings, in half again. Note: It is important to cut through the bones so that marrow will be released when the stew is cooking. Heat one tablespoon of olive oil in large non-stick or cast iron skillet. Add chicken pieces and fry on High until brown. Remove from skillet and set aside.

Add 1 tablespoon of olive oil to skillet and heat. Sauté onion until transparent. Then add garlic and sauté. Add mushrooms and sauté slightly, until they release moisture into the skillet. Add the chicken broth, tomato paste, wine, herbs, olives, salt, and pepper to the skillet. Stir the mixture well until it heats through. Add chicken pieces. Simmer 10 to 40 minutes, uncovered.

Prepare several hours in advance to allow flavors to "marry." Reheat and serve on bed of white rice or soft polenta. Accompany with green vegetable. Serves six.

Pollo Cacciatore Bianco
Hunter's Chicken Stew with "White" Sauce

Bob's sister Gloria Riccardi developed this version of the traditional Chicken Cacciatore without the tomato sauce. She sometimes expands the recipe to serve as many as two dozen guests at her festive holiday dinners. Here is my interpretation of the recipe she shared.

1 frying chicken cut into serving pieces
1/4 cup all-purpose flour
½ teaspoon salt
1/8 teaspoon ground black pepper
2 tablespoons olive oil, divided
1 large onion, chopped
1 large shallot, chopped (optional)
3 cloves garlic, finely chopped
1 pound fresh mushrooms, sliced
1 bunch green onions, chopped
3 tablespoons chopped fresh Italian parsley
1 teaspoon finely chopped fresh rosemary
1 teaspoon finely chopped fresh thyme
1 10-ounce can Oberti pitted green olives*
1/4 cup brine from olives
3/4 cup white wine
1/4 cup marsala
1-1/2 teaspoons beef boullion
1 tablespoon arrowroot
1 tablespoon water

Wash chicken and rinse out cavity. Pat dry. Cut into serving size pieces. Combine flour with salt and pepper and place on dinner plate. Dredge chicken in flour and set aside. Heat large cast iron or cast aluminum skillet and 1 tablespoon olive oil. Add chicken pieces and fry on High until brown. Set aside.

Add 1 tablespoon olive oil to skillet and heat. Sauté onion and shallot until transparent. Then add garlic and sauté. Add mushrooms and sauté slightly, until they release moisture into the skillet. Add green onions, herbs, olives, brine, wine, marsala and bouillon. Stir mixture well as it heats through. Return chicken to skillet. Cover and simmer slowly for 30 minutes. Remove lid, turn chicken pieces over. Simmer for 30 additional minutes uncovered. Remove chicken from skillet. To thicken sauce, mix arrowroot with water and add, simmering about 10 minutes until thick. Return chicken to skillet. Prepare several hours in advance to allow flavors to "marry." Reheat and serve on bed of white rice or soft polenta. Accompany with a green vegetable. Serves six.

* If your market does not have, buy green olives in bulk from your delicatessen.

Chicken With Artichokes

Bob could present chicken in so many tempting and elegant ways. Here is one of my favorites.

1 four - pound chicken
½ cup all-purpose flour
½ teaspoon salt
1/8 teaspoon ground black pepper
½ pound fresh mushrooms, washed
2 tablespoons virgin olive oil
1 9 - ounce package frozen artichoke hearts, thawed and drained
½ cup dry white wine

Remove giblet packet from chicken cavity and set aside for another use. Rinse chicken thoroughly inside and out. Pat dry with paper toweling. Cut into serving-size parts. Combine flour with salt and pepper. Dredge chicken pieces in flour mixture. Pat mushrooms dry and cut into quarters or slices.

In large non-stick skillet, heat olive oil on High. Add chicken pieces and sauté, turning occasionally until well browned. Remove chicken from skillet and set aside. Add mushrooms to skillet and sauté briefly. Return chicken to skillet. Add artichoke hearts and wine. Reduce heat to Low and cover skillet. Simmer on Low 10 to 15 minutes until chicken is no longer pink in center. Serves 2 to 4. Accompany with steamed rice and a green vegetable.

"Busy – Day" Roast Chicken

I coined the title "Busy-Day" for Bob's roast chicken because he could conjure up this "dinner in a dish" upon short notice. This does not mean, however, that dinner guests would find this menu at all casual. Bob's presentation on the plate gave the meal a festive note every time we enjoyed it. As an added plus, the leftovers are delicious served either hot or cold.

1 4 - pound chicken
Salt
Pepper
2 or three stems of fresh rosemary
1 tablespoon olive oil
3 large Idaho potatoes, peeled and cut into quarters
3 large onions, peeled and cut in half lengthwise (through the
    "stem end")
4 large carrots, peeled and cut into thirds
1/4 cup dry white wine
Several sprigs of Italian parsley for garnish

Remove giblet packet from chicken cavity and discard or set aside for another use. Wash chicken well, inside and out. Cut fat, if any, from neck and cavity opening. Discard fat. Blot dry with paper toweling. Sprinkle salt and pepper inside cavity. Rinse rosemary stems and place inside cavity. Truss chicken according to your favorite method and tie with cooking twine. Rub all over with olive oil. Place in center of well oiled large roasting pan.

Arrange potatoes and onions around chicken, largest cut side down. Place carrots in between or on top, as room allows. Place roasting pan on lower shelf of pre-heated 350° oven. Roast for 35 minutes, until chicken starts to brown. "Spritz" the chicken with wine. Return to the oven for 10 minutes. "Spritz" the chicken a second time with any remaining wine. Using a bulb baster, baste chicken and vegetables with pan juices. Return to oven. Ten minutes later, baste a second time. After 10 more minutes, test chicken for doneness (leg should jiggle easily). When done, baste one more time. Remove from oven and cover with foil. Let stand 10 minutes.

Heat dinner plates in warm oven.

Remove chicken carefully from pan to large carving board. Remove rosemary from cavity and discard. To carve, carefully remove wings and legs at their joints. Set aside. Carve breast into slices. Place two or three slices on each plate. Accompany with 2 or 3 sections of potato, several carrot pieces, and half an onion. Using bulb baster, drizzle pan juices over chicken. Garnish plates with parsley. Guests who prefer wings or legs to the breast have the option to choose them instead of the breast, of course.

Bob checks chicken on the barbecue on our deck in Lafayette while Mike Cornell looks on

Teriyaki Chicken

Shortly after Bob and I married, he asked me to collaborate with him on a barbecue. He asked me to come up with something not in his repertoire. I suggested marinating the chicken in a teriyaki sauce for a few hours and then barbecuing it. We liked this so well that it became a day-off favorite. Bob would prod me to hurry with my breakfast and get the chicken into the marinade.

1 four - pound chicken
2/3 cup soy sauce
1/4 cup dry white wine
1 cup orange juice
2 cloves garlic, peeled and crushed through a garlic press
2 tablespoons brown sugar, firmly packed
1 teaspoon ground ginger
2 tablespoons virgin olive oil

Remove giblet packet from chicken cavity and save for another use. Rinse chicken well with cool water. Cut chicken into serving-size pieces. Skin breast pieces, wings, legs and thighs. In large mixing bowl, combine remaining ingredients for marinade and mix well. Add chicken, making sure to coat each piece and immerse it in the marinade. Cover with plastic wrap and refrigerate 2 to 6 hours. Remove chicken from marinade. Grill 4 to 5 inches from hot coals, 12 to 15 minutes, or until chicken is no longer pink in center. Baste and turn over occasionally. Serves 2 to 4.

Bob's Chili

As Bob and I fine-tuned our kitchen collaborations, we found that we gravitated to the arrangement set up by his mother and father, Chef Leo and Jean Pochini. Bob would do the major dishes while I would work around the edges, so to speak. For everyday meals, as well as for guests, I would prepare the salads and Bob would produce the entrées and vegetables. Most of the time, I would make the desserts. We'd share honors on the appetizers as appropriate.

We had another unwritten rule. I was allowed to serve as sous chef to Bob and help out as necessary. He would do the same for me, of course. But he allowed me to prepare only the main courses that I specialized in, such as shish kebab, curry, enchiladas, tamale pie, chili, etc. I could learn his classic cuisine as a student, but he did not allow me to tamper with it. Bob, on the other hand, felt free to ask me for the recipes and dishes he'd like to try and then to play around with the ingredients. Did I object? Certainly not. Years of daily cooking appeared on my personal resumé. I gladly stepped aside for the master. So it was that Bob took my chili recipe and made it his. I had started out inspired by a version of the famous chili from Chasen's, a popular Los Angeles restaurant now closed. Gradually, I had added more vegetables and omitted most of the beef. Bob kept the taste and improved on it. I hope you enjoy it.

2 pounds dry pinto beans, washed and sorted, free of dirt and rocks

2 yellow onions, peeled and chopped

6 cloves garlic, peeled and finely chopped

6 tablespoons chili powder

2 tablespoons ground cumin seed

1 teaspoon pepper

2 teaspoons salt

½ pound salt pork, "pancetta," or thick- sliced bacon, chopped

4 fresh ortega or pasilla chiles, washed, seeded, and chopped

3 jalapeño peppers, washed, seeded and chopped

2 15-ounce cans cut-up tomatoes

1 6-ounce can tomato paste

1 cup dry red wine

½ bunch fresh cilantro, washed and chopped

Chopped fresh red onion

Grated cheddar or jack cheese

First "de-gas" the beans to prevent the gastrointestinal distress normally associated with beans. To do this, place the beans in a large stock pot. Cover with water. On High, bring uncovered pot to a full rolling boil. Cover pot and remove from fire. Let stand one hour. Drain beans into a colander, discarding cooking water.

Return beans to pot. Add onions, garlic, chili powder, cumin, pepper, salt, and enough water to cover. Bring to a boil. Cover pot and simmer 2 to 3 hours. Add meat, chiles, tomatoes, tomato paste, and wine. Cover pot. Simmer 1 hour. Remove lid. Continue simmering until beans are well done and sauce has thickened. Stir in cilantro. Simmer 10 minutes longer. Serve in large soup bowls topped with chopped fresh onion and grated cheese. Accompany with homemade cornbread and you'll have a true "down home" meal.

Cooks note: You may substitute dry kidney beans or dry black beans if you wish. The tiny dry "pinquito" baby beans from Santa Maria also taste delicious in this chili.

Roast Rock Cornish Hens

In the northern Italian city of Perugia, the capital of Umbria, roast wild pigeon is a classic dish. Here in the U.S., we favor Rock Cornish hens over pigeons. Bob would roast them stuffed with the classic Swiss chard dressing he learned from Chef Leo. With the hens, Bob would serve wild rice with mushrooms as well as tender green beans. Our guests would sigh in happy satisfaction after enjoying such a festive dinner.

1 bunch Swiss chard
½ stale sourdough baguette
2 tablespoons olive oil, divided
1 large yellow onion, peeled and finely chopped
6 cloves garlic, peeled and finely chopped
1/4 teaspoon salt
1/8 teaspoon pepper
1/4 teaspoon dried thyme
1 9-ounce package frozen artichoke hearts, thawed and drained, or 1 13-3/4 ounce can artichoke hearts, drained (frozen preferred)
1 cup grated Parmesan cheese
6 large eggs
3 tablespoons butter
6 small Rock Cornish hens, 1-1/4 to 1-1/2 pounds each, thawed, rinsed, and patted dry
½ teaspoon paprika
1/4 cup dry white wine
Sprigs of fresh rosemary for garnish

Remove stems from chard and set aside for soup. Wash leaves well. Drain on paper towels. Place in steamer over ½ inch of water. Cover. Steam on High until chard wilts. Remove from fire and drain well in colander.

In large bowl, break stale bread into chunks. Cover with water and soak until saturated.

In large nonstick skillet, heat 1 tablespoon olive oil. Add onion and sauté on High until it becomes translucent and golden. Add garlic and sauté slightly. Stir in salt, pepper, and thyme. Place in large mixing bowl.

Place chard on chopping board. Cut into bite-size sections with knife. Add to bowl. Cut artichoke hearts into eighths. Add to bowl. Add grated cheese. In a separate bowl, whisk eggs lightly. Do not beat. Add to the vegetables and mix well.

Thoroughly squeeze water from bread. In sauté pan melt butter. Place bread in sauté pan and stir to pick up butter and pan drippings. Add to other ingredients and mix thoroughly.

Rinse hens and pat dry. Set aside giblets for another use. Spoon this mixture into cavity of each bird. Pull legs across filled cavity and truss tightly.

Brush each bird with remaining olive oil and rub with paprika. Place on lower rack in large roasting pan breast side up in preheated 375° oven. Roast 1 hour and 15 minutes. After the first 30 minutes, "spritz" hens with the wine. Ten minutes later, baste with pan juices using bulb baster. Hens are done when an instant-read thermometer placed in the thigh registers 180°. Remove from oven and let stand for 10 minutes. Serve on heated plates, one hen per person, with wild rice and mushrooms and green beans. Garnish each plate with a sprig of rosemary.

Lamb Cacciatore

Our friend Mara Mortensen from Hungary threw down a cook – off gauntlet to Bob. "I love Italian dishes, and I hear you're a master of the cuisine. If I prepared my Chicken Paprikash for you, would you cook Italian for me?"

Accepting Mara's challenge, Bob delved into his memory of special dishes and came up with this one. He served it with soft polenta and green beans cooked until just al dente and finished in olive oil.

He opened the dinner with a zucchini frittata, and I offered Scala's Salad for a first course. Bob finished with zabaglione. The Mortensens still rave about that dinner.

1 ½ - 2 pounds lamb from leg or shoulder
1 teaspoon salt, divided
1/4 teaspoon pepper, divided
2 tablespoons virgin olive oil
1 pound mushrooms, washed and sliced
1 medium onion, finely chopped
3 cloves garlic, finely chopped
1 6-ounce can tomato paste
3 6-ounce canfuls (18 ounces) dry red wine
1 16-ounce can pitted small ripe olives, drained
1 14 ½ -ounce can beef broth
1 tablespoon finely chopped Italian parsley
1 tablespoon finely chopped fresh rosemary

Cut meat into bite-size chunks. Sprinkle with 1/8 teaspoon pepper. In large nonstick skillet, brown meat in olive oil. Remove from pan to plate. Set aside.

Sauté onion until translucent. Add garlic and sauté briefly. Add mushrooms and sauté briefly. Add optional lamb broth, beef broth, tomato paste, wine, olives, parsley, and rosemary. Simmer for 30 minutes. Add lamb and simmer 20 minutes. Sauce should be rich and thick, not watery. Serve on bed of rice or polenta. Serves 4 - 6.

Cook's note: An optional broth may be made from the bones, reduced, and then added. In saucepan combine lamb bones, ½ medium onion, chopped, ½ teaspoon salt, 1/8 teaspoon pepper, 2 cups water. Simmer on Low one to two hours. Reduce to 1 ½ cups.

Roast Leg of Lamb

Bob favored offering roast lamb leg for family celebrations. One large leg will serve a crowd of 10 to 12, and it doesn't take long to prepare. We found that the leftovers make excellent sandwiches.

Bob considered a supply of fresh rosemary essential for this dish and many others. Shortly after we married, I gave him a gallon-can size rosemary plant. He used so much of it he just about killed the plant. I could almost see that plant cringe whenever Bob approached it with a knife. Finally, I planted rosemary as a ground-cover and later, in another garden, as a large hedge!

1 whole bone-in leg of lamb (7 to 8 pounds)
2 teaspoons salt
1 tablespoon ground black pepper
2 teaspoons finely minced fresh rosemary
4 large cloves of garlic, peeled and cut lengthwise into slivers
3 tablespoons olive oil
1 large lemon, optional

Trim excess fat and membrane from the lamb. Rinse well. Pat dry with paper toweling.

Position rack in lower third of oven. Preheat oven to 450°. In small bowl, mix salt, pepper and rosemary. Cut slits 1" deep and ½" wide on all surfaces of lamb, about 12 slits. Using demitasse spoon, "pour" rosemary and seasoning mixture into a slit. Then push in a piece of garlic. Fill all slits. Rub the surface of the lamb with olive oil. Place meaty side up on a rack in a large roasting pan.

Reduce oven temperature to 325°. Roast 1-1/4 hours for medium-rare (instant-read meat thermometer will say 125° to 130°) or 1-3/4 hours for medium (instant-read thermometer will say 135° to 145°). Remove from oven and cover loosely with aluminum foil. Let stand for 15 minutes before carving.

If you wish, squeeze lemon over the platter of sliced lamb to offset any perceived "mutton" taste.

Bob's Meatloaf

So many meatloaf recipes exist that taste delicious. We always welcome one more, and I enjoyed Bob's loaf-pan version. He often made it on chilly winter days when we longed for a fire in our woodstove and "comfort food" for dinner — meatloaf, baked potatoes, and baked acorn squash.

2 slices stale bread torn into small crumbs
1-1/2 pounds lean ground beef
½ pound ground pork sausage
1 large yellow onion, peeled and finely chopped
1 large egg
1 teaspoon olive oil
Topping:
2 tablespoons brown sugar, firmly packed
1/4 cup ketchup

In food processor, pulse hunks of bread into medium-fine crumbs.

Place meat in large mixing bowl and, with your clean hands, mix together well. Add onion, bread crumbs, and egg and mix well. Oil 9" x 5" x 3" loaf pan with olive oil. Put meatloaf mixture in loaf pan. Stir brown sugar into ketchup. Spread on top of loaf mixture. Place on lower rack of preheated 350° oven. Roast 1 hour. Remove from oven and let stand for 10 minutes. Cut into 1" thick slices and serve.

Mother's Meat Loaf

My dad, my sister, and I never tired of Mother's meat loaf. Mother prepared this as a special treat, suitable for Sunday dinners or festive Friday night suppers. To save energy, she also baked scalloped potatoes along with her meat loaf. By the time I was eight, Mother had me help her prepare this special treat. Any "meat and potatoes" man will warm to this combination. Much the texture of a country style pâté, this dish has special appeal as a "comfort food." The cold meat loaf makes gourmet sandwiches for lunch the next day.

1-1/2 pounds lean ground beef
½ pound ground pork sausage
1 medium yellow onion, peeled and finely chopped
1 large bell pepper, washed, seeded, and finely chopped
3/4 cup rolled oats
1 large egg
Olive oil
1/4 cup ketchup, optional
2 slices bacon, optional

In large mixing bowl, mix together the beef and pork with your clean hands. Add onion and bell pepper and mix well, until vegetables are evenly distributed throughout the meat. Add the rolled oats and mix well. Add egg and mix until mixture holds well together.

Oil a large baking pan or dish (9" x 13"). Mold meat mixture into one or two oval loaves and place in dish. Leave plenty of room between the loaf and the sides of the pan or dish. Bake at 350° on lower shelf for 1 hour. Loaf or loaves should be deep brown in color. As an option, spread ketchup on the top of the loaf and place one or two strips of bacon down the center before baking. Carve into 1" thick slices. Serve with scalloped potatoes.

Roast Pork Loin

Bob preferred to roast a bone-in loin of pork rather than the boneless tenderloin which has now become so popular. Leave the layer of fat on the roast to baste it as it cooks.

5 to 7 - pound pork loin roast, bone-in
Olive oil
Black pepper
Leaves from several sprigs of fresh rosemary, finely chopped
Dry white wine
Rosemary sprigs for garnish

Rinse roast under cool water. Pat dry. Rub with olive oil. Sprinkle black pepper over entire roast. Roll in chopped rosemary. Place in oiled baking dish or pan fat side up. Bring to room temperature, then place in preheated oven. Roast at 325° for 35 to 40 minutes per pound, about 2-2/3 hours. After 2 hours, spritz the roast with white wine. Continue roasting, basting with pan drippings about every 10 minutes. Roast is medium done when meat thermometer reads 150°. For well done, roast until thermometer reads 160-165°. Remove from oven and baste once again with pan drippings. Cover loosely with a tent of aluminum foil and let roast rest on the counter or range top for 10 minutes.

To carve the roast, turn rib side up. Run knife blade along close to backbone and remove bone. With backbone side toward you, start at right hand side of roast and slice between the ribs.

To serve, place a slice on the plate and baste with pan drippings. Accompany with rice or potatoes and a vegetable. Garnish with sprigs or flowers of rosemary.

Veal Marsala

By the time I met Bob, I had enjoyed many noteworthy dinners of Veal Scaloppine in several of the Bay Area's upscale Italian restaurants. Occasionally, Bob did make the classic Veal Scaloppine with mushrooms with which I was familiar, and it was outstanding, of course. But Bob favored Veal Marsala, a dish which does not appear on restaurant menus quite as often. With Bob's expert preparation, Veal Marsala became our favorite special - occasion dish, certain to please and impress even the most sophisticated guests.

1-1/2 to 2 pounds veal steak, cut thin and pounded on boh sides
**   with a meat tenderizer (usually sold as "scaloppine-style" veal)**
All-purpose flour
Salt (about ½ teaspoon)
Pepper (about 1/8 teaspoon)
1/4 cup olive oil
2 cloves garlic, peeled and finely chopped
½ cup Marsala

Cut pounded veal into serving-size pieces. Place a generous layer of flour on a large dinner plate. Add salt and pepper and mix well. In large nonstick skillet, heat olive oil on Medium. Sauté garlic for a short time. Dip veal slices into flour, shaking off excess. Place in skillet and fry slowly until golden on both sides. Fry in batches if necessary, holding the cooked portions on a plate lined with a paper towel. When all veal has been browned, return to skillet. Add marsala. Cook on Low 10 to 20 minutes, until veal is tender. Serve immediately on heated plates. Makes 4 to 6 servings.

Cook's Note: Because veal can be pricey, you can prepare a similarly elegant dish using cutlets cut from pork loin or turkey breast.

Accompany with Fettuccine Alfredo or Fettuccine with Pesto Sauce.

Veal Piccata

Bob enjoyed preparing piccata as a special occasion entrée. When our budget didn't allow for veal, he substituted pork cutlets or turkey breast cutlets with equal kudos from our guests.

1 pound "scaloppine style" thinly sliced veal round steak, pounded to tenderize if necessary.
All-purpose flour
Salt (about ½ teaspoon)
Pepper (about 1/8 teaspoon)
1/4 cup olive oil
2 cloves garlic, peeled and finely chopped
1 large lemon, washed and cut into thin slices, seeds removed
1/4 cup dry white wine
1/4 cup capers, well drained
Sprigs of Italian parsley

Cut veal into serving-size pieces. Place a generous layer of flour on a large dinner plate. Add salt and pepper and mix well. In large nonstick skillet, heat olive oil on Medium. Add garlic and sauté until golden. Dip pieces of veal in flour. Fry slowly until golden brown on each side. Lift veal from skillet and place on plate. Add lemon slices and sauté briefly until partially cooked. Remove from skillet. Return veal to skillet and place a lemon slice on each piece. Add wine and capers. Simmer for 5 to 10 minutes, until veal tastes fully cooked and lemons have reached *al dente* stage.

Serve on heated plates with rice and baby green beans. Garnish with parsley. Look pardonably proud as you receive raves.

Veal Scaloppine

Among the dining memories that stand out in my mind, I enjoy remembering how tempting orders of Veal Scaloppine looked on our plates as we awaited the accompanying servings of Fettuccine Alfredo deftly prepared tableside by the head waiter at Amelio's (sadly now closed) in San Francisco.

Veal Scaloppine was also one of Bob's favorite dishes and he often invited family and friends to come into the kitchen and watch him prepare it.

1 pound "scaloppine style" thinly sliced veal * round steak, pounded to tenderize if necessary
All-purpose flour
Salt (about ½ teaspoon)
Pepper (about 1/8 teaspoon)
1/4 cup olive oil, divided
2 cloves garlic, peeled and finely chopped
2 tablespoons butter
½ pound mushrooms, scrubbed, blotted dry, and sliced lengthwise
½ cup dry white wine
Sprigs of Italian parsley

Cut veal into serving-size pieces. Place a generous layer of flour on a large dinner plate. Add salt and pepper and mix well. In large nonstick skillet, heat 3 tablespoons olive oil on Medium. Add garlic and sauté briefly. Dip pieces of veal in flour and fry slowly until golden brown on each side.

Meanwhile, while veal is frying, in a separate skillet, melt butter. Add 1 tablespoon olive oil. On High heat, sauté mushrooms until just barely cooked. Do not overcook. When veal has browned, top with mushrooms. Add wine. Simmer gently for five minutes. Taste-test veal for doneness. Serve immediately on heated plates. Accompany with a serving of fettuccine or with rice and a green vegetable. Garnish with parsley. Serves 4.

* Cutlets of pork loin or turkey breast may be substituted for veal.

Vegetable
Dishes

Baby Artichokes

The artichoke "hearts" we see frozen and canned in our markets often are baby artichokes or buds, not the "hearts" of larger ones. The secret to preparing the babies is to strip all green leaves away until only the white core is left. This takes time but the effort pays off.

15 to 20 fresh baby artichokes
2 lemons, divided
2 garlic cloves (optional), peeled and sliced

Rinse artichokes. With sharp knife, cut off about 1 inch of the tips and discard tips. Starting on the outside of the artichoke bud, remove leaves, rotating the artichoke as you do. Do this until only the pale green center remains. In this way, you eliminate the indigestible, tasteless outer portion. As you finish "undressing" each artichoke, cut off the stem and then drop the artichoke into a large bowl of water that is "acidulated," that is, treated with several tablespoons of lemon juice or white vinegar.

When all artichokes have been prepared, place them in a steamer with the juice and rind of 1 lemon and the garlic slices, and water in the base of the pot. Bring to a boil, then steam on Low until artichokes test soft and tender when you insert a skewer.

Add to pasta dishes, or use in frittata or salad.

Bess' Stuffed Artichokes

I owe this recipe to Bess Cuchini DePaola, the mother of my close friend Cecilia Fonner. Bess, Cecilia, and I were discussing favorite dishes one evening and they shared this family pleaser with me. Our family now enjoys it, too.

2 large artichokes, washed
½ lemon
1/4 cup dry bread crumbs
3 tablespoons finely chopped Italian parsley
½ teaspoon finely chopped garlic
1/4 cup grated Parmesan cheese
2 tablespoons extra virgin olive oil

Remove stems from artichokes. Cut off the thorn from each leaf. Soak artichokes in cool water. Drain. Smack the center of each artichoke with a heavy French knife, spatula, or the flat of your hand to open the center and spread the leaves. Mix the bread crumbs, parsley, garlic, and grated cheese. Fill each leaf opening with a little of the stuffing until all is used. In 2 - quart saucepan, place steamer. Add 1-1/2" water to pan. Place artichokes close to each other in steamer. Squeeze lemon juice on artichokes. Add lemon to pan. Drizzle olive oil over artichokes. Cover pan. Steam on low heat 30 to 40 minutes, until artichokes pierce easily with a fork or skewer. Serve either hot or cold.

Asparagus With Mayonnaise Dip

Fresh asparagus comes into season in March, so Mother always served steamed asparagus with butter for my March 16 birthday dinners. That marked the beginning of Spring during my growing-up days in Arizona and California.

When I first met Bob, he entertained me along with daughters Liane, Jan, and Gina one evening and fresh asparagus was on the menu. Instead of the butter, Bob accompanied each plate with a small bowl of mayonnaise dip. I started to cut off a section of asparagus and dip it into the mayonnaise. But the Pochinis had another way, I quickly learned, for family dining. They picked up each spear with their hands, dipped it into the sauce, and bit off a section. Yes, casual, but so effective.

½ cup mayonnaise
Juice of ½ lemon
1 bunch asparagus, about 1 pound
1/3 cup water

Mix mayonnaise with lemon juice and place in small bowls. Rinse asparagus. Break off stems at the point where they no longer are tender. (Each stem has its own particular breaking point.) Discard tough ends or set them aside for soup.

In large skillet unfold steaming rack until it covers the bottom. Place water in skillet; it should not rise above steamer rack. Lay asparagus on rack with half of the stems facing one direction and half facing the other direction (to avoid crowding). Cover skillet. Steam on Low until asparagus is just barely fork tender, about 5 minutes. Lift steamer out of skillet and place in sink. Drench with cold water to stop cooking process and keep asparagus bright green. Serve immediately with mayonnaise dip.

Asparagus Parmesan

For dressier meals, Bob liked to present asparagus in this way.

1 bunch asparagus, about 1 pound
Wedge of Parmesan cheese

Prepare and serve asparagus as above. Place on plates. Shave curls of Parmesan cheese on top of asparagus. Serve immediately.

Stuffed Bell Peppers

Up until I tasted Bob's version of this dish, I always equated stuffed bell peppers with fillings of rice and ground beef or tuna topped with tomato sauce. Bob's stuffing turns this dish into an accompaniment for a meat course.

Two large bell peppers, washed
Virgin olive oil
1/4 pound fresh button mushrooms, finely chopped
4 slices fresh bread, torn into crumbs
1 large egg
1 teaspoon chopped fresh thyme
2 tablespoons chopped fresh Italian parsley
1/4 cup grated parmesan cheese, divided
1/4 cup water

Split peppers vertically and remove seeds. Steam over boiling water for 10 minutes. Place in oiled baking dish small enough that sides of peppers touch.

In large mixing bowl, combine chopped mushrooms, bread crumbs, egg, thyme, parsley, and 2 tablespoons parmesan cheese. Mix well . Spoon into pepper halves. Top with 2 tablespoons grated parmesan. Add water to baking dish. Bake at 375° until peppers are tender and the filling hot, about 25 minutes. Serves 4 as a side dish.

Buttered Carrots

Gina Pochini developed this dish, which is as easy on the budget as it is delicious. Carrots take on a more glamorous appeal.

½ medium yellow onion, peeled and finely chopped
1 tablespoon unsalted butter
2 pounds carrots, peeled and sliced 1/4" thick
1/4 teaspoon salt
½ cup water

In 2 - quart saucepan, sauté onion in butter until translucent. Add carrot slices and salt and stir. Add water. Cover pan. Simmer on Low, stirring occasionally, until carrots are fork tender, 45 to 60 minutes. Serves 4 to 6.

Fried Celery Root

Bob introduced me to the Pochinis' distinctive holiday meal accompaniment, tasty fried vegetables. Now it doesn't seem like Christmas for me until I can prepare and serve a platter of these special treats.

1 celery root, medium or large size
1 teaspoon salt
1 large egg
½ to 1 cup dry bread crumbs Italian style
All-purpose flour
2 tablespoons virgin olive oil

Wash celery root and brush well to remove dirt. Place in 2 -quart sauce pan with salt and enough water to cover. Cover pot. Simmer on Low for 10 minutes to soften celery root. Remove from pot and cool. Peel to remove stringy outer layer. Cut in two vertically. Then cut into 1/4" slices.

In flat bowl, whisk egg until well mixed. Place crumbs in a plate or flat bowl. Place flour in a flat plate. Heat oil in large nonstick skillet.

Dip celery root first into flour, then into egg, then into bread crumbs, to coat well. Fry on Low until browned on both sides. Drain on paper toweling.

Fried Zucchini

2 medium size zucchini, rinsed, stems removed, sliced lengthwise
1 large egg
½ to 1 cup dry bread crumbs, Italian style
All-purpose flour
2 tablespoons virgin olive oil

Prepare zucchini. In a flat bowl, whisk egg until well blended. Place crumbs in a plate or flat bowl. Place flour into a flat bowl. Heat oil in large nonstick skillet.

Dip zucchini slices first into flour, then into egg, then into bread crumbs, to coat well. Fry in oil until brown on both sides. Drain on paper toweling.

Fried Eggplant

1 large eggplant or 2 Japanese eggplants
1 tablespoon salt
2 large eggs
1 cup dry bread crumbs, Italian style
All-purpose flour
2 - 4 tablespoons virgin olive oil

Rinse eggplant well and remove green "stem." Do not peel. Slice large eggplant crosswise into 3/8" to ½" wide sections. Cut sections in half to make half circles. Or slice Japanese eggplants lengthwise. Place on paper toweling. Sprinkle with salt. Cover with a layer of paper toweling. Weight with one or two heavy plates. Let sit for 30 to 60 minutes; this helps the eggplant release its moisture.

In flat bowl, whisk eggs until well blended. Place crumbs in a plate or flat bowl. Place flour on a plate. Heat 2 tablespoons olive oil in large nonstick skillet.

Dip eggplant slices first into flour, then into egg, then into bread crumbs to coat well. Fry in oil until brown on both sides. Eggplant soaks up lots of oil so you may need to add oil as you fry. Drain eggplant on paper toweling.

On large platter, arrange eggplant, then zucchini, then celery root. May be served slightly warm or at room temperature. Serves a crowd.

Barbecued Corn

The secret to this dish is to soak the corn, including the husks, in water just before placing the ears over the coals. Another fresh corn secret that seems to escape some cooks is to keep the corn in the husk until just before preparing it, in order to keep the corn fresh and full of sugar. If you husk the corn at the market, as many shoppers do these days, you hasten the conversion of sugar to carbohydrates within the kernels. This reduces the delicious sweet flavor of the corn. True corn afficionados grow their own at home. Just before serving, they set the pot of water to boil on the stove and then pick and husk their treasured corn.

Fresh "roasting ears" of corn (allow 1 – 2 per person)

Soak the unhusked ears of corn in water for 30 to 60 minutes. Light the barbecue and prepare it for cooking. Remove the corn from the water and peel the husks away from the ear, leaving husks attached. Remove all silk. Pull husks back over the ear, covering the ear completely. Roast for 10 to 20 minutes. Serve immediately in the husks. Let your guests have the fun of husking their own corn, in whatever way they choose.

Eggplant Parmigiana

This dish is one of my favorites for casual dining. For vegetarians, or those of us who limit our meat consumption, it offers a satisfying amount of protein and yet presents a dressy main course.

6 tablespoons virgin olive oil, divided
½ yellow onion, peeled and chopped
2 - 3 Roma tomatoes, washed and sliced
1 clove garlic, peeled and put through garlic press
1 8 - ounce can tomato sauce
½ teaspoon dried oregano, crumbled
1 small spray Italian parsley, chopped
1 large eggplant or several smaller Japanese eggplants rinsed and
**   unpeeled**
1 tablespoon salt
2 large eggs
1 cup dry bread crumbs, Italian style
All-purpose flour
1 pound mozzarella cheese, cut into slices
½ cup grated Parmesan cheese

In large nonstick skillet, heat 2 tablespoons olive oil. Sauté onion until golden. Add tomatoes and garlic and sauté slightly. Stir in tomato sauce, oregano, and parsley. Simmer for 1 hour.

Slice eggplant crosswise into 3/8" sections. (Slice Japanese eggplants lengthwise.) Place on paper toweling. Sprinkle with salt. Cover with paper toweling. Place one or two heavy plates on top to press out any moisture. Let stand for 30 minutes. This helps eggplant release its moisture.

In flat bowl, whisk eggs until well blended. Place crumbs on a plate. Place flour in a flat bowl. Heat 2 tablespoons olive oil in a large nonstick skillet.

Dip eggplant slices first into flour, then into egg, then into bread crumbs to coat well. Fry in oil on both sides until brown and tender.

Eggplant soaks up lots of oil, so you may need to add oil as you fry. Drain eggplant on paper toweling.

Place a thin layer of sauce on the bottom of a well oiled baking dish. Top with eggplant, then with the slices of mozzarella, then with the remaining sauce. Sprinkle grated parmesan over all. Bake in preheated 350° oven until cheese melts. Serves 4 to 6.

Fennel With Cheese

Bob occasionally served fennel, or finocchio, to accompany one of his special-occasion dinners. It was a new taste treat for me, and I enjoyed his version.

1 bunch fennel, stems only, rinsed and cleaned, coarse "threads" removed
½ lemon, juiced
Olive oil
Fontina cheese, grated

Cut stems into 2 - inch lengths. Sprinkle with lemon juice. Place fennel stems in saucepan with steamer. Cook on Low until fork tender. Remove from pan and drain on paper towels. Prepare baking dish by rubbing with olive oil. Place stems in dish concave side up. Spoon grated fontina into each stem. Warm in preheated 350° oven until cheese melts and is bubbly. Serve immediately.

Sautéed Mushrooms

Ray, our first income tax preparer, kept his bill to a minimum if Bob and I would have him over for dinner once or twice during tax season. Grilled or barbecued steak smothered with mushrooms got raves from Ray, so we often treated him to that. The trick is to sauté the mushrooms quickly after the steak is ready, then top the steak with the mushrooms.

Large firm mushrooms, about 6 per person
1 tablespoon olive oil

Scrub mushrooms well with a brush. (Do not peel.) Blot with paper toweling. Place on cutting board stem side up. Slice 3/8" thick. Heat nonstick skillet. Add olive oil and heat. Sauté mushrooms on High until just brown. **Do not overcook.** Mushrooms should not release juice into pan. Immediately, top the grilled steak with the mushrooms.

Peas With Pesto

Pesto sauce gives the glamour touch to a favorite green vegetable.

1 pound fresh peas, shelled
 or 1 14 - ounce package frozen peas
½ teaspoon salt
½ cup pesto sauce (See Page 275.)

Steam fresh peas in a small amount of salted water until *al dente*. Drain in colander. Rinse with cold water to stop cooking process. Or cook frozen peas according to package directions. Drain and rinse as with fresh peas.

Return peas to saucepan. Stir in pesto sauce. Set aside until ready to serve. Then heat on Low until peas and pesto are warmed through.

Peapods or Edible Pod Peas Stir~fried With Mushrooms

Like today's chefs, Bob liked to engage in what has been termed "fusion cooking," that is, borrowing dishes from another culture and cuisine to complement your own favorites. Bob enjoyed wok cooking, and such dishes often would appear on the plate along with an Italian veal dish or American style roast beef.

1 pound Chinese peapods or garden - fresh edible pod peas
½ pound button mushrooms, washed and scrubbed
2 tablespoons virgin olive oil

Wash peas in colander. Remove stems and any "pointy" tips. Blot dry on paper toweling. Cut mushrooms into vertical slices.

Heat oil in wok on High. Toss in peapods. Stir as the pods cook, continuing to cook and stir until pods are tender. Add mushrooms. Continue cooking and stirring until mushrooms are just tender. Serve immediately.

Potatoes Mashed With Carrots

Imagine my surprise when Bob accompanied a meal with orange colored mashed potatoes. They taste as good as they look and vary the ubiquitous mashed potatoes we enjoy so often.

2 large Idaho potatoes, peeled and cut up
4 large carrots, peeled and sliced
Salt
½ cup milk
2 tablespoons unsalted butter

In separate saucepans, boil potatoes and carrots in salted water until they are mushy. Add carrots to potatoes with the milk and mash until well combined. Add butter in chunks and continue mashing until butter is evenly distributed throughout. Serve immediately.

Potatoes With Green Beans

This was one of Bob's favorite dishes to serve with a barbecue. It can be prepared in advance and served chilled or at room temperature when the barbecue is ready.

8 - 10 baby new potatoes, preferably red, well scrubbed
3/4 teaspoon salt, divided
3 tablespoons extra virgin olive oil, divided
½ pound fresh green beans, washed

Cut potatoes lengthwise, then crosswise, into 1" to 1-1/2" chunks. Boil with water to cover and ½ teaspoon salt until *al dente*. Drain. In large bowl, toss with 2 tablespoons olive oil and set aside.

Trim off ends of beans and string if necessary. Cut diagonally into 2" lengths. Steam with water and 1/4 teaspoon salt until *al dente*. Place in colander and cool with running water to stop cooking process and keep beans green. Cool in bowl for 10 to 20 minutes. Add to potatoes. Toss with 1 tablespoon olive oil. Cool. Serve at room temperature or chilled. Any leftovers make a delicious accompaniment with lunch the next day.

Oven - Fried Potatoes

Bob prepared this dish many times for me and for our guests. It always got raves for visual appeal coupled with melt-in-the-mouth texture. And yet, it's so easy to make.

Baby new potatoes, scrubbed and cut into bite-sized pieces
2 or 3 tablespoons of olive oil
1 spray of Italian parsley, finely chopped

In large bowl, toss potato pieces with olive oil until well coated. Add chopped parsley and toss. Transfer potatoes to well oiled baking dish. Roast at 350° until you can pierce potatoes easily with a fork. Hold in warm oven until ready to serve. Allow 2 or 3 potatoes per person.

Baked Acorn Squash

Once you learn the secret of baking winter squash, you'll serve it often on chilly days. Bob and I treated ourselves to squash to accompany meatloaf.

Medium size acorn squash (Allow ½ squash per person.)
Brown sugar
Unsalted butter

Preheat oven to 350°. Wash squash and cut in half lengthwise. Scoop out seeds and membrane and discard. Put ½" water in glass baking dish. (Size of dish will depend on how many squash you are cooking.) Place squash halves cut side down in dish. Bake for 30 minutes. Remove from oven. Turn squash cut side up. Fill each cavity with 1 tablespoon crumbled brown sugar topped with ½ tablespoon butter. Adjust water level in baking dish. Return squash to oven and bake 30 minutes longer, until pierced easily with skewer or fork.

Bob's Mixed Vegetable Frittata

Bob developed this recipe based on his family's classic dish, transforming it from an appetizer into a hearty side dish. The corn gives it a "down home" American touch.

8 ounces of kernel corn, canned, frozen or fresh
Olive oil
1 large onion, peeled and chopped
Salt and pepper
1 medium zucchini
½ pound green beans
½ red bell pepper, rinsed and chopped
½ cup grated parmesan cheese
3 large eggs

Drain corn and place in large bowl. Slice zucchini crosswise and then into halves. Wash and stem green beans. Remove any strings. Cut into fourths.

Heat 1 tablespoon oil in nonstick skillet. Sauté onion until golden. Season with salt and pepper.

Steam or microcook zucchini until *al dente*. Rinse with cold water. Drain in colander.

Steam or microcook green beans until *al dente* (about 4 - 8 minutes on High in microwave). Rinse with cold water. Drain well in colander.

Add onions, zucchini, bell pepper and beans to bowl. Add parmesan cheese. Break eggs into bowl. Mash yolks and whites into vegetables. Fold mixture well. Turn into oiled baking dish – 8 x 8 or 7 x 9. Bake in preheated 350° oven for 35 minutes until set and browned. Makes 9 servings. Serve warm as a side dish.

Sauces

Arnoldi's Sauce Pomodoro

When friends of mine took over the venerable Arnoldi's Restaurant, a Santa Barbara landmark, they brought into our taste pleasures this distinctive Sauce Pomodoro, a vibrant red concoction that tastes as delicious as it looks. This is my adaptation.

1/4 cup extra virgin olive oil
6 cloves of garlic, peeled and sliced
1 28-ounce can San Marzano peeled tomatoes*
Salt to taste
Pepper
Tabasco Sauce

Heat olive oil, add garlic slices and sauté slightly. Remove from heat and set aside. Allow to stand 1 hour to infuse oil with garlic essence. Remove garlic and discard.

Purée tomatoes. Strain to remove seeds. Combine with garlic-infused oil. Heat on Low while stirring, to combine flavors. Add salt, pepper and Tabasco sauce to taste. Sauce should be bright red.

*Or 1 26-1/2- ounce package of Italian strained tomatoes.

Marinara Sauce

This is the all-purpose "red sauce" used in many dishes, from Seafood Vongole to Pasta Primavera to lasagne to pizza. Bob would set aside a morning to make this sauce, ladling it into pint or quart jars to freeze for later use. This enabled him to conjure up a meal in minutes from our freezer and our pantry.

1 tablespoon olive oil
2 medium yellow onions, peeled and coarsely chopped
1 head garlic, peeled and finely chopped
½ teaspoon salt
1/8 teaspoon black pepper
2 tablespoons chili powder
1 6 - ounce can tomato paste
2 8 - ounce cans tomato sauce
3 cups dry red wine
8 Roma tomatoes, washed and coarsely chopped
3 or 4 stems of fresh thyme, destemmed and chopped
½ bunch fresh basil leaves, chopped
5 or 6 stems of Italian parsley, chopped (stems and leaves)

Heat olive oil in large nonstick skillet or stock pot. Sauté onions until soft and translucent. Add garlic and sauté. Add salt, pepper, and chili powder. Stir well. Add remaining ingredients and simmer until flavors blend, about one to two hours. Purée, using an in-batch electric blender or other method. Taste. Correct seasoning as necessary. Makes about 2 quarts.

Meat Sauce for Pasta

The "gravy" in Italian cuisine refers to the savory red sauce produced along with a pot roast. The meat is removed from the "gravy" and served separately or later. The "gravy" goes as well with mashed potatoes as it does with pasta.

(1) 3 - to 4 - pound 7-bone roast, bone-in
Flour
Same ingredients as for Marinara Sauce (See Page 272.)

Rinse roast and pat dry. Dredge with flour. Heat olive oil in large stock pot or Dutch oven. On High heat, brown roast on both sides. Remove from pot and set aside. Sauté onions until soft and translucent. Add garlic and sauté. Add salt, pepper, and chili powder. Stir well. Add remaining ingredients and stir. Return roast to pot. Cover pot and simmer on Low until meat falls off the bone, one to two hours. Remove meat from pot. Taste sauce. Correct seasoning if necessary. Makes about 2 quarts.

Bob's Pasta Sauce With Sausage

Chef Leo passed along to Bob his prejudice against ground beef. "Americans may use it in their spaghetti and their casserole dishes, but it doesn't belong in my family's cuisine," Bob told me. In this sauce which serves a crowd, Bob used sausage. This recipe will wean you away from ground beef.

1 large onion, peeled and chopped
3 cloves garlic, peeled and finely chopped
5 Italian sausages, meat removed from casings
1 pound mushrooms, washed and sliced
1 spray Italian parsley (about half a bunch), washed and chopped
4 Roma tomatoes, washed and coarsely chopped
1 6 - ounce can tomato paste
2 8 - ounce cans tomato sauce
12 ounces (1-1/2 cups) red wine
12 ounces (1-1/2 cups) water
1 tablespoon chili powder
1-1/2 teaspoons dried oregano
1-1/2 teaspoons dried basil
2 tablespoons olive oil
Grated parmesan cheese

In large skillet heat olive oil. Brown onion until translucent and golden. Add garlic and sausage and brown. Add mushrooms and stir-fry until slightly browned. Add remaining ingredients. Simmer 1 hour and 15 minutes. Taste and correct seasonings in necessary. Serve with cooked pasta of your choice. Pass grated parmesan cheese. Serves 4 - 6.

Pesto Sauce

Bob liked to prepare more pesto than we normally used for one dinner. He would freeze the rest for later use.

2 cups water
1 tablespoon salt
2 bunches basil, leaves only, washed
½ cup extra virgin olive oil
1 head garlic, peeled

In 2 - quart saucepan, bring the water and the salt to a boil. Immerse basil leaves for 30 seconds or less, to blanch them. Empty into colander and drain. Shock with ice water and drain. Squeeze dry with paper toweling. (Blanching the basil will keep the pesto bright green.)

Put olive oil in blender. Add garlic and purée until it forms an emulsion. Add basil. On Low, chop until basil is fine and distributed throughout the sauce.

To serve, toss pasta with sauce, toasted pine nuts, and grated parmesan cheese.

To freeze, place a double thickness of plastic wrap in several small freezer containers, such as cream cheese tubs. Add pesto mixture in a layer ½" to 1" thick. Cover with more plastic wrap, then with container cover. Freeze. When solid, remove from containers and place in freezer bags for ease of storage (less bulk). To use, with a serrated knife, cut off a 2" - square cube from a block of frozen pesto (unwrapped). Place in microsafe measuring cup and cover with 2 tablespoons extra virgin olive oil and 1 tablespoon butter (optional). Allow to thaw, naturally or in microwave. Toss with cooked pasta, toasted pine nuts, and 2 tablespoons grated parmesan cheese. Serves 2.

Pomodoro Sauce for Pizza and Pasta

Caught with no sauce on hand and a pizza or pasta dish underway? Try this quick and easy no-cook concoction. This works well with chicken or eggplant parmesan also.

1 6 - ounce can tomato paste
1-1/2 cans (9 ounces) red cooking wine
1/4 teaspoon dried oregano leaves, crumbled
1/4 teaspoon dried thyme leaves

Combine ingredients in bowl. Stir until blended. Fresh oregano and/or thyme may be used for the dried; increase amount to 1 teaspoon chopped fine.

Reduction Sauces

After years of cooking, Bob and I finally learned of reduction as the way to intensify flavor.

With this "recipe," I invite you to reduce the pan drippings, wine, or broth that you use in putting a sauce or gravy together. Many instructions may say, for example, "Add wine and simmer until volume is reduced by half." Or something to that effect. This simple trick for preparing a sauce for such a dish as cacciatore makes it easy to intensify the flavor of the sauce for a hard-to-identify undertone. It can elevate your sauce from ordinary to classic.

Bob's Velouté Sauce

This is the Pochini version of a sauce often combined with seafood. Bob used it to give a rich accent to his seafood crepes.

3 tablespoons unsalted butter
3 tablespoons flour
1 cup bouillon
1/4 teaspoon salt
1/8 teaspoon white pepper
½ cup cream
Yolks of 2 eggs

In nonstick skillet, melt butter. Stir in flour and cook until a roux forms. Do not brown. Stir in bouillon. Cook, stirring, until thick. Stir in seasonings and cream. Beat egg yolks. Add some sauce to the beaten yolks and stir well. Add warmed yolk mixture to the sauce, stirring gently. Cook for 1 minute. Remove from heat.

Classic White Sauce

Bob refused to consider any recipe or sauce using a canned cream soup as base. "Definitely not in the cuisine," he would maintain. This eliminated so many of my American style main dish recipes that I felt compelled to find an acceptable substitute. I decided to substitute the classic white sauce using corn starch, and Bob approved. To make the process simple, I adopted the microwave method of preparing the sauce. With this easy-to-make substitution, my recipes earned the Pochini "seal of approval."

1 tablespoon corn starch
1 cup milk, whole or nonfat
2 tablespoons unsalted butter
1/4 teaspoon salt
1/8 teaspoon pepper

In a large Pyrex measuring cup, stir the corn starch into the milk until smooth. Add butter, salt, and pepper. Microcook on High 3 to 5 minutes, stirring twice with a fork or wire whisk. When mixture boils, microcook 1 additional minute. Makes 1 cup sauce.

Pizza

Pizza

Over the many years since pizza first became a home menu staple, I have made my own shells from mixes, pre-prepared raw dough, and pre-baked pizza shells. For the ease of preparing a quick pizza at home, I now favor some sort of pre-baked shell or simple focaccia on which I add my choice of topping ingredients.

When I first started to introduce innovative pizza toppings into our casual dining, Bob would ignore my need to be creative. To him, pizza meant marinara sauce, plenty of cheese, slices of salami, ham, olives, and any other goodies he could find – shredded chicken, onion slices, mushrooms, peppers. In other words, "Dagwood style." He trumped my ace every time I dealt a "pizza hand." No simplicity for him, and I did tease him about it.

Finally, he came to lunch late one day, just as I was pulling from the oven a pizza topped with a simple combination. Once he tried that first one, he became a convert to the simpler style. Here are a few topping combinations I enjoy. Try experimenting to see what you find tasty. Imagination pays delicious dividends.

1) Pierce pizza shell all over with a fork. Brush with 1 tablespoon extra virgin olive oil. Top with crumbled gorgonzola cheese, chopped green onions, coarsely chopped walnuts, and grated parmesan cheese. Bake at 450° for 10 minutes until well heated. (Inspired by takeout at Bette's Oceanview Diner in Berkeley's Fourth Street bistro area.)

2) Pierce pizza shell all over with a fork. Brush with 1 tablespoon extra virgin olive oil. Top with vertical slices of Roma tomatoes, fresh arugula leaves, bite-size pieces of solid tuna canned in olive oil, and grated parmesan cheese. Drizzle with a little olive oil from the tuna can. Bake at 450° 10 minutes, until well heated. (Inspired by a memorable pizza slice served at the bar in Rome's airport.)

3) Pierce pizza shell all over with a fork. Brush with 1 tablespoon extra virgin olive oil. Top with dollops of ricotta cheese, fresh mushroom slices, chopped green onions, and grated parmesan cheese. Bake at 450° 10 minutes, until well heated.

4) Pierce pizza shell all over with a fork. Brush with 1 tablespoon extra virgin olive oil. Top with crumbled goat cheese, shredded radicchio, cherry tomato halves, chopped fresh oregano, grated light Havarti cheese, and grated romano or parmesan cheese. Bake at 450° 10 minutes, until well heated.

5) Pierce pizza shell all over with a fork. Brush with 1 tablespoon extra virgin olive oil. Top with pitted ripe olives cut in half lengthwise, 1/8 pound (6 tablespoons) grated light Havarti cheese, 3 tablespoons julienned sundried tomatoes in olive oil, 3 tablespoons chopped prosciutto, and 3 tablespoons grated parmesan cheese. Bake in preheated 450° oven until brown and bubbly. Remove from oven. Sprinkle on 2 tablespoons of chiffonade of fresh basil leaves.

6) Pierce pizza shell all over with a fork. Brush with 1 tablespoon extra virgin olive oil. Top with 1/4 cup shredded cheese - light Havarti, fontina, provolone, or a mixture of all three. Add 1/4 to ½ cup "pulled" barbecued chicken, 1/4 cup coarsely chopped red onion, 2 tablespoons of barbecue sauce, and 3 tablespoons grated parmesan cheese. Bake at 450° for 10 minutes until well heated.

7) Pierce pizza shell all over with a fork. Brush with 1 tablespoon extra virgin olive oil. Spread with 1/4 to ½ cup prepared marinara sauce. Top with 1/4 cup shredded light Havarti, fontina, and provolone mixture. Add slices of mushrooms, zucchini, and bell peppers and leaves of baby spinach. Top with 3 tablespoons of grated parmesan cheese. Bake at 450° for 10 minutes until well heated.

Desserts

Apple Torte

This easy-to-make treat is a favorite of my interior design colleague Gloria Scillacci. After one taste, I begged her to share her recipe and she obliged. I like to use D'Anjou or Bosc pears as a variation.

4 cups sliced, peeled firm apples,* Granny Smith or Fuji
2 cups sugar
2 cups sifted flour
1-1/2 teaspoons baking soda
2 teaspoons cinnamon
1 teaspoon salt
2 large eggs
3/4 cup vegetable oil
2 teaspoons vanilla
1 cup chopped walnuts
Fresh berries for garnish

In large mixing bowl, mix apples with sugar. Sift flour. Add baking soda, cinnamon, and salt and sift once again. Add to apple mixture. In separate bowl, beat eggs until frothy. Add oil and vanilla. Fold into apple mixture. Add nuts. Turn into well oiled 9" x 13" baking dish. Bake at 350° for 50 minutes. Serve warm or chilled. Cut into squares and place on dessert plates. Garnish with fresh berries.

* Note: When I use pears instead of apples, I then substitute chopped almonds for the walnuts.

Noni's Biscotti

This is Jean Pochini's recipe for a firm cookie, good for dipping in coffee or liqueur.

½ cup butter
1 cup granulated sugar
3 large eggs
3 cups flour
½ teaspoon salt
3 teaspoons baking powder
1 teaspoon vanilla
1 cup nuts, toasted and coarsely chopped

Preheat oven to 300°. In large mixing bowl, cream butter with sugar. Add eggs and beat well. Sift flour and measure. Add remaining dry ingredients to flour and sift together. Add dry ingredients to wet mixture by thirds. Add vanilla and chopped nuts. Turn onto floured board. Knead lightly until smooth. Divide dough into four parts. Roll each half as wide and as long as your cookie sheet. Place on greased and floured cookie sheets . Bake at 300° for 30 minutes, or until firm to touch. Remove from oven and while still warm cut crosswise into 3/4" thick slices. Lay slices on their sides on the cookie sheets . Return to oven and bake at 300° for about 10 minutes, until browned. Watch the biscotti closely; it's easy to scorch them. Cool. Store in cookie jar or tin. May be frozen.

Toni's Biscotti

I shocked the Pochinis when I presented these softer biscotti for a family party, but they devoured them with joy. Former Calabrian Toni Hagg shared the recipe with me.

1 cup butter
1 cup granulated sugar
4 large eggs
1 teaspoon vanilla
1 teaspoon anise flavoring
4 cups flour
4 teaspoons baking powder
1 teaspoon salt
1 tablespoon anise seeds
Granulated sugar for topping

Preheat oven to 350° Cream butter and sugar. Beat in eggs. Add flavorings. Sift flour and measure. Sift with baking powder and salt. Add by thirds to wet mixture. Stir in seeds. Roll into two or three rolls 1-1/4" thick. Place on greased, floured cookie sheet. Sprinkle with additional granulated sugar. Bake at 350° for 25 minutes. Remove from oven. Cool to room temperature. Cut crosswise into 3/4" slices. Place back on cookie sheet cut sides up. Toast *briefly* under broiler (watch closely). Turn and toast other side. Cool. Store in cookie jar or tin. May be frozen.

Botrytis Cheesecake

Each time Bob and I traveled on 101 between Santa Barbara and the Bay area, we would stop at Monterey Vineyard (now closed) along the highway in Gonzales to replenish our wine cellar. One day the tasting room hostess encouraged us to try a new offering — 1978 Botrytis Sauvignon Blanc, a dessert wine made from grapes frost-bitten before harvest and then infected with botrytis, or "noble rot." Monterey had decided to turn their proverbial "lemons" into lemonade by producing botrytis dessert wine with the ruined grapes. It had a complex sweetness that we enjoyed, so we decided to purchase a bottle.

Then the hostess leaned across the counter and whispered, "I even have a slice of botrytis cheesecake for you to try — left over from last night's dinner for our wine merchants." She also shared the recipe with us, and we served it many times at dinners for our wine connoisseur friends. She credited Chef Michael R. Clark, C.E.C., MICHAEL'S Catering on the Monterey Peninsula, for this innovative version of an old favorite.

<u>Graham Cracker Crust</u>
20 graham crackers, crushed into crumbs (1-1/2 cups)
1/4 pound unsalted butter, melted
1 teaspoon cinnamon
1 tablespoon sugar

Combine all ingredients in large bowl. Press into 9" springform pan.

<u>Filling</u>
1 cup sugar
2 pounds cream cheese, softened
3 large eggs
1/4 pound butter, softened
1/4 bottle (750 ml) (4/5 cup) Botrytis Sauvignon Blanc*

In large mixing bowl, add sugar 1/3 cup at a time to the cream cheese until well mixed. Add one egg at a time, mixing well. Blend in softened butter. Add wine and blend well. Pour into graham cracker crust lined springform pan. Bake at 350° for one hour. Remove from oven. Cake should appear wobbly in the center, but don't worry. It will continue to cook while cooling and will firm up.

Serve chilled accompanied by a liqueur glass of botrytis wine.

* Check with your wine merchant to find a botrytis wine.

Noni's Chocolate Cake

Jean Pochini, a thoroughly modern home cake baker, used a mix for this crowd-pleasing dessert. She transformed the mix so thoroughly one would swear she had concocted a "scratch" cake.

Cake

1 package Duncan Hines moist devil's food cake mix
Eggs as recommended on package
Vegetable oil as recommended on package. Use canola, corn,
  safflower, soybean, or sunflower.

Mix according to directions. Pour into two 9-inch buttered and floured layer cake pans. Bake per directions on package until it springs back when lightly pressed with your finger and just starts to pull away from the sides of the pans. Remove the pans from the oven and place them on a rack to cool for 20 minutes. Run a sharp knife around the edge of each layer and invert them onto a rack to complete cooling, 20 minutes more.

Meanwhile, prepare the filling and the frosting.

Filling

1 package fresh strawberries
1 cup heavy whipping cream
1 tablespoon sugar
½ teaspoon vanilla extract

Wash, stem, and slice strawberries into bowl. Set aside. In separate bowl, whip cream until peaks form. Stir in sugar and vanilla. Set aside in refrigerator. Bananas may be sliced and used in place of berries.

Frosting

1-1/2 cups water
4-1/2 tablespoons butter
1-1/2 cups sugar
9 tablespoons cocoa
6 tablespoons cornstarch
1-1/2 teaspoons salt
1-1/2 teaspoons vanilla extract

Combine water and butter in small saucepan. Place on medium heat to boil. While water and butter are coming to boil, mix dry ingredients in medium saucepan. Add a small amount of water to make a paste. When water and butter come to a boil, add to paste. Place pan over medium heat. Stir constantly, 5 to 10 minutes, until spreadable. Remove from heat. Stir in vanilla. Cool before spreading on cake.

<u>Assembly</u>

After the cake layers have cooled, slice off the domed tops; this will keep the layers from sliding around. If you wish, you may cut each layer in half horizontally with a string or a long carving knife to get four layers.

Place bottom layer on cake plate. Top with one-third of the whipped cream, taking care to keep the cream well inside the edge so that it will not bulge out from the perimeter as you add layers. Top with one-third of the berry slices. Alternate layers and filling. Frost with cooled but spreadable frosting. Refrigerate until serving time.

Roast Chestnuts

At the end of our first Christmas dinner together, Bob tossed a dozen or so hot roast chestnuts directly onto the center of the tablecloth. "Merry Christmas," he sang out. "But, Bob you tossed the chestnuts directly onto the cloth!" I exclaimed. "Enjoy. It has to be washed anyway." He then showed me how to peel and eat the warm chestnuts, with a glass of amaretto, of course. This was my first time to experience the slightly sweet mealy texture of chestnuts. I considered them delicious, especially in the context of a happy Christmas celebration.

About two years later , Bob and I served a menu of Cornish Game Hens with all the trimmings at a Christmas Eve dinner for his three daughters Liane, Jan, and Gina, along with my friend Kay Peakes. The diminutive and enquiring octogenarian expressed joy at every nuance of our Italian American celebration. When Bob threw the roast chestnuts on the table, she embraced this new experience with enthusiasm. "You know, in all my years, I've never had roast chestnuts. I'm eager to try them." She peeled one and took a bite. "Eeuw! This is not a taste I like. I'm sorry." We told her she didn't have to eat it and she didn't. But she enjoyed the amaretto. So — try them. You may like them.

Use the tip of a sharp paring knife to cut an X on the flat side of each nut. Place on a flat baking sheet. Roast at 400° for 30 minutes. Serve at once.

Mini Cream Puffs

Because Jean Pochini liked to show off her baking skills, she many times would offer not just one dessert, but two. One Sunday she treated Bob and me to these mini cream puffs, as well as to her specialty chocolate cake. This finale came after a full Sunday dinner menu which included roast lamb. Bob and I did not complain.

Cream Puffs
½ cup unsalted butter
1 cup water
1 cup all-purpose flour, sifted
4 large eggs

Preheat oven to 400°.

In large saucepan, heat butter with water until mixture boils. Turn heat to Low. Add flour and stir constantly until mixture leaves the sides of the pan and forms a ball, about 1 minute. Remove from heat. Add eggs one at a time, beating after each addition and then continuing to beat until smooth and velvety. (This is a lot of beating.) Drop in portions the size of a walnut onto ungreased baking sheet. You will have 18 portions. Bake until puffed, golden brown and dry, about 15 to 20 minutes. Remove from oven and cool slowly, away from drafts, at least 10 minutes. May be frozen for next-day use.

Custard Filling
½ cup sugar
½ teaspoon salt
6 tablespoons all-purpose flour
2 cups half-and-half
2 eggs, beaten
2 teaspoons vanilla

In saucepan, mix together sugar, salt, and flour. Stir in the half-and-half. Cook on Low, stirring constantly until mixture boils. When mixture boils and cannot be stirred down, boil 1 minute. Remove from heat. Stir in 1 or 2 tablespoons of the mixture into the beaten eggs. Add that blended mixture into the saucepan. Bring just to the boiling point. Remove from heat and cool. Stir in vanilla. Continue to cool.

Cut tops off cream puffs and scoop out any soft dough. Fill with cooled custard. Replace tops. Frost with thin chocolate icing. Place 2 or 3 puffs on a dessert plate. Decorate perimeter with icing.

Icing
2 tablespoons unsalted butter
2 squares (2 ounces) baking chocolate
1 cup sifted powdered sugar
2 tablespoons boiling water

In large Pyrex measuring cup, microcook butter and chocolate on High 1 to 2 minutes until melted. Blend in sugar and water. Beat until smooth and spreadable.

Stuffed Dates

Our family friends Hans and Gladys Hansen grew dates on their ranch near Tempe, Arizona; and Gladys made stuffed dates rolled in powdered sugar for Christmas gifts every year. This was a favorite holiday treat during my growing-up period. Many years later, I found that the same confectionary delight was also a Pochini holiday favorite.

1 pound Medjool dates, pitted
1 walnut or pecan for each date
Powdered sugar

Split nut halves. Fit into date cavities. Roll dates in powdered sugar to coat. Place on waxed paper. Re-roll in sugar if necessary. Store in refrigerator.

Dates may also be stuffed with cream cheese or a mixture of cream cheese and chopped nuts.

Hard Sauce

Serve this with a holiday dessert such as persimmon pudding. Place the warm pudding in the dessert dishes and then use a melon-baller to scoop out the chilled sauce and put it on top. Decorate with holly or an edible herb such as rosemary.

1 cup powdered sugar
5 tablespoons butter
1/8 teaspoon salt
1 teaspoon vanilla, or 1 tablespoon rum, bourbon, brandy, coffee
    or lemon juice as desired
1/4 cup cream

Sift powdered sugar. In mixing bowl, beat butter until soft. Add powdered sugar by thirds until well mixed with butter. Add salt and vanilla. Beat in the cream until sauce is smooth. Chill thoroughly. Serve with pudding or cake, either warm or chilled.

Bob's Mock Napoleons

My cousin Bob Hogan would marvel at Bob's agility and enthusiasm for preparing and serving food. "He's amazing," he told me between courses as Bob bustled like a mercurial genie between the kitchen and the dining room. "Where does he get the energy for it all?"

The more I got to know Bob, the more I came to realize it was knowledge and inventiveness as well as energy that gave Bob his oomph as a host. Here's a dessert he could conjure up on his way to work and have ready to serve that evening when he arrived home.

12 2" x 3" or 2-1/2" x 2-1/2" graham crackers
Puréed applesauce
Whipped cream, from a pressure dispenser
Chocolate syrup or frosting mix

Place 4 graham crackers in a small baking dish. Top with a layer of applesauce, then a layer of whipped cream. Top with another graham cracker, a layer of applesauce, a layer of whipped cream. Top with another graham cracker, applesauce, and whipped cream, then top that with a drizzling of chocolate syrup. Refrigerate 4 to 8 hours. Makes 4 Napoleons.

Orange Pie

I like to serve this citrus treat in winter or spring, when navel oranges are in season.

Crust
1 1/4 cups flour
3/4 cup (1 ½ sticks) butter or margarine, softened
1/4 cup powdered sugar, sifted
1 tablespoon grated orange peel

Combine all ingredients and press on the bottom and sides of a 10-inch pie plate. Bake at 375° for 15 - 18 minutes. Cool. Note: You can buy a pre-prepared crust, but it must be a 10-inch crust or the amount of filling will overflow.

Filling
6 tablespoons cornstarch
1 ½ cups fresh orange juice, divided
½ cup sugar
2/3 cup orange marmalade
1 teaspoon vanilla
1 teaspoon cinnamon
1 teaspoon nutmeg
6 navel oranges, skinned and sectioned (white membrane removed)
whipped cream, sweetened

Dissolve cornstarch in ½ cup of the orange juice. Add remaining juice and all of the other ingredients except oranges to saucepan. Cook, stirring constantly until thick and clear. Add orange sections and mix gently. Pour into cooled piecrust. Chill three to four hours. Serve with slightly sweetened whipped cream. Serves 7 - 8.

Peach or Apricot Cobbler

Among my Grandmother Rose's favorite desserts to make and serve on hot summer days were her fresh fruit cobblers. Easy to prepare and assemble, these cousins to the deep-dish pies could bake in the oven along with Grandma's dinner biscuits or cornbread. Over my growing-up years I helped prepare many cobblers. Grandma's secret was to use tapioca as a thickener for the fruit. Served warm or cold, with heavy cream, these treats always brought delight to our palates. The term cobbler derives from "cobble up," to put together in a hurry; thus the cobbler makes a handy addition to a cook's repertoire of quick and easy desserts

The Fruit:

3 cups ripe peaches, peeled and cut up (pits removed) or 3 cups apricots, washed, stoned, and cut up
2/3 cup sugar
1 tablespoon cornstarch
1 cup boiling water
½ tablespoon butter
½ teaspoon cinnamon
1 tablespoon tapioca

Prepare fruit. In large saucepan, mix together sugar and cornstarch. Gradually stir the boiling water into this mixture. Bring to a boil. Boil 1 minute, stirring gradually. Add fruit and any juice. Pour into a 9" x 9" or 7" x 11" baking dish or pan. Dot with butter. Sprinkle with cinnamon and tapioca.

The Dough:

1 cup sifted flour
1 tablespoon sugar
1-1/2 teaspoons baking powder
1 teaspoon salt
3 tablespoons butter, well chilled, cut up
½ cup milk

Sift together the flour, sugar, baking powder and salt. With pastry blender, cut butter into dry ingredients until fine. Add milk. Stir in to form soft dough. Drop by spoonfuls onto fruit. Bake at 400° for 30 minutes. Serve warm, in bowls, with cream or vanilla ice cream. Makes 6 servings.

Fresh Pear Slices in Mango Purée

In the middle of summer, most of us prefer light desserts. Here's a fruit combination Bob and I devised that's a winner.

**4 Bartlett or D'Anjou pears, washed, cored, and cut into 8 slices
each**
Juice of one lemon
1 ripe mango
2 tablespoons cointreau

Prepare pear slices. Place in serving dishes. Sprinkle with lemon juice to prevent browning. Peel mango. Cut into cubes and place in bowl. Purée with sharp knife. Mash with fork. Add cointreau and blend. Spoon over sliced pears. Chill. Serves 4.

Persimmon Pudding

If you or a friend has a persimmon tree decorating the garden you want to find ways to use the fruit. This pudding often appears on holiday menus. Preparation is simple, and it adds an exotic finale to your meal.

4 to 6 ripe Japanese persimmons, Fuyu or Hachiya variety, to yield 2 cups pulp
3 large eggs
1-1/4 cups sugar
1-1/2 cups all-purpose flour
1 teaspoon baking powder
1 teaspoon soda
½ teaspoon salt
½ cup melted butter
2-1/2 cups milk
2 teaspoons cinnamon
1 teaspoon ginger
½ teaspoon nutmeg
Sprigs of holly

Peel fully ripe, soft persimmons. Purée in a blender. Place in a large mixing bowl. Beat in remaining ingredients in the order given. Pour into greased 9"x 9" baking dish. Bake in a preheated 325° oven until firm — about 1 hour. Serve warm with Hard Sauce. May be stored in refrigerator and then reheated at serving time. Garnish individual servings with holly sprigs.

"Russian" Pie

This favorite recipe was handed down from one generation to another by the Walnut Creek ranching family of Bee Koontz. She would stir it up on short notice for impromptu occasions, and I'm glad she did. I enjoyed it and asked for the recipe. Bob and I served it often as a finale to our company dinners.

1 large egg
3/8 cup brown sugar, firmly packed
3/8 cup granulated sugar
1 teaspoon vanilla
1 cup sifted flour
1-1/2 teaspoons baking powder
½ cup chopped walnuts
1-1/2 cups apples, peeled, cored, and diced
½ cup whipping cream
½ teaspoon vanilla
1 tablespoon sugar

In large mixing bowl, whisk egg until frothy. Add sugar and vanilla. Sift flour. Add baking powder and sift together. Stir dry ingredients, by thirds, into egg mixture. Fold in nuts and apples. Pour into buttered layer cake pan or pie plate. Bake in preheated oven at 350° for 35 minutes. Cut into wedges and serve warm or at room temperature, topped with a spoonful of vanilla-flavored sweetened whipped cream.

Marinated Strawberries

Bob and I were preparing a special dinner for two when I pulled out the strawberries. Deciding that shortcake would be too rich after Veal Scaloppine, we opted to serve them plain. Bob told me to hull them and then let him look at the situation. Musing, he chopped the berries slightly. Then he added a tablespoon of sugar. After that, he carried the bowl to the bar. A splash of cointreau and one of triple sec and a stir. Into the refrigerator they went. An hour later they provided the perfect after-dinner treat.

1 box strawberries, rinsed and hulled
1 tablespoon sugar
2 tablespoons cointreau
2 tablespoons triple sec

Cut strawberries into quarters. Place in bowl. Stir in sugar. Add cointreau and triple sec. Refrigerate for 1 hour or more. Serves 2.

Four~Star Dining at Home
(Suggested Menus)

Four ~ Star Dining at Home
Suggested Menus

Now that you have the stories and the recipes which tell you the Pochinis' approach to dining, you also might like a few ideas for fitting them together into menus.

When I came up with the idea for *The Frittata Affair*, an exposition of the family cuisine, I turned to my treasured diary of our entertainments. Before Bob and I would begin to prepare a meal for guests, we would collaborate on a menu. Then I would write it out for us to refer to as we cooked. Soon I realized we were turning out meals comparable to, if not better than, what one could order at a fine restaurant. I realized we were preparing and serving four-star cuisine in our own home. Our guests, with their compliments, ratified my realization.

Soon I picked up an album at a stationery store, and I started entering the dishes served at our dinners, as well as the guests present, in its pages. By the time Bob and I had spent twelve years entertaining family and friends, each page was filled.

About that time, from these many pages, I then selected the recipes to include in our book. Bob went over my choices and gave his approval. I then started upon my long journey to research and write this book. Bob passed away a few months after I started, but he had approved the direction I was taking. Since then, Daughter Liane, Son Bud, and Daughter Gina have helped me with details about the cuisine and the family. (Sadly, Daughter Jan passed away a year before Bob did.)

In the years without Bob, I have continued to prepare and present his cuisine to family and friends. And I have kept these menus in Album Number 2. From these many parties, I have selected favorites to give you an idea of how to incorporate the cuisine into your own repertoire. Yes, by now, we do have more convenience foods available. Don't hesitate to experiment and include these gourmet prepared foods in your dinners along with your "from scratch" dishes. After all, even if some of us "farm types" know how to raise chickens from fertilized egg to the dinner on the table, few of us do it now. We accept the conveniences, so long as the producers use earth-friendly, humane methods.

Best of all, we now have cooking methods, recipes, and inspiration available to us from many sources. We still can enjoy cooking and entertaining at home *and* find time for other pleasures.

Please let these suggested menus inspire you. Enjoy the fun of mixing and matching appetizers, soups, salads, entrées, and desserts. Use the menus as a guide, then create your own. Your guests will love you for it.

Mangia! Mangia!

Judy

New Year's Day Dinner for Six

Go festive and formal with an elaborate menu to pamper your favorite guests. (Procure the pâté from your favorite deli.)

Country Style Liver Pâté   **Water Wafers**
Champagne

Composed Spinach Salad
tossed with White Wine Vinaigrette
topped with
Slices of Avocado and Whites of Eggs
garnished with Sieved Egg Yolks

Potato - Leek Soup

Roast Cornish Game Hen
with
Artichoke Heart / Chard Stuffing
Risotto Milanese
Sautéed Zucchini Slices
Cabernet

Brie   **Sourdough Pugliese**
Old Vines Zinfandel

Noni's Chocolate Cake
Coffee

Roast Chestnuts
Zinfandel Port

305

Festive January Dinner for Four

Gather around the fire for hearty fare and warm conversation.

Celery Root Frittata

Brie   **Water Wafers**

Potato - Leek Soup

Spinach Salad
with
Baby Shrimp and Avocado
Balsamic Vinaigrette Dressing

Fettuccine Alfredo

Lamb Cacciatore on Bed of Polenta
Buttered Carrots with Sautéed Onion
Sourdough French Bread

Persimmon Pudding   **Hard Sauce**

Roast Chestnuts
Port

Special Occasion Dinner

Here's an example of a Pochini styled menu suitable for a birthday, Valentine's Day, or wedding anniversary. Set out your fine china and best linens and dine by candlelight.

Asparagus Frittata

**Baby Greens Tossed with Winter Pear Slices,
Crumbled Gorgonzola, and Chopped Roasted Almonds
with
Champagne Vinegar / Balsamic Dressing
Pugliese Bread with Olive Oil**

**Veal Marsala
Sautéed Mushrooms
Green Beans Sautéed with Olive Oil
Bob's Perfect Rice**

**Strawberries and Papaya
in
Triple Sec Marinade**

Thanks to the Hunter

Bob's close friend Bill enjoys hunting, and he often would share his bounty of duck, pheasant, or venison with his friends. To thank him, Bob would prepare a dinner featuring the game, on this occasion, pheasant. The chicken cacciatore recipe adapts well to any fowl — pheasant, duck, goose, etc. If you yearn to prepare cacciatore with pheasant but don't know a generous and successful hunter, check with your service butcher. (Although my local butcher doesn't sell pheasant, he referred me to a ranch which raises and sells them.)

Artichoke Leaves Stuffed With Baby Shrimp
Sauvignon Blanc

Broccoli Soup

Orange / Avocado / Red Onion Salad

Pheasant Cacciatore
on
Polenta
Amador County Zinfandel

Apple Torte
with
Fresh Raspberries
Orange Muscat

Baby Shower for Liane

Women relatives and friends from all over the Bay Area converged on our house in Lafayette one slightly rainy April day to celebrate the impending arrival of daughter Liane's first baby. Daughter Jan, Daughter Gina, and I decided to collaborate on the luncheon menu and share the work. First we offered a simple appetizer buffet. Then we served a festive salad buffet. Bob and the men guests stayed downstairs in the game room to play pool for the afternoon, venturing up to snitch plates of food after the ladies had been served. Such a joyous occasion it was, and Andrew John Cornell was born the following June 5.

Bruschetta
Mortadella Pinwheels
Crudités   **Lemon Mayonnaise**
Champagne

Marinated Asparagus Bundles
in Red Bell Pepper Rings
Dilled Baby Shrimp in Butter Lettuce "Boats"
Pasta Salad with Sundried Tomatoes and Olives
Chardonnay

"Welcome Baby Cornell" Decorated Sheet Cake
Coffee   **Tea**

Bob with grandson "Drew" Cornell, age six months

Dinner for the Tax Man

Bob's tax man, Ray, came onto the scene soon after Bob and I married. Rough hewn and outspoken, as well as a former IRS agent, Ray gave us invaluable assistance. The hearty eater liked Bob's cooking and repaid our generous hospitality by keeping his charges within reason. Here is a typical menu.

Celery Root Frittata
Country Pâté Water Wafers

Bacon, Tomato, Avocado, and Spinach Salad

Grilled Steak
Smothered in Sautéed Mushrooms
Oven Fried Potatoes
Green Beans With Pesto

Orange Pie

A Special Birthday

For this five-course birthday dinner we served four prized wines, in keeping with Bob's policy of "special fare for special folks." You can choose your own based on these suggestions.

Polenta Squares with Gorgonzola
Henry Estates Blended Oregon White

Spinach Salad with Avocado and Egg
White Wine Vinaigrette

Bob's Gnocchi with Pesto Sauce
Gundlach-Bundschuh Zinfandel

Roast Pork Loin with Rosemary
Artichokes Bordelaise
Topolos Cabernet

Chocolate Cake
Moscato Amabile

Guaranteed to Impress

When Bob and I entertained his sister Gloria and her husband Mel Riccardi, Bob did his best to show his talented older sister that he also could cook. Over the years, Gloria acknowledged Bob's risotto as closely duplicating Chef Leo's savory masterpiece. Bob had taken possession of the antique aluminum pot used at Pochini's Restaurant for preparing risotto, and he always used it for that special dish.

Green Bean Frittata
Melon Wrapped with Prosciutto

Marinated Tomatoes on Butter Lettuce
Garnished With Dilled Baby Shrimp

Roast Duckling
Risotto Milanese
Chinese Pea Pods Stir-fried with Mushrooms

Botrytis Cheesecake
Botrytis

Casual Dinner on the Patio

When the weather turns hot in midsummer we look for easy, delicious dishes that take a minimum of preparation and fuss. Make the cake, devil the eggs, put the chicken in the marinade, and assemble the salad in the morning. In the afternoon, swim or play tennis with the family. Then fire up the barbecue as the day begins to cool and enjoy the ambiance of your patio or deck for a convivial gathering.

Deviled Eggs

Caesar Salad

Barbecued Teriyaki Chicken
Corn on the Cob
Rotelle Pasta Salad

Vanilla Bundt Cake
with
Strawberries and Whipped Cream

Fourth of July Barbecue

The Pochinis like to gather family and friends around the pool or on the patio or deck for a casual outdoor feast. Here's a menu featuring some of our favorite picnic fare.

Asparagus Frittata　　　　**Zucchini Frittata**
Sauvignon Blanc

Barbecued Teriyaki Chicken
Bob's Potato Salad
Ceci and Kidney Bean Salad
With Red Onion and Garlic
Marinated Tomatoes
Slices of Lemon Cucumber
Marinated in Olive Oil and White Wine Vinegar
with Celery Seed
Foppiano Zinfandel

Peach Slices and Blueberries
Vanilla Bean Ice Cream

Picnic at the Concert

Our favorite picnic venue, the lawn above the Concord Pavilion, drew us many times. We enjoyed our gourmet lunch or dinner while listening to world class jazz. This menu stands out as one of our favorites. We adjourned to our home nearby for dessert.

Marinated Tomatoes

Veal Pocket Stuffed with Swiss Chard
and
Artichoke Hearts
Bob's Potato Salad
Zucchini Frittata

Fresh Comice Pears in Mango Purée and Triple Sec
over
Vanilla Ice Cream

Dinner with Convivial Guests

My cousin Bob Hogan liked to entertain, and his wife, Helen, was an accomplished cook. As our social relationship blossomed, we quite often enjoyed dinners at each other's homes. For this particular party, Bob instructed me to engage our guests in conversation while he worked his kitchen magic between courses. I presided over the conversation from the "host chair" while Bob hustled back and forth from dining room to kitchen. Bob Hogan watched with awe and amusement. Then he turned to me and said, "What a genius with food! Where ever did you find him?" The Hogans and I chuckled with delight as Bob served the next course and then sat down in the "hostess chair." Note that the Risotto Milanese is served as a separate course for this dinner.

Celery Root Frittata

Avocado Halves Stuffed with Baby Shrimp
on
Butter Lettuce

Risotto Milanese

Calamari Steak
Sautéed Asparagus

Pear / Almond Torte
Vanilla Ice Cream
Late Harvest Moscato

Hail the Visiting Children

Bob prided himself on serving the best cuisine always, to family as well as friends. We served this dinner for Daughter Liane and her husband Kevin when they visited from Fresno.

Brie with Sourdough Baguette Slices
Mixed Greek Olives

Baby Spinach Salad with Slices of Comice Pears
and Toasted Walnuts

Crab Jambalaya
Cherry Tomatoes

Bob's Mock Napoleons

Fall Celebration

Many years ago, I took the lead from noted Minneapolis hostess Helen Bossing, who reported that she gardened with an eye to growing unique produce for her dinner parties. Ever since, whenever I plant a vegetable garden or an orchard, I aim to grow the fruit, vegetables, and herbs that give an off-beat flavor to my menus. Here is a dinner that features what I harvested one fall from our garden in Danville.

Proscuitto with Mission Figs and Kadota Figs
Fried Baby Zucchini and Zucchini Blossoms

Chilled Cucumber Soup

Caprese Salad of Heirloom White, Green, and Purple Tomatoes
with Fresh Mozzarella, Fresh Basil, and Balsamic Vinaigrette
on a Bed of Baby Greens

Barbecued Chuck Blade Roast
Sautéed Italian Green Beans
Perry Creek Zinfandel

Soft Fontina   **Manchego**   **St. André**
Sourdough Pugliese
Amador Foothill Zinfandel

Harvest Season Barbecue

Whether you grow your own produce or pick it up at a farmer's market, celebrate the warmth of early October with a harvest picnic at home. For this menu, everything but the steak and the salad dressing came from our own garden.

Golden Zucchini Frittata

Golden Zucchini Soup

Salad of Sliced Heirloom Tomatoes on Baby Lettuce Mix, with Balsamic Vinaigrette and Basil

Barbecued Chateaubriand
Baby Red Potatoes Tossed with Italian Green Beans

Peach Cobbler

Dinner for Bob's Sister

Shortly after Bob and I learned how to approximate the Caravaggio we had enjoyed at Spiedini in Walnut Creek, we decided to share the treat with guests. Bob's sister Gloria and her husband Mel seemed the most likely candidates. Their finely tuned palates would savor such a treat, we reasoned. Note that we served the Caravaggio as a separate "sit-down" appetizer course.

Truffle Pâté   **Water Wafers**

Caravaggio

Spinach Salad with Bacon and Egg
Henry Estates Oregon Chardonnay

Broccoflower Soup

Petrini's Top Sirloin Roast
Wild and Brown Rice with Mushrooms
Italian Green Beans
Lytton Springs Zinfandel

Pear / Almond Torte
Coffee

Sunday Dinner for the Family

The oak leaves were falling and sunny days had a brisk fall feeling. We enjoyed the warmth of our kitchen and the fire in the fireplace stove as we prepared this dinner for Mel and Gloria.

**Trader Joe's Tahini
Lavosh**

**Composed Salad of Tomato and Avocado Slices
Baby Shrimp Garnish
on
Butter Lettuce
Balsamic Vinaigrette**

**Bob's Spinach Fettuccine
with
Pesto Sauce**

**Roast Leg of Lamb
Brown Rice accented with Curry
Stuffed Zucchini**

**Apple / Walnut Torte
Whipped Cream**

Christmas Dinner With Friends

When family members all live a distance away, that's the time to host a holiday dinner for friends in a similar situation. After this particular dinner in Santa Barbara, my friend Sheila led us all in a hilarious game of old-fashioned charades. Note that the pasta is a separate course, a Pochini holiday tradition.

Prosciutto with Melon
Cauliflower Frittata
Country Pâté Water Wafers

Shrimp Louis Salad

Tortelloni with Pesto Sauce

Roast Rock Cornish Hens Stuffed With
Artichoke Hearts, Chard, and Mushrooms
Chinese Pea Pods with Baby Carrots
Fried Eggplant   Fried Celery Root

Pumpkin Pie with Whipped Cream
Coffee

Kitchen
Equipment

Kitchen Equipment

When Bob and I merged forces we each brought to our union a full complement of pots, pans, utensils, bowls, serving pieces, etc. "My, he's a homey guy," I thought as I became aware of the many food preparation gadgets he owned. We used our extras to outfit our RV and later a second home.

Whether you're just now outfitting your kitchen or are reviewing what you have and filling in some blanks, here is a guide for you to consider.

Pots and Pans

Saucepans - 1 - quart and 2 - quart with lids
Large stock pot with lid
6- to 7- inch frying pan with lid
12 - inch heavy skillet with lid
    non-stick cast aluminum or cast iron
1-1/2 - quart double boiler
Cast aluminum griddle, preferably non-stick surface
Roasting pan with rack
Steamer insert for stock pot, or separate steamer, optional

Measuring Tools

Set of measuring spoons
Set of measuring cups for liquids - 1- cup, 2- cup, and quart
Nest of measuring cups for dry ingredients

Mixing Tools

Nest of bowls - small, medium, and large
Whisks - small, medium, and large
Large stirring spoon, preferably for nonstick surfaces
Slotted stirring spoon, preferably for nonstick surfaces

Cooking and Serving Tools

Ladle, preferably for nonstick surfaces
Pancake turner, perforated, preferably for nonstick surfaces
Pasta serving fork
Ravioli lifter, optional

Knives

6 - inch paring knife
6 - inch serrated edge tomato knife
Large bread knife with sawtooth edge
French knife for chopping
Carving knife and fork
Straight-edge knives, short, medium, long
Boning knife
Curved-bladed serrated knife for grapefruit and pineapple
Sharpening stone, and honing steel

Baking Tools and Containers

9 - inch square pan or dish, 2 inches deep
9- x 13- inch oblong pan, or dish, 2 inches deep
2 round cake layer pans, 8-inches x 1-1/4 inches deep,
   or 9 inches x 1-1/2 inches deep
8 -inch or 9 -inch pie plate
2 cooky sheets without sides
Muffin pan
Pizza pan or stone
2 - quart Pyrex casserole with cover
Large tube-center spring form mold, optional
10 - inch diameter x 4 - inch deep tube-center pan, optional
Assorted molds for puddings, optional
Pastry blender for cutting in butter or shortening, optional
Rolling pin
Large bread or pastry board
Flour sifter

Miscellaneous

Flat metal spatula for spreading
Pastry brush
Potato masher
Pie server
2 funnels - 1 large, 1 small
2 strainers - 1 large, 1 small

Cheesecloth
Kitchen twine
Teakettle, preferably one that whistles
Large colander
Set of small metal skewers
Folding steamer insert
Grater with fine to coarse blades
Rubber spatula
Small scrub brush for vegetables
Potholders
Teapot
Tongs
Timer with alarm
Candy thermometer
Salad bowl and servers
Tomato press
Ice cream maker, optional
Egg-slicer
Mandoline
Metal Trivets
Refrigerator storage bowls
Storage cannisters
Ice pick
Ice cream scoop
Garlic press
Instant-read meat thermometer
Kitchen scissors
Poultry shears, optional
Apple-corer
Can opener
Jar opener
Bottle opener
Corkscrew
Pastry tube with assorted tips, optional
Foley food mill for puréeing and straining
Lemon juicer that fits over cup or bowl

Cherry pitter, optional
Melon baller, optional
Ravioli cutter
Ravioli press
Pizza cutter
Bulb baster
Nutcracker
Large shakers for salt and pepper
Pepper grinder
Turkey lacing skewers
Meat slicer, optional

Appliances

Toaster or toaster oven
Electric can opener, optional
Coffee maker
Food processor
Mixer, hand held
Mixer on stand with bowls, optional
In-pot blender
Blender with strong motor
Electric juicer for citrus fruit
Hot tray, optional
Slow cooker, optional
Electric bean pot, optional
Pasta machine
Waffle iron
Electric skillet, optional
Electric slicer, optional

About
Ingredients

About Ingredients

Every "ethnic" cook book needs a few words about the key or offbeat ingredients and where to find them. Here are a few suggestions.

Balsamic Vinegar – Like good sherry, good balsamic vinegar is aged in a solera system. The Italian city of Modena near Bologna earned fame for bringing this process to full development. The longer the aging, the more the vinegar can cost. For everyday use, a less expensive quality will do. Use the 25-year old balsamic to flavor fresh strawberries.

Specialty Cold Cuts and Cheeses – Look for these items at your Italian deli. Some markets carry them as well. If you have your heart set on the less popular varieties, such as braesola, copacola, or burrata cheese, you may find it possible to place a special order.

Porcini Mushrooms – Forest mushrooms picked fresh, then sliced and dried. Sometimes, but rarely, available fresh. Sold by the ounce because you need only a small amount to flavor risotto or other dishes. Expect to pay $42 per pound or more. Japanese forest mushrooms might be an acceptable substitute, but I have not found it necessary to check this out. Find porcini mushrooms at an Italian deli or in the ethnic foods section of your market.

Olive Oil – Extra virgin quality comes from the first cold pressing of the olives by the giant millstones. Virgin olive oil comes from subsequent pressings, also done cold. Olive oil that is not extra virgin or virgin is the product of final pressings in which the mill uses heat to extract the last drops of oil from the olives and even from the pits. Tastes vary depending on the regions from which the olives come. Most Mediterranean regions produce delicious olive oil. Here in California, many of our wineries now grow olives and produce and market small quantities of extra virgin artisanal oil. Let your taste buds guide you in your preferences.

Pasta, Dry – The best dry pasta is made from semolina flour from the hard, durum wheat. This type of pasta does not release its starch when cooked and then become "gluey." Most modern day pasta factories here in the U.S. extrude the spaghetti and noodles through plastic molds. This keeps the price of the pasta affordable for the mass market, but the resulting smooth surface of the pasta allows the sauce to slide off and the spaghetti or noodles to become slippery and resistant to lifting off the plate with your fork. Artisan pasta makers, on the other hand, pass the dough through bronze molds. This gives the pasta the slightly coarse texture that gets the sauce to cling and bring out its flavor.

Most artisanal dry pasta is made in Italy. Look for it in the dry pasta section of your Italian deli. Also available in limited quantities at other markets. It can come in angel hair or spaghetti type strands or in varied shapes, such as bow-ties, shells, little ears, etc.

Mastro Pepe operates the coiling machine

Mastro Pepe with his spaghetti making machine.

Artisanal Pasta making: Mfd. by: Pastificio Artigiano "Cav. Giuseppe Cocco"
snc. Zona Artigianale n 15 Fara S. Martino Abruzzi - Italy
The dough is then passed through bronze moulds to give the pasta just the
right slightly coarse texture that gets the sauce to cling and brings out its flavor.
The coiling machine rolls the pasta out into sheets, and with its wooden rollers,
like traditional rolling pins, draws it out to the desired thickness. The pasta has
now taken shape and then the most difficult and delicate stage begins – drying the
pasta at natural temperatures.
Photos courtesy of www.pastacocco.com

Pasta, Fresh – Once we Americans tasted fresh pasta noodles, such as fettuccine, we became addicted to them. Fettuccine Alfredo became an instant hit, a dining delicacy we savored. We also bought house made ravioli from our favorite delis. It came all cooked, sauced, and ready to heat and eat. Most of us did not wonder about how the cooks made it; we just ate and enjoyed it. When Mrs. Molino of Pleasant Hill, my favorite ravioli maker, initiated me into the mysteries I became fascinated at the complicated production process. I felt awe at Mrs. Molino's expertise, but I did not aspire to learn how to make ravioli.

Now the Atlas pasta machine (about a $30 investment) helps make it possible to produce pasta at home, just as the Italians do. Most of us, however, still prefer to buy fresh pasta already made. We find it at some (but not all) Italian delis and in our markets. Fresh pasta is more delicate than the dried versions and usually takes less time to cook.

Polenta – Modern day Italians use stone-ground corn meal. This gives more texture to the dish than our domestic U.S. corn meal, but you can substitute regular corn meal. Prior to the arrival of corn in Italy from the New World, after 1492, Italians made polenta from spelt, an ancient grain popular in Roman times and now returning to use.

Canned Tomatoes, Imported – For that special appeal of a bright red sauce, use San Marzano plum tomatoes, peeled and then canned with a purée of San Marzano tomatoes. Edith at the Italian Grocery in Santa Barbara recommends Cento brand in the can or Pomi brand strained farm fresh tomatoes by Parmalat. Both come from Italy.

Imported Tuna in Olive Oil – This delicacy seldom appears on the shelves of mainstream markets. Look for it at your Italian deli. The higher price puts this tuna into the gourmet category, but it's worth it. Use the oil in your salad dressing or pasta sauce.

Breast of Baby Veal – Bob and I found we could not buy this veal cut at any meat market in the Coachella Valley, and none would place a special order. The reason: They said they would have to order a complete side of veal and then break it down, a process most modern butchers avoid. If you live in such a community, you may have to wait until you visit a metropolitan area where at least a few butchers cater to an ethnic market.

Recipes

LaVergne, TN USA
20 November 2009
164867LV00003B/4/A